AUDUBON READER

AUDUBON READER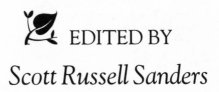
The Best Writings of John James Audubon

EDITED BY

Scott Russell Sanders

Indiana University Press  *Bloomington*

*No part of this book may be reproduced or utilized in any form
or by any means, electronic or mechanical, including photocopying
and recording, or by any information storage and retrieval system,
without permission in writing from the publisher. The Association
of American University Presses' Resolution on Permissions constitutes
the only exception to this prohibition.*

Manufactured in the United States of America

Library of Congress Cataloging-in-Publication Data

Audubon John James, 1785–1851.
  Audubon reader.

  Bibliography: p.
    1. Audubon, John James, 1785–1851.   2. Birds—
North America.   3. Ornithologists—North America—
Biography.   4. Artists—North America—Biography.
I. Sanders, Scott R. (Scott Russell), 1945–
II. Title.
QL31.A9A34   1986   598.092′4 [B]   85-45773
ISBN 0-253-31081-4
ISBN 0-253-20384-8 (pbk.)

1 2 3 4 5 90 89 88 87 86

For Patrick Parrinder

CONTENTS

Part 🍃 Three

LETTERS AND JOURNALS

AUDUBON READER

Introduction

I know that I am a poor writer, that I scarcely can
manage to scribble a tolerable English letter, and not a
much better one in French, though that is easier to me.
I know I am not a scholar, but . . . no man living has
studied our birds as much as I have done . . . so I shall
set to at once.

We are all familiar with Audubon the painter. Reproductions of his
vivid birds and beasts hang in our courthouses, lie in slick books on
our coffee tables, decorate our bedrooms and greeting cards. Say his
name, and in the minds of most listeners a colored print will arise.
But Audubon was also a writer, and a remarkable one, despite his
misgivings. During the years when he was feverishly painting the illustrations that made him famous, he was equally busy writing journals,
letters, autobiographical essays, and volumes of natural history. Taken
together, these pages summon up for us the retreating wilderness and
the boisterous frontier, and they display the appealing figure of Audubon himself, out in the fields and woods, observing it all with
passion.

Audubon did not *think* of himself as a writer. Although he was
second to none of his contemporaries in field experience, he was
lacking in book knowledge, in the formal armor of schooling, and that
made him feel vulnerable. He also felt insecure in his grasp of English,
which he did not use until the age of eighteen. At the time he began
learning his adopted language, in the first decade of the nineteenth
century, American English was in a state of ferment, stirred up by the
break from the old country and by the revolutionary conditions in the
new one. Vigorous, polyglot, rambunctious, America's newfangled
speech deserved a dictionary of its own, and Noah Webster soon
provided one. Audubon's use of this mercurial language was enthusiastic, expressive—and erratic. Like Thomas Jefferson and many another worthy, he was a phonetic speller. The waywardness of his
spelling was aggravated by the fact that he spoke English with a heavy
French accent. He used punctuation in a carefree and bewildering

fashion, or did without it altogether in his pell-mell rush of words. He wrote as he spoke and lived—impulsively, headlong—launching himself into sentences before he had any clear notion of how to exit from them; and consequently, his syntax was often as tangled as the Ohio River canebrakes he knew so well.

For these reasons, when it came time for him to publish his writings, Audubon had the good sense to seek out collaborators. After his death, most of the letters and journals that he left unpublished were either "improved" or destroyed by his widow and a tidy-minded granddaughter. The initial problem one encounters in assessing his writing, therefore, is in identifying what, amid the several thousand pages appearing under his name, may actually be attributed to Audubon.

The text of the book on mammals, The Viviparous Quadrupeds of North America (1846–1854), although informed by Audubon's notes was in fact largely written by his capable, long-suffering friend John Bachman, and thus provides only indirect evidence of Audubon the writer. The nearly five hundred life histories of birds and the sixty "episodes" published in the five volumes of the Ornithological Biography (1831–1839), on the other hand, are substantially the work of Audubon. In this case, as well, he was fortunate in his choice of collaborator. The Scottish scientist William Macgillivray was responsible for most of the technical material in the bird biographies, and likewise for "smoothing down the asperities" of Audubon's style, as Audubon himself declared in the introduction.

By comparing the original text for "Pitting of the Wolves" with the version published in the Ornithological Biography, we can see that Macgillivray was generally faithful to the shape and texture of Audubon's prose, limiting himself for the most part to the unsnarling of syntax and polishing-up of diction. Thus, where Audubon wrote, "the mangled remains of his companion lay scattered around on the blooded snow," Macgillivray substituted, "the mangled remains of his comrade lay scattered around on the snow, which was stained with blood." "Winter once more had come dreary, sad, cold and forbidding," from the original, was reduced to, "Winter had commenced, cold, dark, and forbidding." Where Audubon indulged himself in romantic excess, writing that the "silence of night was as dismal as that of the tomb," Macgillivray wrote simply, "the silence of night was dismal." The colloquial "nag" was transformed into the polite "horse," "lugged" into "carried." Where Audubon, in frontier slang, said that a cornered wolf fighting a pack of dogs "showed game," his editor wrote, "showed some spirit." Two men out courting, described in the manuscript as "seminocturnal young sparks," in the published version were elevated into "ardent youths."

In the process of scrubbing Audubon's language and putting it through a wringer of Victorian prose, Macgillivray also washed out some of its color and idiosyncrasy. It became less American and more British, in part because of Macgillivray's background, but also in part because that was the language deemed proper at the time for an educated audience, on either side of the Atlantic. We might regret Macgillivray's scrubbing and ironing, yet we can at least be grateful that he did not distort the essential vision of the text. What we read in the *Ornithological Biography* preserves Audubon's way of seeing, his quality of attention and turn of mind, which are the items of chief importance in any writer.

The journals were not so kindly treated. Audubon kept them almost continually from 1820 until the mid-1840s, writing next to campfires, in wayside inns, in the holds of ships. Serving the functions of diary, confessional, field notebook, and family epistle, they were the chief source for his bird biographies and informal essays. With a few exceptions, the only versions of these voluminous journals that we now possess are those published by his granddaughter Maria R. Audubon in 1897. In her preface she indicates that from the mass of papers in her possession, she used "perhaps one-fifth," without specifying how she chose what to include, and she makes no mention of altering what she *did* include.

We gain an insight into her method, however, when she insists that, contrary to published opinions, her grandfather was neither vain nor selfish; and, in all of the writings she examined, "there is not one sentence, one expression, that is other than that of a refined and cultured gentleman. More than that, there is not one utterance of 'anger, hatred or malice.' " That is flatly untrue, as we can see from other sources. Audubon was a far more complicated, flawed, and intriguing figure than the one his wife and granddaughter wished for us to see. In the best Victorian tradition of scouring the icons of dead celebrities, Maria censored, prettified, and quietly rewrote the journals in such a way as to fit her image of Audubon as a "refined and cultured gentleman," immune to anger or jealousy or vanity. Having given her doctored portrait to the world, she burned most of the manuscripts.

Fortunately, some of the manuscript journals have been preserved, including the fascinating one from 1826, the pivotal year during which Audubon left Lucy and America behind and launched *The Birds of America* in England. We can judge the extent of Maria's surgery by comparing, say, her account of the ocean crossing with Audubon's. She did not content herself with correcting grammar, punctuation, and spelling. She also cut out unseemly references to mice, maggots, and cockroaches, cabins sour with sweat, and stomachs growling with hunger. When Audubon wrote something as inoffensive as, "I smelt the putrid weeds on the shore" (a stench he subsequently traced to the on-deck latrine), Maria altered it to, "I smelt the 'land smell' " (and made no mention of the latrine). At one point he described a steward whose red flannel shirt stuck out of an open fly in a suggestive manner; Maria erased both shirt and sailor entirely. More than once, addressing Lucy, the lonely husband hinted at his sexual longings; but Maria would not let that pass her censor. In fact, whenever *any* feeling, any smell or sound or taste, struck hard on Audubon's senses, Maria either expunged it or toned it down, as if strength of feeling, and anything to do with a man's rude flesh, were taboo.

Likewise, she doctored all passages that register Audubon's dizzy swings of mood, his swift slipping back and forth between elation and black despair. For instance, the following characteristic entry does not appear in her version:

> I know only the acuteness of the feeling that acts through my whole frame like an electric shock. I immediately feel chilled, and suddenly throw my body on my mattress and cast my eyes towards the azure canopy of heaven, scarce able to hold the tears from flowing.

There was ample precedent for such emotional gushing in the romantics, especially Byron, whose poetry Audubon had been reading on this voyage. Whatever objections Maria might have had to such passages on stylistic grounds, she almost certainly excluded them because of what they revealed about the moodiness of her famous grandfather.

Since it would hardly do for a "cultured gentleman" to be revealed as a bastard, of course she omitted Audubon's few sly allusions to his illegitimate birth. In keeping with her image of him as the sober gentleman-artist, she cut out his numerous references to wine, whiskey, and other "spiritous liquors," as well as the several maudlin, comical, semihysterical passages written while he was under the influence.

Borrowing a metaphor from the anthropologists, we can distinguish, therefore, between Audubon "raw" and Audubon "cooked"; between the private voice of the letters and unedited journals, on the one hand, and the public voice of the *Ornithological Biography* and the expurgated journals, on the other. In the raw, Audubon is more colorful, sensuous, and opinionated. He is more likely to lapse into backwoods slang—describe a crowded ship by saying that "we will have to Pig together on the floor"; or proclaim his enthusiasm by saying that "with me it is *Neck or Nothing!*"; or advise a young woman "not to fritter herself with visionary fears"; or excuse himself at the end of a letter as "too dumpish to write any more." The unretouched man is more vain and moody, more outrageous in ambition and self-doubt, more feisty, more complex. Yet even in his cooked form, he is a highly original observer of both nature and humanity. He is large-hearted, omnivorously curious, fond of gossip, vigorous in his storytelling, and filled with zest. Through his eyes we see the swirl and ferment of frontier America; we meet a huge cast of characters, bird and beast and human, glimpsed during that once-on-a-continent moment when all wilderness east of the Rocky Mountains was on the point of vanishing.

Audubon was most candid in his letters, which were composed hastily, often late at night after a dozen hours of painting or exploring or canvassing for subscribers. Hundreds of letters have survived from the years 1826–1840—Audubon's great period, which included the creation of *The Birds of America* and the *Ornithological Biography*. Because these letters have been published without alteration, they enable us to form an impression of the unedited writer. Filled with chat and strong emotion, often confessional, by turns exuberant and despairing, they make lively reading, for their insight into the man and for their untamed language. Thus we overhear him confiding to Lucy:

> I dreamed a few nights ago that I was shooting Ducks with William in the Pond Settlement and that we had so many killed that our Horses were scarcely able to walk under the load and that it was so pichy Dark when we returned that every tree came in contact with my own noble Nose!

We share his excitement upon glimpsing a strange bird: "I have not shot but have seen a Hawk of great size entirely *new*—may perhaps kill him tomorrow." We observe him fulminating against his detractors—"I really care not a fig—all such stuffs will soon evaporate being mere smoak from a Dung Hill"—or against a politician—"If I was not a good Man and a Christian I would have wished him under Way to the '*Sulphur Springs*,' and in the sulphur to have been *upset*, yes upset and up to his lips in burning Lava!"

The letters reveal more strikingly than any of the other writings his stormy changes of mood. In one place we find him complaining about the "blue devils":

> I . . . have had the horrors all around me—Dreams of sinking & burning ships at night.—fears of lost Drawings & failures of subscribers by day have ever and anon been my companions—Not even the Bustle of this Large town can dissipate these unpleasant fancies—I walk the streets it is true, but neither hear nor see any thing but my fancies dancing about through the atmosphere like so many winged Imps resembling in shapes, colour, & capers all the *beau ideal* of the Infernal regions!

In another place we find him crowing:

> So you see or do not you see how lucky the "Old Man" is *yet!* and why all this Luck?—Simply because I have laboured like a cart Horse for the last thirty years on a Single Work, have been successful almost to a miracle in its publication thus far, and now am thought a—a—a—(I dislike to write it, but no matter here goes) a Great Naturalist!!!

The exclamations that pepper the letters are the mark of an enthusiast, a man who lurches from boasting to begging; a romantic, tossed by the extreme weathers of emotion; a lady's man, fond of music and dancing; a showman, a salesman, a doting—if wandering—father and husband. The letters show us, more clearly even than the journals, the impulses that drove him through his long travels and sustained him through his grueling labors: the desire for fame, the dread of failure, the hunger for knowledge, the sheer enjoyment of the hunt and the trek and the out-of-doors. The Audubon of the letters is a man obsessed, lured on by the gargantuan enterprise of his science and his art as powerfully as ever Ahab was lured on by the whale.

Written for the most part while Audubon was absent from his family on birding expeditions and subscription tours, the journals are usually addressed to his wife, Lucy, or to his sons. They are reports about what he observes in the woods, where he sleeps, whom he meets, how he feels; but they are also apologies, justifying his long absences and chronicling his slow rise from obscurity to fame.

Even in Maria Audubon's expurgated version, the journals have an on-the-spot freshness about them, catching Audubon's impressions as they form. For example, here is a passage from the 1826 journal:

> My drawing finished, I caught four Dolphins; how much I have gazed at these beautiful creatures, watching their last moments of life, as they changed their

hue in twenty varieties of richest arrangement of tints, from burnished gold to silver bright, mixed with touches of ultramarine, rose, green, bronze, royal purple, quivering to death on our hard broiling deck. As I stood and watched them, I longed to restore them to their native element in all their original strength and vitality, and yet I felt but a few moments before a peculiar sense of pleasure in catching them with a hook to which they were allured by false pretences.

That is an archetypal moment for Audubon. We see him delicately balanced among four rival identities—the hunter, exulting in triumph over his prey; the artist, enjoying the play of colors; the scientist, observing behavior; and the nature lover, regretting the death of something beautiful. In Audubon's own day, you could have found more accomplished hunters or scientists; in our time you could find more zealous conservationists and finer artists. What makes Audubon extraordinary and what charges his writings with inner drama is the *fusing* of these roles, the fierce interplay of identities.

The European journals, covering the period 1826–1829, show Audubon's transformation from backwoods shopkeeper to cosmopolitan artist. They are full of turmoil, because Audubon had been uprooted from the woods after more than two decades of tramping; and he had also been separated by an ocean from his family. In the learned and wealthy circles where his work carried him, he felt uneasy about the paltriness of his education and the emptiness of his purse. Thus, upon meeting an Englishwoman, he wrote, "Her eyes reached my very soul, and I feared her presence. I know that at one glance she had discovered my great inferiority." London, where he was forced to spend most of his time while completing The Birds of America, never suited him. He was tormented by the size of the city and its crowds, and by "the constant evidence of the contrast between the rich and the poor." Uprooted, lonely, and insecure, he alternated between giddy hope for his project and suffocating dread of failure:

I disengaged my Birds and looked at them with pleasure and yet with a considerable degree of fear that they never would be published. . . . Some dark thoughts came across my mind. I feared thee sick, perhaps lost forever to me, and felt deathly sick. . . . I felt tears frequently about my eyes, and I forced myself out of the room to destroy this painful gloom that I dread at all times and that sometimes I fear may do more.

No doubt there is a certain degree of romantic posturing here, but there is also a note of genuine anguish, which sounds repeatedly in the European journals.

The general theme of these early journals, however, is success—
the swift, miraculous rise to celebrity:

> Now to me this is all truly wonderful. I came to this Europe fearful, humble,
> dreading all, scarce daring to hold up my head and meet the glance of the
> learned, and I am praised so high. It is quite unaccountable and I still fear it
> will not last. These good people certainly give me more merit than I am entitled
> to. It is only a mere glance of astonishment or surprise operating on them,
> because my style is new and different from what has preceded me.

His style *was* new, both on the page and in person, and this fact had
a great deal to do with his initial success. By luck and by shrewd
performance, he fitted to perfection the role of the American woodsman, which at that moment the public on both sides of the Atlantic
was eager to behold. In his Leatherstocking novels, James Fenimore
Cooper was appealing to this same curiosity; he unveiled his noble
frontiersman, Natty Bumppo, in 1823, three years before Audubon's
arrival in England, and continued the enormously popular series
through *The Deerslayer*, which appeared in 1841, two years after Audubon's return to America. Daniel Boone and David Crockett had
long since become folk heroes, and supplied models for both Cooper
and Audubon. Andrew Jackson, a man of the western country and a
symbol of the frontier, was elected president in 1828.

The European journals show Audubon playing the woodsman's
role in the drawing rooms of England with gusto and self-irony, imitating bird calls and Indian yells, singing Ohio River songs, eating
corn on the cob and raw tomatoes (which his English hosts imagined
to be poisonous), answering endless questions about the wilderness,
the beasts, the "aborigines." In keeping with his image, he often
sported fringed buckskins, brandished a walking stick, and wore his
chestnut hair long, thereby inspiring the ladies to gaze at him with
curiosity and provoking a servant boy to stare at him "like an ass at
a fine thistle." To his way of seeing, by contrast, a judge's powdered
wig—that utterly civilized headdress—"might make a capital bed for
an Osage Indian during the whole of a cold winter on the Arkansas
River."

Anticipating Mark Twain, Audubon also played the role of innocent abroad, wondering at the wealth and decadence he found in
Europe, comparing the manicured landscape of the Old World with
America's unruly wilderness. What the English called trees put him
in mind of Louisiana saplings; their pears and apples were the size of
green peas. Beside the mighty Ohio, the Thames was a puny brook,

across which "a Sand-hill Crane could easily wade . . . without damping its feathers." As for London's new zoological gardens, they contained fewer natural curiosities than one might find on a single morning in an American swamp.

Audubon was himself a natural curiosity, and made the most of it. But of course, play-acting alone did not enable him to sustain his enormous project of writing and painting and selling. In addition to artistic gifts and personal charm, it took dogged labor, as Audubon noted in a characteristic (and immodest) analogy: "Since Napoleon became, from the ranks, an Emperor, why should not Audubon be able to leave the woods of America a while and publish and sell a *book?*"

His later journals, recounting trips to Labrador (1833) and the Yellowstone country (1843), are less dramatic than those from the period in Europe, but they exhibit even more starkly his almost fanatical will. By the time he made those journeys, Audubon was no longer living in constant fear of failure; he knew what his mission was, and stuck to it with fierce determination. His official purpose was to observe the behavior of birds and beasts, and to gather specimens. Unofficially, he was escaping into the open air, sleeping in ships and forts and tents, exploring the continent. Although lacking the inner tumult of the earlier journals, these later ones are still interesting for what they show about Audubon's powers as a reporter, and about his growing ecological anxiety.

They provide keen observations on the Indians, on landscape and crops, on patterns of settlement, roads, and wild foods. Broiled dog, for example, struck him as surprisingly good—"no sooner had the taste touched my palate than I changed my dislike to liking, and found this victim of the canine order most excellent"; hashed eider duck and herons' eggs proved to be tasty, and likewise raw buffalo liver in moderate portions; but he could not bring himself to try the hunter's favorite delicacy, steaming buffalo brains. What Audubon observed of the Indians was often at variance with the flowery records left by "poetical travellers." He wrote memorable accounts of once-powerful tribes fallen on hard times—the Seminoles of Florida, where the government was bent on a policy of extermination; the demoralized Indians of Maine; the horse warriors of the plains, reduced to begging or to jumping in the river after the rotting carcasses of buffaloes; entire western tribes decimated by smallpox.

In passage after passage in these Labrador and Missouri journals,

Audubon captured the "wonderful dreariness" of the Far North and the intoxicating desolation of the Far West. He described flocks of gannets, their white bodies swirling in the air like blown snow, and buffaloes pouring in a furious brown river across the plains. But amid this abundance of wildlife, where he hunted with as much gusto as ever, he also began to worry about how long nature would be able to support so much slaughter. In the north, trappers were destroying the fur-bearing animals, and eggers were annihilating the birds. "In less than half a century," he predicted, "these wonderful nurseries will be entirely destroyed, unless some kind government will interfere to stop the shameful destruction." White men intent on profit had already driven away the Indians:

> Nature herself seems perishing. Labrador must shortly be depeopled, not only of aboriginal man, but of all else having life, owing to man's cupidity. When no more fish, no more game, no more birds exist on her hills, along her coasts, and in her rivers, then she will be abandoned and deserted like a worn-out field.

This fearful vision led him to lament, "Where can I go now, and visit nature undisturbed?"

In the Yellowstone country, traveling as a celebrity, beginning to wear out after decades of tramping and laboring, Audubon wrote obsessively about the "sport" and "frolic" of killing. He and his men shot everything with a skin around it—buffalo, rabbits, elk, deer, bighorn sheep, all manner of birds. Yet he also protested against the mayhem. Surveying the prairies littered with the skulls of buffalo, most of them killed for sport, with perhaps no more than their tongues harvested, he complained in his journal, "What a terrible destruction of life"; if it kept up, he prophesied, the buffalo would go the way of the great auk to extinction.

In their capacity as field notebooks, the journals reveal another source of Audubon's enduring significance. No one before him in America had *looked* at the woods and wildlife so closely, or recorded in such exhaustive detail what they had seen. He paid attention to the behavior of birds, to habitats, mating rituals, the shape and placement of nests, the contents of crops and gizzards, patterns of migrations, and dozens of other matters. Audubon's field experience, faithfully recorded in the journals, distinguished both his paintings and his nature writings from those of the stay-at-homes, whom he dismissed as "crazed naturalists of the closet." When attacked by critics, as he frequently was, he appealed to the journals as proof of his truthfulness to nature:

> The World is well aware that it is not necessary for any one inclined to publish falsehoods or form tales of Wonder, to travel as I constantly do, at an (I am sorry to say) enormous expense, keeping a regular Journal of all my actions and the whole of my observations connected with the Science which I am studying, when on the contrary I might with ten fold ease settle myself in some corner of London and write nolens volens all such fables as might cross my brains and publish these without caring one Jot about the consequences.

With so many of his rivals busily publishing falsehoods and tales of wonder, he exclaimed, countless "niny tiny Works are in progress to assist in the mass of confusion already scattered over the World." Those who never left their studies might accuse him of extravagance, but Audubon insisted, "I write as I . . . see, and that is enough to render me contented with my words."

The transition from hastily jotted letters and journals to the publication of scientific studies was a difficult one, and Audubon undertook it with trepidation. When he resolved, during his first year in England, "to attempt the being an author," he confided to his journal: "It is a terrible thing to me; far better am I fitted to study and delineate in the forest, than to arrange phrases with suitable grammatical skill." When halfway through the composition of the *Ornithological Biography*, he wrote to John Bachman:

> God preserve you, and save you the trouble of ever publishing Books on Natural Science! for my part I would rather go without a shirt or any inexpressibles through the whole of the florida swamps in musquito time than labour as I have hitherto done with the pen.

Written over nearly a decade, from 1830–1839, running to five fat volumes and covering roughly five hundred birds, the *Ornithological Biography* was an enormous undertaking. Despite Audubon's misgivings, it earned him a considerable reputation both as a writer and as a scientist. In all the works of Charles Darwin, only two authorities are cited more often than Audubon. Spencer Fullerton Baird, a young friend of Audubon's who was to become secretary of the Smithsonian Institution, said he found the essays about birds to be as engrossing as his favorite novels. Thoreau declared that he "read in Audubon with a thrill of delight."

As we have seen already, the *Ornithological Biography* owes its stylistic polish and a good deal of its technical information to the painstaking editor, William Macgillivray. But the energy, the wit, the sheer exuberance of detail come straight from Audubon. He justly prided himself on working from field notes:

> I possess the knowledge that every word which I have published or shall publish is truth and nothing but the result of my own observations in fields and forests where neither of my enemies ever have or ever will tread with as firm a foot & step as I have done and still do.

More important than the accuracy of observation is the observer's fearless, passionate, indefatigable presence, which shows through all the pages of the *Ornithological Biography*, offering us a personal encounter with nature:

> I still see the high rolling billows of the St. Lawrence breaking in foaming masses against the huge Labrador cliffs where the Cormorant places its nest on the shelves. I lay flat on the edge of a precipice, a hundred feet above the turbulent waters. By crawling along carefully I came within a few yards of the spot where the parent bird and her young, quite unconscious of my nearness, were fondling each other.

Or again: "I have approached trees whilst these Woodpeckers were thus busily employed in forming their nest, and by resting my head against the bark, could easily distinguish every blow given by the bird." Audubon takes us inside hollow trees to count chimney swifts, into caves to tie silver threads around the legs of phoebes, onto cliffs in search of eggs, through swamps and waist-high waters. He tells us how he nearly perished in quicksand while pursuing a great horned owl, how his fingers froze one December midnight while he awaited the arrival of Canada geese, how cactus spines scratched his feet when he hunted for the nests of white ibis, how he worked so feverishly on the painting of a golden eagle "that it nearly cost me my life," how he backpedaled furiously and leapt in the river to escape a wounded heron.

The *Ornithological Biography* shows us the life of birds through the lens of a man's emotions. When fledgling water turkeys are pushed from their nest prematurely, Audubon feels despondent; swans flying make him feel carefree and buoyant. Like Whitman, he might have claimed, "I am the man, I suffer'd, I was there." Many species he kept for pets, and he tells us about living with them for months or years as with intimate friends. A pet heron was suffered to stalk the family cat, and a trumpeter swan to chase the children. The birds are also granted the full range of human feeling. In Audubon's eyes, they betrayed courage and cowardice, innocence and guilt, hope and despair; when courting, they seemed to him coy or jealous, pompous or pugnacious. We are told, for instance, that after the turkey hens lay their eggs,

> the males become clumsy and slovenly, if one may say so, cease to fight with each other, give up gobbling or calling so frequently, and assume so careless a habit, that the hens are obliged to make all the advances themselves. They *yelp* loudly and almost continually for the cocks, run up to them, caress them, and employ various means to rekindle their expiring ardour.

When describing birdcalls, he searched high and low for analogy. The cry of the gannet is "wolfish," that of the bald eagle like "the laugh of a maniac"; that of the ivory-billed woodpecker like "the false high note of a clarionet"; the cormorant grunts like a pig, the golden eagle barks like a dog, and the great horned owl's call sounds "like the last gurglings of a murdered man." In describing the birds' behavior, he quite often appealed to human parallels. Thus, Atlantic puffins chase one another under water "with so much speed as to resemble the ricochets of a cannon ball"; and bluejays hammer "at a grain of corn like so many blacksmiths paid by the piece."

By comparison with modern scientific writing, that is all exceedingly messy and subjective. When Audubon chose, he could be as precise as any present-day ornithologist. For example, he could provide an exact description of the ibis's eye, explaining, "I am thus particular in stating these matters, because it is doubtful if anyone else has paid attention to them." But it is Audubon's *personal* encounter with nature, more so than his science, that has kept his writing so pertinent and so fresh.

Probably the best known of Audubon's writings are the sixty informal essays, or "episodes," which are interspersed through the first three volumes of the *Ornithological Biography*. Dealing with his frontier experiences from the period 1818–1834, these interludes were designed, he told his readers, "to relieve the tedium which may be apt now and then to come upon you, by presenting you with occasional descriptions of the scenery and manners of the land which has furnished the objects that engage your attention." In his letters he was more forthright, saying that the episodes were "food for the Idle!" They were a literary analogue to his long hair and beard, his fringed buckskins and drawing-room high jinks, a way of satisfying his readers' appetite for a taste of the wilderness.

Audubon knew those first readers very well. He had met nearly all of his subscribers, his scientific rivals, his patrons and judges; they made up the audience he imagined as he wrote. For the most part they were indoor types, rich and well-read, the denizens of high society. To defend himself against the skepticism of those who would peruse his "episodes" in their cozy parlors, Audubon insisted on the truthfulness of his accounts. "I shall not lead you into the region of romance," he assured his readers. And elsewhere: "This is no tale of fiction, but the relation of an actual occurrence, which might be embellished, no doubt, but which is better in the plain garb of truth."

Tales of fiction were, however, among the patterns he bore in mind for his writing, as this journal entry about Sir Walter Scott would suggest:

> Oh Walter Scott, where art thou? Wilt thou not come to my country? Wrestle with mankind and stop their increasing ravages on Nature, and describe her now for the sake of future ages. Neither this little stream, this swamp, this grand sheet of flowing water, nor these mountains will be seen in a century hence as I see them now. Nature will have been robbed of her brilliant charms.

The most influential literary models at this time in America were—aside from the novels of Scott—the works of Washington Irving and James Fenimore Cooper. Irving's *The Sketch Book* (1819–1820) included American lore amid its genteel essays on England; and his *Tours on the Prairies* (1835) and *Astoria* (1836) set an example for writing about the West. Cooper established the pattern for writing about wilderness, Indians, and pioneers. The influence of fictional romance can be seen in Audubon's portraits of frontier characters, the drunken trappers and renegades, the charlatans and eccentrics. Literary landscapes appear to have influenced his descriptions of the Kentucky forests, the Atlantic coast, the Florida Keys, the wastes of Labrador, the Ohio canebrakes, and the Mississippi River with "its mighty mass of waters rolling sullenly along, like the flood of eternity." However, by contrast with Scott and Irving and Cooper, who were merely armchair explorers, Audubon knew the ground and the frontier types very well. He was not as refined a writer, but he was better informed.

Like the romantics, Audubon was attracted by the picturesque and the dramatic in nature—earthquake and hurricane, foxfire and forest fire, floods and cataracts; and he had a soft spot for melodrama and tear-jerking sentimentality. He was also fascinated by the workaday lives of those who settled along the frontier. Thus, in the "episodes" he memorialized the festivals, the cornhuskings and July Fourth picnics, the ox-plowing contests, the fancy-dress balls. True to the

practical outlook of his adopted homeland—as symbolized by his hero, Benjamin Franklin—he paid close attention to the way people *did* things. He reported in detail on how to trap beaver or set a trotline for catfish, how to dry cod, butcher a buffalo, make maple sugar, or build a boat of hide; he instructed us in the firing of a flintlock, the poling of a keelboat, the locating of turtle eggs.

Although the "episodes" contain some of his finest writing, Audubon himself thought of them as "very so so indeed." Much of the material came straight from journals or memory, but much of it was also a recounting of stories that had been told to him. Thus he could ask John Bachman, "Can you send me some good stories for Episodes? Send quickly and often." All the while he was traveling, Audubon was collecting lore about frontier toughs, about Indians and beasts, along the same heartland rivers where Samuel Clemens and William Faulkner would later gather material of their own. He heard an unending chorus of stories—on riverboats, around campfires, inside forts, on cross-country horseback rides, on hunts, in wayside inns. He gathered tales about the hunting of moose in Maine, buffalo in the Yellowstone country, and alligators in Florida; about desperadoes and vigilantes, pirates and runaway slaves; and he retold these tales in his "episodes." In a few cases, such as the essay about his shooting expedition with Daniel Boone or the one about his near-murder in a settler's cabin on the Illinois prairie, he placed himself at the center of stories that he had most likely heard other people tell.

As in the life histories of the birds, so in these "episodes" Audubon created a persona for himself. We see him penniless and downcast at the falls of Niagara, paying for his meals with quick portraits; and we see him, years later, grown so famous that settlers in the wilds of Labrador learned of his arrival from the newspapers. Through it all he preserved "a heart as true to Nature as ever." This public Audubon is fond of music and dancing, abstemious about food and drink; he is industrious, cheerful, as honest as the day is long; he rivals the Indians in his woodland skills; and he is driven by an "irrepressible desire of acquiring knowledge." He is a patient, keen-eyed messenger, bringing us news from nature.

As a writer, Audubon belongs to a distinguished American band of roving nature reporters. The earliest representatives were the Jesuit missionaries of the seventeenth century. They were followed, in the eighteenth century, by a host of vagabond naturalists, including Mark

Catesby and the famous Bartrams, father John and son William; and in the early nineteenth century by those intrepid explorers Meriwether Lewis and William Clark, and by the first great artist of American birds, Alexander Wilson. These men scoured the land, curious about everything, recording their observations in journals and letters, often publishing their findings in travel narratives. In the earliest days there was little distinction between rumor and fact; but gradually the more scientific observations of nature were separated from the background of anecdote and folklore. William Bartram's *Travels* (1791) influenced the next generation of poets, including Wordsworth and Shelley. Alexander Wilson's *American Ornithology* (1808–1814) was the standard against which Audubon measured his own achievement. Those who followed Audubon in this tradition of nature reporting include Thoreau, John Muir, John Burroughs, Aldo Leopold, and Rachel Carson. More recently, the essays of Loren Eiseley, Annie Dillard, Edward Hoagland, and Peter Matthiessen show how vital this literary form continues to be. All of these writers confront nature not as aloof observers, seeking facts, but as participants seeking meaning. That was Audubon's strength as a writer, not system building but on-the-spot reporting, bearing his keen sensibility through uncharted territory.

He should also be read within the context of that burst of literary creativity that Van Wyck Brooks aptly called the "flowering of New England." While Audubon was reluctantly pushing his quills and his iron-tipped pens, in the East a remarkable cluster of young men was rapidly growing to maturity, including Emerson, Thoreau, Whitman, and Melville. By mid-century, they would supply America with its first great literature. One feature common to their masterworks—*Walden* (1854), *Moby Dick* (1851), *Leaves of Grass* (1855), and Emerson's *Nature* (1836)—was a preoccupation with the encounter between the human and the nonhuman, between society and nature. Their obsession was also Audubon's: to see, to question, to understand the wild milieu. In fact, that has been one of the central themes of our literature, from the very beginnings up to the present. All along, what has distinguished America from the Old World has been the juxtaposition of civilization and wilderness.

Like the great figures of the American Renaissance, Audubon was encyclopedic, in ambition and method—as if, by spanning the continent, seeing and reporting it all, he could somehow make sense of it, take on its grand scale. The following passage, an ecstatic aside from his biography of the raven, is a typical specimen of the American sublime:

Who is the stranger to my own dear country that can adequately conceive of the extent of its primeval woods, the glory of its solemn forests that for centuries have waved before breeze and tempest, of its vast Atlantic bays, of its thousands of streams, vast lakes and magnificent rivers? There is the diversity of our Western plains, our sandy Southern shores with their reedy swamps; protecting cliffs; rapid Mexican Gulf currents; rushing tides of the Bay of Fundy; majestic mountains; and thundering cataracts. Would I might delineate it all. . . .

When an English sea captain proposed to him, at the outset of his writing career, that he record his knowledge in a "little book," Audubon protested, "I cannot write at all, but if I could how could I make a *little* book, when I have seen enough to make a dozen *large* books?"

Although he felt a sympathy for the displaced Indians and fretted over the destruction of the wilderness and its creatures, that did not prevent him from identifying enthusiastically with the energies of settlement. He embodied, in his life and his work, the sheer joy of exploration, traversing the continent, testing himself against the wilds, the beasts, the border people. His ambition, he declared, was "to search out things hidden since the creation of this wondrous world," and in that he succeeded admirably. The emphasis here belongs on *wonder*, which was the keynote of his writing as of his painting. If he lacked the powerful sense of evil that would characterize the next generation of writers—especially Melville, Poe, and Hawthorne; if he ignored the wounds of slavery that were festering all around him; if he painted human emotions too freely onto nature, Audubon nonetheless provided us with the most comprehensive view of our continent anyone had ever achieved. His writings preserve for us glimpses of a pristine America, a landscape and a way of life that were altering even as he observed them.

Chronology of
John James Audubon's Life and Work

1785 Born Jean Rabine on April 26 in Les Cayes, Sainte-Domingue (later Haiti); illegitimate son of Captain Jean Audubon and Jeanne Rabine. Mother soon dies; father returns to France, later becomes naval officer for revolutionary government.

1791 In June, because of slave uprising in Sainte-Domingue, the boy is shipped to Nantes, France, along with half-sister, Rose. The children are reared by stepmother, Anne Moynet Audubon.

1791–1800 Erratic schooling in Nantes and nearby Couëron; witness to most violent years of French Revolution, including public guillotining.

1794 March 7, adopted by Captain and Mme Audubon, as Jean-Jacques-Fougère Audubon.

1796 August, enrolls in naval academy at Rochefort, where his father is an officer.

1800 March, failing as cadet, returns to Couëron.

1803 To avoid Napoleon's draft, is sent to Mill Grove, Captain Audubon's estate near Philadelphia. In America, calls himself John James Audubon.

1804 At Mill Grove, begins study of American birds; banding of phoebes. Meets Lucy Bakewell, who lives on neighboring estate of Fatland Ford.

1805 March, returns to France, seeking permission to marry Lucy. Parents insist he wait until he proves himself in business.

1806 April, back to the United States, bound in commercial partnership to Ferdinand Rozier.

1807 With Rozier, opens store in Louisville.

1808 April 5, marries Lucy Bakewell; they set up house in Indian Queen Hotel, Louisville.

1809 June 12, son Victor Gifford Audubon born.

1810 March, meets ornithologist Alexander Wilson, who is peddling a volume of bird portraits. Louisville store fails; Audubon family and Rozier move downriver to Henderson, Kentucky, where they set up new shop.

1811 Partners split up; Rozier settles in Missouri. Audubon runs store in Henderson on his own.

1812 July 3, becomes American citizen.

November 30, son John Woodhouse Audubon born.

1815–1819 Invests in land, lumber, steam mill, steamship, and other enterprises.

1815 Winter, daughter Lucy born.

1817 Winter, daughter Lucy dies.

1818 Father dies in France. Because of illegitimacy, Audubon receives no legacy.

1819 Summer, failure of investments, then bankruptcy; sells everything except gun, dog, clothes, and drawings. Briefly jailed for debt. Autumn, daughter Rosa born; dies seven months later.

1820 Works as taxidermist, portraitist, and sign painter in Cincinnati to support family.

October 12, sets out down Ohio and Mississippi rivers in search of birds to fill out his portfolio, with visions of publishing a book.

1820–1829 Lucy supports herself and the two boys by working as governess and teacher, mainly in Louisiana.

1821 Lucy and the boys join Audubon in New Orleans.

1821–1826 In Louisiana and Mississippi, drawing birds; earns meager income as tutor in painting, violin, dancing, fencing.

1823–1824 Travels to Philadelphia and New York, fails to secure a publisher for *Birds of America*.

1826 June, departs for England, leaving Lucy and boys in America to wait until he has succeeded in his publishing scheme. Arrives in Liverpool, where he is soon celebrated as the "American Woodsman," and his drawings are exhibited.

November, William Home Lizars engraves first plates of *The Birds of America* in Edinburgh.

1827 Audubon begins selling subscriptions—at roughly $1,000 each—through England and Scotland. Arranges for Robert Havell, Jr., in London, to engrave remainder of *Birds*.

1829 May, returns to United States, to draw additional birds and retrieve Lucy. Already a celebrity, he is entertained by President Andrew Jackson; his movements are reported in newspapers.

1830 April, returns with Lucy to England. Assisted by Scottish scientist William Macgillivray, begins work in Edinburgh on *Ornithological Biography*.

1831 February, first volume of *Onithological Biography* published.

September, collecting trip to the United States.

October, meets John Bachman in Charleston. Victor goes to England to oversee production of *The Birds of America*.

1831–1834 Selling subscriptions in America. Collecting and drawing in Florida and Labrador.

1834 May, returns to England. Resumes work on *Ornithological Biography*.

1836 October, on collecting trip to the United States, secures skins of birds, including some new to science, from western expedition of John Kirk Townsend and Thomas Nuttall.

1838 June, last plates of *The Birds of America* are engraved.

1839 *Synopsis of the Birds of America* and last volume of *Ornithological Biography* are published.

September, final departure from England for the United States. Begins work on compact edition of *Birds* and, in collaboration with John Bachman, on *The Viviparous Quadrupeds of North America*.

1842 Family moves into Minnie's Land, estate on the Hudson upriver from Manhattan.

1843 March-September, last collecting expedition, to Upper Missouri River.

1845 First volume of *Quadrupeds* published.

1846 His eyes and mind begin to fail. Sons John and Victor take over responsibility for his work.

1848 Can no longer draw, paint, or write.

Third and final volume of *Quadrupeds* published.

1851 January 27, dies at Minnie's Land.

Part ✍ One

After each five articles about birds in the first three volumes of the Ornithological Biography, Audubon inserted an essay concerning American "scenery and manners." Written between 1830 and 1835, these sixty informal "episodes"—although filtered, like all of the Ornithological Biography, through the editorial screen of William Macgillivray—show Audubon at his most lively and acute. The fifteen essays in my selection have been rearranged, to reflect not the sequence of composition or publication but the rough chronological order of the experiences on which they were based.

The Ohio

To render more pleasant the task which you have imposed upon yourself, of following an author through the mazes of descriptive ornithology, permit me, kind reader, to relieve the tedium which may be apt now and then to come upon you, by presenting you with occasional descriptions of the scenery and manners of the land which has furnished the objects that engage your attention. The natural features of that land are not less remarkable than the moral character of her inhabitants; and I cannot find a better subject with which to begin, than one of those magnificent rivers that roll the collected waters of her extensive territories to the ocean.

When my wife, my eldest son (then an infant), and myself were returning from Pennsylvania to Kentucky, we found it expedient, the waters being unusually low, to provide ourselves with a *skiff*, to enable us to proceed to our abode at Henderson. I purchased a large, commodious, and light boat of that denomination. We procured a mattress, and our friends furnished us with ready prepared viands. We had two stout Negro rowers, and in this trim we left the village of Shippingport, in expectation of reaching the place of our destination in a very few days.

It was in the month of October. The autumnal tints already decorated the shores of that queen of rivers, the Ohio. Every tree was hung with long and flowing festoons of different species of vines, many loaded with clustered fruits of varied brilliancy, their rich bronzed carmine mingling beautifully with the yellow foliage, which now predominated over the yet green leaves, reflecting more lively tints from the clear stream than ever landscape painter portrayed or poet imagined.

The days were yet warm. The sun had assumed the rich and glowing hue, which at that season produces the singular phenomenon called there the "Indian Summer." The moon had rather passed the meridian of her grandeur. We glided down the river, meeting no other ripple of the water than that formed by the propulsion of our boat. Leisurely we moved along, gazing all day on the grandeur and beauty of the wild scenery around us.

Now and then, a large cat-fish rose to the surface of the water in pursuit of a shoal of fry, which starting simultaneously from the liquid element, like so many silvery arrows, produced a shower of light, while the pursuer with open jaws seized the stragglers, and, with a splash of the tail, disappeared from our view. Other fishes we heard uttering beneath our bark a rumbling noise, the strange sounds of which we discovered to proceed from the white perch, for on casting our net from the bow we caught several of that species, when the noise ceased for a time.

Nature, in her varied arrangements, seems to have felt a partiality towards this portion of our country. As the traveller ascends or descends the Ohio, he cannot help remarking that alternately, nearly the whole length of the river, the margin, on one side, is bounded by lofty hills and a rolling surface, while on the other, extensive plains of the richest alluvial land are seen as far as the eye can command the view. Islands of varied size and form rise here and there from the bosom of the water, and the winding course of the stream frequently brings you to places, where the idea of being on a river of great length changes to that of floating on a lake of moderate extent. Some of these islands are of considerable size and value; while others, small and insignificant, seem as if intended for contrast, and as serving to enhance the general interest of the scenery. These little islands are frequently overflowed during great *freshets* or floods, and receive at their heads prodigious heaps of drifted timber. We foresaw with great concern the alteration that cultivation would soon produce along those delightful banks.

As night came, sinking in darkness the broader portions of the river, our minds became affected by strong emotions, and wandered far beyond the present moments. The tinkling of bells told us that the cattle which bore them were gently roving from valley to valley in search of food, or returning to their distant homes. The hooting of the Great Owl, or the muffled noise of its wings as it sailed smoothly over the stream, were matters of interest to us; so was the sound of the boatman's horn, as it came winding more and more softly from afar. When daylight returned, many songsters burst forth with echoing notes, more and more mellow to the listening ear. Here and there the lonely cabin of a squatter struck the eye, giving note of commencing civilization. The crossing of the stream by a deer foretold how soon the hills would be covered with snow.

Many sluggish flat-boats we overtook and passed: some laden with produce from the different head-waters of the small rivers that pour their tributary streams into the Ohio; others, of less dimensions, crowded with emigrants from distant parts, in search of a new home. Purer pleasures I never felt; nor have you, reader, I ween, unless indeed you have felt the like, and in such company.

The margins of the shores and of the river were at this season amply supplied with game. A Wild Turkey, a Grouse, or a Blue-winged Teal, could be procured in a few moments; and we fared well, for, whenever we pleased, we landed, struck up a fire, and provided as we were with the necessary utensils, procured a good repast.

Several of these happy days passed, and we neared our home, when, one evening, not far from Pigeon Creek (a small stream which runs into the Ohio, from the State of Indiana), a loud and strange noise was heard, so like the yells of Indian warfare, that we pulled at our oars, and made for the opposite side as fast and as quietly as possible. The sounds increased, we imagined we heard cries of "murder;" and as we knew that some depredations had lately been committed in the country by dissatisfied parties of Aborigines, we felt for a while extremely uncomfortable. Ere long, however, our minds became more calmed and we plainly discovered that the singular uproar was produced by an enthusiastic set of Methodists, who had wandered thus far out of the common way, for the purpose of holding one of their annual camp meetings, under the shade of a beech forest. Without meeting with any other interruption, we reached Henderson, distant from Shippingport by water about two hundred miles.

When I think of these times, and call back to my mind the grandeur and beauty of those almost uninhabited shores; when I picture to myself the dense and lofty summits of the forest, that everywhere spread along the hills, and overhung the margins of the stream, unmolested by the axe of the settler; when I know how dearly purchased the safe navigation of that river has been by the blood of many worthy Virginians; when I see that no longer any Aborigines are to be found there, and that the vast herds of elks, deer and buffaloes which once pastured on these hills and in these valleys, making for themselves great roads to the several salt-springs, have ceased to exist; when I reflect that all this grand portion of our Union, instead of being in a state of nature, is now more or less covered with villages, farms, and towns, where the din of hammers and machinery is constantly heard; that the woods are fast disappearing under the axe by day, and the fire by night; that hundreds of steam-boats are gliding to and fro, over the whole length of the majestic river, forcing commerce to take root and to prosper at every spot; when I see the surplus population of Europe coming to assist in the destruction of the forest, and transplanting civilization into its darkest recesses;—when I remember that these extraordinary changes have all taken place in the short period of twenty years, I pause, wonder, and, although I know all to be fact, can scarcely believe its reality.

Whether these changes are for the better or for the worse, I shall not pretend to say; but in whatever way my conclusions may incline, I feel with regret that there are on record no satisfactory accounts of the state of that portion of the country, from the time when our people first settled in it. This has not been because no one in America is able to accomplish such an undertaking. Our Irvings and our Coopers have proved themselves fully competent for the task. It has more probably been because the changes have succeeded each other with such rapidity, as almost to rival the movements of their pen. However, it is not too late yet; and I sincerely hope that either or both of them will ere long furnish the generations to come with those delightful descriptions which they are so well qualified to give, of the original state of a country that has been so rapidly forced to change her form and attire under the influence of increasing population. Yes; I hope to read, ere I close my earthly career, accounts from those delightful writers of the progress of civilization in our western country. They will speak of the Clarks, the Croghans, the Boons, and many other men of great and daring enterprise. They will analyze, as it were, into each component part, the country as it once existed, and will render the picture, as it ought to be, immortal.

Louisville in Kentucky

LOUISVILLE in Kentucky has always been a favourite place of mine. The beauty of its situation, on the banks of *La Belle Rivière*, just at the commencement of the famed rapids, commonly called the Falls of the Ohio, had attracted my notice, and when I removed to it, immediately after my marriage, I found it more agreeable than ever. The prospect from the town is such that it would please even the eye of a Swiss. It extends along the river for seven or eight miles, and is bounded on the opposite side by a fine range of low mountains, known by the name of the Silver Hills. The rumbling sound of the waters, as they tumble over the rock-paved bed of the rapids, is at all times soothing to the ear. Fish and game are abundant. But, above all, the generous hospitality of the inhabitants, and the urbanity of their manners, had induced me to fix upon it as a place of residence; and I did so with more pleasure when I found that my wife was as much gratified as myself, by the kind attentions which were shown to us, utter strangers as we were, on our arrival.

No sooner had we landed, and made known our intention of remaining, than we were introduced to the principal inhabitants of the place and its vicinity, although we had not brought a single letter of introduction, and could not but see, from their unremitting kindness, that the Virginian spirit of hospitality displayed itself in all the words and actions of our newly-formed friends. I wish here to name those persons who so unexpectedly came forward to render our stay among them agreeable, but feel at a loss with whom to begin, so equally deserving are they of our gratitude. The Croghans, the Clarks (our great traveller included), the Berthouds, the Galts, the Maupins, the Tarascons, the Beals, and the Booths, form but a small portion of the long list which I could give. The matrons acted like mothers towards my wife, the daughters proved agreeable associates, and the husbands and sons were friends and companions to me. If I absented myself on business or otherwise, for any length of time, my wife was removed to the hospitable abode of some friends in the neighbourhood until my return, and then I was several times obliged to spend a week or more with these good people, before they could be prevailed upon to let us return to our own residence. We lived for two years at Louisville, where we enjoyed many of the best pleasures which this life can afford; and whenever we have since chanced to pass that way, we have found the kindness of our former friends unimpaired.

During my residence at Louisville, much of my time was employed in my ever favourite pursuits. I drew and noted the habits of every thing which I procured, and my collection was daily augmenting, as every individual who carried a gun always sent me such birds or quadrupeds as he thought might prove useful to me. My portfolios already contained upwards of two hundred drawings. Dr. W. C. Galt, being a botanist, was often consulted by me, as well as his friend Dr. Ferguson. M. Gilly drew beautifully, and was fond of my pursuits. So was my friend, and now relative, N. Berthoud. As I have already said, our time was spent in the most agreeable manner, through the hospitable friendship of our acquaintance.

One fair morning I was surprised by the sudden entrance into our counting-room of Mr. Alexander Wilson, the celebrated author of the "American Ornithology," of whose existence I had never until that moment been apprised. This happened in March 1810. How well do I remember him, as he then walked up to me! His long, rather hooked nose, the keenness of his eyes, and his prominent cheek-bones, stamped his countenance with a peculiar character. His dress, too, was of a kind not usually seen in that part of the country; a short coat, trowsers, and a waistcoat of grey cloth. His stature was not above the middle size. He had two volumes under his arm, and as he approached the table at which I was working, I thought I discovered something like astonishment in his countenance. He, however, immediately proceeded to disclose the object of his visit, which was to procure subscriptions for his work. He opened his books, explained the nature of his occupations, and requested my patronage.

I felt surprised and gratified at the sight of his volumes, turned over a few of the plates, and had already taken a pen to write my name in his favour, when my partner rather abruptly said to me in French, "My dear Audubon, what induces you to subscribe to this work? Your drawings are certainly far better, and again, you must know as much of the habits of American birds as this gentleman." Whether Mr. Wilson understood French or not, or if the suddenness with which I paused, disappointed him, I cannot tell; but I clearly perceived that he was not pleased. Vanity and the encomiums of my friend prevented me from subscribing. Mr. Wilson asked me if I had many drawings of birds. I rose, took down a large portfolio, laid it on the table, and showed him, as I would show any other person fond of such subjects, the whole of the contents, with the same patience with which he had shown me his own engravings.

His surprise appeared great, as he told me he never had the most distant idea that any other individual than himself had been engaged in forming such a collection. He asked me if it was my intention to publish, and when I answered in the negative, his surprise seemed to increase. And, truly, such was not my intention; for, until long after, when I met the Prince of Musignano in Philadelphia, I had not the least idea of presenting the fruits of my labours to the world. Mr. Wilson now examined my drawings with care, asked if I should have any objections to lending him a few during his stay, to which I replied that I had none: he then bade me good morning, not, however, until I had made arrangement to explore the woods in the vicinity along with him, and had promised to procure for him some birds, of which I had drawings in my collection, but which he had never seen.

It happened that he lodged in the same house with us, but his retired habits, I thought, exhibited either a strong feeling of discontent, or a decided melancholy. The Scotch airs which he played sweetly on his flute made me melancholy too, and I felt for him. I presented him to my wife and friends, and seeing that he was all enthusiasm, exerted myself as much as was in my power, to procure for him the specimens which he wanted. We hunted together, and obtained birds which he had never before seen; but I did not subscribe to his work, for, even at that time, my collection was greater than his. Thinking that perhaps he might be pleased to publish the result of my researches, I offered them to him, merely on condition that what I had drawn, or might afterwards draw and send to him, should be mentioned in his work, as coming from my pencil. I at the same time offered to open a correspondence with him, which I thought might prove beneficial to us both. He made no reply to either proposal, and before many days had elapsed, left Louisville, on his way to New Orleans, little knowing how much his talents were appreciated in our little town, at least by myself and my friends.

Some time elapsed, during which I never heard of him, or of his work. At length, having occasion to go to Philadelphia, I, immediately after my arrival there, inquired for him, and paid him a visit. He was then drawing a White-headed Eagle. He received me with civility, and took me to the Exhibition Rooms of Rembrandt Peale, the artist, who had then portrayed Napoleon crossing the Alps. Mr. Wilson spoke not of birds or drawings. Feeling, as I was forced to do, that my company was not agreeable, I parted from him; and after that I never saw him again. But judge of my astonishment some time after, when, on reading the thirty-ninth page of the ninth volume of American Ornithology, I found in it the following paragraph:

> "*March 23d,* 1810.—I bade adieu to Louisville, to which place I had four letters of recommendation, and was taught to expect much of every thing there; but neither received one act of civility from those to whom I was recommended, one subscriber, nor one new bird; though I delivered my letters, ransacked the woods repeatedly, and visited all the characters likely to subscribe. Science or literature has not one friend in this place."

The Eccentric Naturalist

"WHAT an odd looking fellow!" said I to myself, as while walking by the river, I observed a man landing from a boat, with what I thought a bundle of dried clover on his back; "how the boatmen stare at him! surely he must be an original!" He ascended with a rapid step, and approaching me, asked if I could point out the house in which Mr. Audubon resided. "Why, I am the man," said I, "and will gladly lead you to my dwelling."

The traveller rubbed his hands together with delight, and drawing a letter from his pocket, handed it to me without any remark. I broke the seal and read as follows: "My dear Audubon, I send you an odd fish, which you may prove to be undescribed, and hope you will do so in your next letter. Believe me always your friend B." With all the simplicity of a woodsman I asked the bearer where the odd fish was, when M. de T. (for, kind reader, the individual in my presence was none else than that renowned naturalist) smiled, rubbed his hands, and with the greatest good humour said, "I am that odd fish I presume, Mr. Audubon." I felt confounded and blushed, but contrived to stammer an apology.

We soon reached the house, when I presented my learned guest to my family, and was ordering a servant to go to the boat for M. de T.'s luggage, when he told me he had none but what he brought on his back. He then loosened the pack of weeds which had first drawn my attention. The ladies were a little surprised, but I checked their critical glances for the moment. The naturalist pulled off his shoes, and while engaged in drawing his stockings, not up, but down, in order to cover the holes about the heels, told us in the gayest mood imaginable that he had walked a great distance, and had only taken a passage on board the *ark*, to be put on this shore, and that he was sorry his apparel had suffered so much from his late journey. Clean clothes were offered, but he would not accept them, and it was with evident reluctance that he performed the lavations usual on such occasions before he sat down to dinner.

At table, however, his agreeable conversation made us all forget his singular appearance; and, indeed, it was only as we strolled together in the garden that his attire struck me as exceedingly remarkable. A long loose coat of yellow nankeen, much the worse of the many rubs it had got in its time, and stained all over with the juice of plants, hung loosely about him like a sack. A waistcoat of the same, with enormous pockets, and buttoned up to the chin, reached below over a pair of tight pantaloons, the lower parts of which were buttoned down to the ancles. His beard was as long as I have known my own to be during some of my peregrinations, and his lank black hair hung loosely over his shoulders. His forehead was so broad and prominent that any tyro in phrenology would instantly have pronounced it the residence of a mind of strong powers. His words impressed an assurance of rigid truth, and as he directed the conversation to the study of the natural sciences, I listened to him with as much delight as Telemachus could have listened to Mentor. He had come to visit me, he said, expressly for the purpose of seeing my drawings, having been told that my representations of birds were accompanied with those of shrubs and plants, and he was desirous of knowing whether I might chance to have in my collection any with which he was unacquainted. I observed some degree of impatience in his request to be allowed at once to see what I had. We returned to the house, when I opened my portfolios and laid them before him.

He chanced to turn over the drawing of a plant quite new to him. After inspecting it closely, he shook his head, and told me no such plant existed in nature;—for M. de T., although a highly scientific man, was suspicious to a fault, and believed such plants only to exist as he had himself seen, or such as, having been discovered of old, had, according to Father Malebranche's expression, acquired a "venerable beard." I told my guest that the plant was common in the immediate neighbourhood, and that I should show it him on the morrow. "And why to-morrow, Mr. Audubon? let us go now." We did so, and on reaching the bank of the river, I pointed to the plant. I thought M. de T. had gone mad. He plucked the plants one after an other, danced, hugged me in his arms, and exultingly told me that he had got, not merely a new species, but a new genus. When we returned home, the naturalist opened the bundle which he had brought on his back, and took out a journal rendered water-proof by means of a leather case, together with a small parcel of linen, examined the new plant, and wrote its description. The examination of my drawings then went on. You would be pleased to hear his criticisms, which were of the greatest advantage to me, for, being well acquainted with books as well as with nature, he was well fitted to give me advice.

It was summer, and the heat was so great that the windows were all open. The light of the candles attracted many insects, among which was observed a large species of Scarabæus. I caught one, and, aware of his inclination to believe only what he should himself see, I showed him the insect, and assured him it was so strong that it would crawl on the table with the candlestick on its back. "I should like to see the experiment made, Mr. Audubon," he replied. Accordingly it was made, and the insect moved about, dragging its burden so as to make the candlestick change its position as if by magic, until coming upon the edge of the table, it dropped on the floor, took to wing, and made its escape.

When it waxed late, I showed him to the apartment intended for him during his stay, and endeavoured to render him comfortable, leaving him writing materials in abundance. I was indeed heartily glad to have a naturalist under my roof. We had all retired to rest. Every person I imagined was in deep slumber save myself, when of a sudden I heard a great uproar in the naturalist's room. I got up, reached the place in a few moments, and opened the door, when, to my astonishment I saw my guest running about the room naked, holding the handle of my favorite violin, the body of which he had battered to pieces against the walls in attempting to kill the bats which had entered by the open window, probably attracted by the insects flying around his candle. I stood amazed, but he continued jumping and running round and round, until he was fairly exhausted: when he begged me to procure one of the animals for him, as he felt convinced they belonged to "a new species." Although I was convinced of the contrary, I took up the bow of my demolished Cremona, and administering a smart tap to each of the bats as it came up, soon got specimens enough. The war ended, I again bade him good night, but could not help observing the state of the room. It was strewed with plants, which it would seem he had arranged into groups, but which were now scattered about in confusion. "Never mind, Mr. Audubon," quoth the eccentric naturalist, "never mind, I'll soon arrange them again. I have the bats, and that's enough."

Several days passed, during which we followed our several occupations. M. de T. searched the woods for plants, and I for birds. He also followed the margins of the Ohio, and picked up many shells, which he greatly extolled. With us, I told him, they were gathered into heaps to be converted into lime. "Lime! Mr. Audubon; why, they are worth a guinea a piece in any part of Europe." One day, as I was returning from a hut in a cane-brake, he observed that I was wet and spattered with mud, and desired me to show him the interior of one of these places, which he said he had never visited.

The Cane formerly grew spontaneously over the greater portions of the State of Kentucky and other western districts of our Union, as well as in many farther south. Now, however, cultivation, the introduction of cattle and horses, and other circumstances connected with the progress of civilization, have greatly altered the face of the country, and reduced the cane within comparatively small limits. It attains a height of from twelve to thirty feet, and a diameter of from one to two inches, and grows in great patches resembling osier-holts, in which occur plants of all sizes. The plants frequently grow so close together, and in course of time become so tangled, as to present an almost impenetrable thicket. A portion of ground thus covered with canes is called a *Cane-brake*.

If you picture to yourself one of these cane-brakes growing beneath the gigantic trees that form our western forests, interspersed with vines of many species, and numberless plants of every description, you may conceive how difficult it is for one to make his way through it, especially after a heavy shower of rain or a fall of sleet, when the traveller, in forcing his way through, shakes down upon himself such quantities of water, as soon reduce him to a state of the utmost discomfort. The hunters often cut little paths through the thickets with their knives, but the usual mode of passing through them is by pushing one's self backward, and wedging a way between the stems. To follow a bear or a cougar pursued by dogs through these brakes, is a task, the accomplishment of which may be imagined, but of the difficulties and dangers accompanying which I cannot easily give an adequate representation.

The canes generally grow on the richest soil, and are particularly plentiful along the margins of the great western rivers. Many of our new settlers are fond of forming farms in their immediate vicinity, as the plant is much relished by all kinds of cattle and horses, which feed upon it at all seasons, and again, because these brakes are plentifully stocked with game of various kinds. It sometimes happens that the farmer clears a portion of the brake. This is done by cutting the stems, which are fistular and knotted, like those of other grasses, with a large knife or cutlass. They are afterwards placed in heaps, and when partially dried set fire to. The moisture contained between the joints is converted into steam, which causes the cane to burst with a smart report, and when a whole mass is crackling, the sounds resemble discharges of musquetry. Indeed, I have been told that travellers floating down the rivers, and unacquainted with these circumstances, have been induced to pull their oars with redoubled rigour, apprehending the attack of a host of savages ready to scalp every one of the party.

A day being fixed, we left home after an early breakfast, crossed the

Ohio, and entered the woods. I had determined that my companion should view a cane-brake in all its perfection, and after leading him several miles in a direct course, came upon as fine a sample as existed in that part of the country. We entered, and for some time proceeded without much difficulty, as I led the way, and cut down the canes which were most likely to incommode him. The difficulties gradually increased, so that we were presently obliged to turn our backs to the foe, and push ourselves on the best way we could. My companion stopped here and there to pick up a plant and examine it. After a while we chanced to come upon the top of a fallen tree, which so obstructed our passage that we were on the eve of going round, instead of thrusting ourselves through amongst the branches, when from its bed, in the centre of the tangled mass, forth rushed a bear, with such force, and snuffing the air in so frightful a manner, that M. de T. became suddenly terrorstruck, and, in his haste to escape, made a desperate attempt to run, but fell amongst the canes in such a way, that he looked as if pinioned. Perceiving him jammed in between the stalks, and thoroughly frightened, I could not refrain from laughing at the ridiculous exhibition which he made. My gaiety, however, was not very pleasing to the savant, who called out for aid, which was at once administered. Gladly would he have retraced his steps, but I was desirous that he should be able to describe a cane-brake, and enticed him to follow me, by telling him that our worst difficulties were nearly over. We proceeded, for by this time the bear was out of hearing.

The way became more and more tangled. I saw with delight that a heavy cloud, portentous of a thunder gust, was approaching. In the mean time, I kept my companion in such constant difficulties, that he now panted, perspired, and seemed almost overcome by fatigue. The thunder began to rumble, and soon after a dash of heavy rain drenched us in a few minutes. The withered particles of leaves and bark attached to the cane stuck to our clothes. We received many scratches from briars, and now and then a twitch from a nettle. M. de T. seriously inquired if we should ever get alive out of the horrible situation in which we were. I spoke of courage and patience, and told him I hoped we should soon get to the margin of the brake, which, however, I knew to be two miles distant. I made him rest, and gave him a mouthful of brandy from my flask; after which we proceeded on our slow and painful march. He threw away all his plants, emptied his pockets of the fungi, lichens, and mosses which he had thrust into them, and finding himself much lightened, went on for thirty or forty yards with a better grace. But, enough—I led the naturalist first one way, then another, until I had nearly lost myself in the brake, although I was well acquainted with it, kept him tumbling and crawling on his hands and knees, until long after mid-day, when we at length reached the edge of the river. I blew my horn, and soon showed my companion a boat coming to our rescue. We were ferried over, and, on reaching the house, found more agreeable occupation in replenishing our empty coffers.

M. de T. remained with us for three weeks, and collected multitudes of plants, shells, bats, and fishes, but never again expressed a desire of visiting a cane-brake. We were perfectly reconciled to his oddities, and, finding him a most agreeable and intelligent companion, hoped that his sojourn might be of long duration. But, one evening when tea was prepared, and we expected him to join the family, he was nowhere to be found. His grasses and other valuables were all removed from his room. The night was spent in searching for him in the neighbourhood. No eccentric naturalist could be discovered. Whether he had perished in a swamp, or had been devoured by a bear or a gar-fish, or had taken to his heels, were matters of conjecture; nor was it until some weeks after that a letter from him, thanking us for our attention, assured me of his safety.

The Prairie

On my return from the Upper Mississippi, I found myself obliged to cross one of the wide Prairies, which, in that portion of the United States vary the appearance of the country. The weather was fine, all around me was as fresh and blooming as if it had just issued from the bosom of nature. My knapsack, my gun, and my dog, were all I had for baggage and company. But, although well moccasined, I moved slowly along, attracted by the brilliancy of the flowers, and the gambols of the fawns around their dams, to all appearance as thoughtless of danger as I felt myself.

My march was of long duration; I saw the sun sinking beneath the horizon long before I could perceive any appearance of woodland, and nothing in the shape of man had I met with that day. The track which I followed was only an old Indian trace, and as darkness overshadowed the prairie, I felt some desire to reach at least a copse, in which I might lie down to rest. The Night-hawks were skimming over and around me, attracted by the buzzing wings of the beetles which form their food, and the distant howling of wolves gave me some hope that I should soon arrive at the skirts of some woodland.

I did so, and almost at the same instant a fire-light attracting my eye, I moved towards it, full of confidence that it proceeded from the camp of some wandering Indians. I was mistaken:—I discovered by its glare that it was from the hearth of a small log cabin, and that a tall figure passed and repassed between it and me, as if busily engaged in household arrangements.

I reached the spot, and presenting myself at the door, asked the tall figure, which proved to be a woman, if I might take shelter under her roof for the night. Her voice was gruff, and her attire negligently thrown about her. She answered in the affirmative. I walked in, took a wooden stool, and quietly seated myself by the fire. The next object that attracted my notice was a finely formed young Indian, resting his head between his hands, with his elbows on his knees. A long bow rested against the log wall near him, while a quantity of arrows and two or three raccoon skins lay at his feet. He moved not; he apparently breathed not. Accustomed to the habits of the Indians, and knowing that they pay little attention to the approach of civilized strangers (a circumstance which in some countries is considered as evincing the apathy of their character), I addressed him in French, a language not unfrequently partially known to the people in that neighborhood. He raised his head, pointed to one of his eyes with his finger, and gave me a significant glance with the other. His face was covered with blood. The fact was, that an hour before this, as he was in the act of discharging an arrow at a raccoon in the top of a tree, the arrow had split upon the cord, and sprung back with such violence into his right eye as to destroy it for ever.

Feeling hungry, I inquired what sort of fare I might expect. Such a thing as a bed was not to be seen, but many large untanned bear and buffalo hides lay piled in a corner. I drew a fine time-piece from my breast, and told the woman that it was late, and that I was fatigued. She had espyed my watch, the richness of which seemed to operate upon her feelings with electric quickness. She told me that there was plenty of venison and jerked buffalo meat, and that on removing the ashes I should find a cake. But my watch had struck her fancy, and her curiosity had to be gratified by an immediate sight of it. I took off the gold chain that secured it from around my neck, and presented it to her. She was all ecstasy, spoke of its beauty, asked me its value, and put the chain round her brawny neck, saying how happy the possession of such a watch should make her. Thoughtless, and, as I fancied myself, in so retired a spot, secure, I paid little attention to her talk or her movements. I helped my dog to a good supper of venison, and was not long in satisfying the demands of my own appetite.

The Indian rose from his seat, as if in extreme suffering. He passed and repassed me several times, and once pinched me on the side so violently, that the pain nearly brought forth an exclamation of anger. I looked at him. His eye met mine; but his look was so forbidding, that it struck a chill into the more nervous part of my system. He again seated himself, drew his butcher-knife from its greasy scabbard, examined its edge, as I would do that of a razor suspected dull, replaced it, and again taking his tomahawk from his back, filled the pipe of it with tobacco, and sent me expressive glances whenever our hostess chanced to have her back towards us.

Never until that moment had my senses been awakened to the danger which I now suspected to be about me. I returned glance for glance to my companion, and rested well assured that, whatever enemies I might have, he was not of their number.

I asked the woman for my watch, wound it up, and under pretence of wishing to see how the weather might probably be on the morrow, took up my gun, and walked out of the cabin. I slipped a ball into each barrel, scraped the edges of my flints, renewed the primings, and returning to the hut, gave a favourable account of my observations. I took a few bearskins, made a pallet of them, and calling my faithful dog to my side, lay down, with my gun close to my body, and in a few minutes was, to all appearance, fast asleep.

A short time had elapsed, when some voices were heard, and from the corner of my eyes I saw two athletic youths making their entrance, bearing a dead stag on a pole. They disposed of their burden, and asking for whisky, helped themselves freely to it. Observing me and the wounded Indian, they asked who I was, and why the devil that rascal (meaning the Indian, who, they knew, understood not a word of English) was in the house. The mother—for so she proved to be, bade them speak less loudly, made mention of my watch, and took them to a corner, where a conversation took place, the purport of which it required little shrewdness in me to guess. I tapped my dog gently. He moved his tail, and with indescribable pleasure I saw his fine eyes alternately fixed on me and raised towards the trio in the corner. I felt that he perceived danger in my situation. The Indian exchanged a last glance with me.

The lads had eaten and drunk themselves into such condition, that I already looked upon them as *hors de combat;* and the frequent visits of the whisky bottle to the ugly mouth of their dam I hoped would soon reduce her to a like state. Judge of my astonishment, reader, when I saw this incarnate fiend take a large carving-knife, and go to the grindstone to whet its edge. I saw her pour the water on the turning machine, and watched her working away with the dangerous instrument, until the sweat covered every part of my body, in despite of my determination to defend myself to the last. Her task finished, she walked to her reeling sons, and said, "There, that'll soon settle him! Boys, kill yon———, and then for the watch."

I turned, cocked my gun-locks silently, touched my faithful companion, and lay ready to start up and shoot the first who might attempt my life. The moment was fast approaching, and that night might have been my last in this world, had not Providence made preparations for my rescue. All was ready. The infernal hag was advancing slowly, probably contemplating the best way of despatching me, whilst her sons should be engaged with the Indian. I was several times on the eve of rising and shooting her on the spot:—but she was not to be punished thus. The door was suddenly opened, and there entered two stout travellers, each with a long rifle on his shoulder. I bounced up on my feet, and making them most heartily welcome, told them how well it was for me that they should have arrived at that moment. The tale was told in a minute. The drunken sons were secured, and the woman, in spite of her defence and vociferations, shared the same fate. The Indian fairly danced with joy, and gave us to understand that, as he could not sleep for pain, he would watch over us. You may suppose we slept much less than we talked. The two strangers gave me an account of their once having been themselves in a somewhat similar situation. Day came, fair and rosy, and with it the punishment of our captives.

They were now quite sobered. Their feet were unbound, but their arms were still securely tied. We marched them into the woods off the road, and having used them as Regulators were wont to use such delinquents, we set fire to the cabin, gave all the skins and implements to the young Indian warrior, and proceeded, well pleased, towards the settlements.

During upwards of twenty-five years, when my wanderings extended to all parts of our country, this was the only time at which my life was in danger from my fellow creatures. Indeed, so little risk do travellers run in the United States, that no one born there ever dreams of any to be encountered on the road; and I can only account for this occurrence by supposing that the inhabitants of the cabin were not Americans.

Will you believe, reader, that not many miles from the place where this adventure happened, and where fifteen years ago, no habitation belonging to civilized man was expected, and very few ever seen, large roads are now laid out, cultivation has converted the woods into fertile fields, taverns have been erected, and much of what we Americans call comfort is to be met with. So fast does improvement proceed in our abundant and free country.

The Earthquake

TRAVELLING through the Barrens of Kentucky (of which I shall give you an account elsewhere) in the month of November, I was jogging on one afternoon, when I remarked a sudden and strange darkness rising from the western horizon. Accustomed to our heavy storms of thunder and rain, I took no more notice of it, as I thought the speed of my horse might enable me to get under shelter of the roof of an acquaintance, who lived not far distant, before it should come up. I had proceeded about a mile, when I heard what I imagined to be the distant rumbling of a violent tornado, on which I spurred my steed, with a wish to gallop as fast as possible to the place of shelter; but it would not do, the animal knew better than I what was forthcoming, and, instead of going faster, so nearly stopped, that I remarked he placed one foot after another on the ground with as much precaution as if walking on a smooth sheet of ice. I thought he had suddenly foundered, and, speaking to him, was on the point of dismounting and leading him, when he all of a sudden fell a-groaning piteously, hung his head, spread out his four legs, as if to save himself from falling, and stood stock still, continuing to groan. I thought my horse was about to die, and would have sprung from his back had a minute more elapsed, but at that instant all the shrubs and trees began to move from their very roots, the ground rose and fell in successive furrows, like the ruffled waters of a lake, and I became bewildered in my ideas, as I too plainly discovered that all this awful commotion in nature was the result of an earthquake.

I had never witnessed any thing of the kind before, although, like every other person, I knew of earthquakes by description. But what is description compared with the reality? Who can tell of the sensations which I experienced when I found myself rocking as it were on my horse, and with him moved to and fro like a child in a cradle, with the most imminent danger around, and expecting the ground every moment to open, and present to my eye such an abyss as might engulf myself and all around me? The fearful convulsion, however, lasted only a few minutes, and the heavens again brightened as quickly as they had become obscured; my horse brought his feet to the natural position, raised his head, and galloped off as if loose and frolicking without a rider.

I was not, however, without great apprehension respecting my family, from which I was yet many miles distant, fearful that where they were the shock might have caused greater havoc than I had witnessed. I gave the bridle to my steed, and was glad to see him appear as anxious to get home as myself. The pace at which he galloped accomplished this sooner than I had expected, and I found, with much pleasure, that hardly any greater harm had taken place than the apprehension excited for my own safety.

Shock succeeded shock almost every day or night for several weeks, diminishing, however, so gradually as to dwindle away into the mere vibrations of the earth. Strange to say, I for one became so accustomed to the feeling as rather to enjoy the fears manifested by others. I never can forget the effects of one of the slighter shocks which took place when I was at a friend's house, where I had gone to enjoy the merriment that, in our western country, attends a wedding. The ceremony being performed, supper over, and the fiddles tuned, dancing became the order of the moment. This was merrily followed up to a late hour, when the party retired to rest. We were in what is called, with great propriety, a Log-house, one of large dimensions, and solidly constructed. The owner was a physician, and in one corner were not only his lancets, tourniquets, amputating-knives, and other sanguinary apparatus, but all the drugs which he employed for the relief of his patients, arranged in jars and phials of different sizes. These had some days before made a narrow escape from destruction, but had been fortunately preserved by closing the doors of the cases in which they were contained.

As I have said, we had all retired to rest, some to dream of sighs and smiles, and others to sink into oblivion. Morning was fast approaching, when the rumbling noise that precedes the earthquake began so loudly, as to waken and alarm the whole party, and drive them out of bed in the greatest consternation. The scene which ensued it is impossible for me to describe, and it would require the humorous pencil of Cruickshank to do justice to it. Fear knows no restraints. Every person, old and young, filled with alarm at the creaking of the log-house, and apprehending instant destruction, rushed wildly out to the grass enclosure fronting the building. The full moon was slowly descending from her throne, covered at times by clouds that rolled heavily along, as if to conceal from her view the scenes of terror which prevailed on the earth below. On the grassplat we all met, in such condition as rendered it next to impossible to discriminate any of the party, all huddled together in a state of almost perfect nudity. The earth waved like a field of corn before the breeze: the birds left their perches, and flew about not knowing whither; and the Doctor, recollecting the danger of his gallipots, ran to his shop-room, to prevent their dancing off the shelves to the floor. Never for a moment did he think of closing the doors, but spreading his arms, jumped about the front of the cases, pushing back here and there the falling jars; with so little success, however, that before the shock was over, he had lost nearly all he possessed.

The shock at length ceased, and the frightened females, now sensible of their dishabille, fled to their several apartments. The earthquakes produced more serious consequences in other places. Near New Madrid, and for some distance on the Mississippi, the earth was rent asunder in several places, one or two islands sunk for ever, and the inhabitants fled in dismay towards the eastern shores.

A Racoon Hunt in Kentucky

THE Racoon, which is a cunning and crafty animal, is found in all our woods, so that its name is familiar to every child in the Union. The propensity which it evinces to capture all kinds of birds accessible to it in its nightly prowlings, for the purpose of feasting on their flesh, induces me to endeavour to afford you some idea of the pleasure which our western hunters feel in procuring it. With your leave, then, Reader, I will take you to a "Coon Hunt."

A few hours ago the sun went down far beyond the "far west." The woodland choristers have disappeared, the matron has cradled her babe, and betaken herself to the spinning-wheel; the woodsman, his sons, and "the stranger" are chatting before a blazing fire, making wise reflections on past events, and anticipating those that are to come. Autumn, sallow and sad, prepares to bow her head to the keen blast of approaching winter; the corn, though still on its stalk, has lost its blades; the wood pile is as large as the woodsman's cabin; the nights have become chill, and each new morn has effected a gradual change in the dews, which now crust the withered herbage with a coat of glittering white. The sky is still cloudless; a thousand twinkling stars reflect their light from the tranquil waters; all is silent and calm in the forest, save the nightly prowlers that roam in its recesses. In the cheerful cabin all is happiness; its inmates generously strive to contribute to the comfort of the stranger who has chanced to visit them; and, as racoons are abundant in the neighbourhood, they propose a hunt. The offer is gladly accepted. The industrious woman leaves her wheel, for she has listened to her husband's talk; now she approaches the fire, takes up the board shovel, stirs the embers, produces a basket filled with sweet potatoes, arranges its contents side by side in front of the hearth, and covers them with hot ashes and glowing coals. All this she does, because she "guesses" that hungry stomachs will be calling for food when the sport is over. Ah! Reader, what "homely joys" there are in such scenes, and how you would enjoy them! The rich may produce a better, or a more sumptuous meal; but his feelings can never be like those of the poor woodsman. Poor I ought not to call him, for nature and industry bountifully supply all his wants; the woods and rivers produce his chief dainties, and his toils are his pleasures.

Now mark him! the bold Kentuckian is on his feet; his sons and the stranger prepare for the march. Horns and rifles are in requisition. The good man opens the wooden-hinged door, and sends forth a blast loud enough to scare a wolf. The racoons scamper away from the cornfields, break through the fences, and hie to the woods. The hunter has taken an axe from the wood-pile, and returning, assures us that the night is clear, and that we shall have rare sport. He blows through his rifle, to ascertain that it is clear, examines his flint, and thrusts a feather into the touchhole. To a leathern bag swung at his side is attached a powder-horn; his sheathed knife is there also; below hangs a narrow strip of home-spun linen. He takes from his bag a bullet, pulls with his teeth the wooden stopper from his powder-horn, lays the ball on one hand, and with the other pours the powder upon it until it is just overtopped. Raising the horn to his mouth, he again closes it with the stopper, and restores it to its place. He introduces the powder into the tube; springs the box of his gun, greases the "patch" over with some melted tallow, or damps it; then places it on the honeycombed muzzle of his piece. The bullet is placed on the patch over the bore, and pressed with the handle of the knife, which now trims the edges of the linen. The elastic hickory rod, held with both hands, smoothly pushes the ball to its bed: once, twice, thrice has it rebounded. The rifle leaps as it were into the hunter's arms, the feather is drawn from the touch-hole, the powder fills the pan, which is closed. "Now I'm ready," cries the woodsman. His companions say the same. Hardly more than a minute has elapsed. I wish, Reader, you had seen this fine fellow—but hark! the dogs are barking.

All is now bustle within and without: a servant lights a torch, and off we march to the woods. "Don't mind the boys, my dear sir," says the woodsman, "follow me close, for the ground is covered with logs, and the grape vines hang everywhere across." "Toby, hold up the light, man, or we'll never see the gullies." "Trail your gun, sir, as General Clark used to say,—not so, but this way—that's it; now then, no danger you see; no fear of snakes, poor things! They are stiff enough, I'll be bound. The dogs have treed one. Toby, you old fool, why don't you turn to the right—not so much there—go a-head, and give us light— What's that?— Who's there?— Ah, you young rascals! you've played us a trick, have you. It's all well enough, but now, just keep behind, or I'll"——
—and in fact, the boys, with eyes good enough to see in the dark, al-

though not quite so well as an Owl's, had cut directly across the dogs, which had surprised a racoon on the ground and bayed it, until the lads knocked it on the head. "Seek him, boys," cries the hunter. —The dogs, putting their noses to the ground, pushed off at a good rate. "Master, they're making for the creek," says old Toby. On towards it therefore we push. What woods, to be sure! No gentleman's park this, I assure you, Reader. We are now in a low flat; the soil thinly covers the hard clay; nothing but beech trees hereabouts, unless now and then a maple. Hang the limbs! say I—hang the supple-jacks too—here I am, fast by the neck—cut it with your knife. My knee has had a tremendous rub against a log—now, my foot is jammed between two roots—and here I stick. "Toby, come back—don't you know the stranger is not up to the woods? Halloo, Toby, Toby!" There I stood perfectly shackled, the hunter laughing heartily, and the lads glad of an opportunity of slipping off. Toby arrived, and held the torch near the ground, on which the hunter cutting one of the roots with his hatchet, set me free. "Are you hurt, Sir?"—no, not in the least. Off we start again. The boys had got up with the dogs, which were baying a Racoon in a small puddle. We soon joined them with the light. "Now, stranger! watch and see!" The Racoon was all but swimming, and yet had hold of the bottom of the pool with his feet. The glare of the lighted torch was doubtless distressing to him; his coat was ruffled, and his rounded tail seemed thrice its ordinary size, his eyes shone like emeralds; with foaming jaws he watched the dogs, ready to seize each by the snout if it came within reach. They kept him busy for several minutes; the water became thick with mud; his coat now hung dripping, and his draggled tail lay floating on the surface. His guttural growlings, in place of intimidating his assailants, excited them the more; and they very unceremoniously closed upon him, curs as they were, and without the breeding of gentle dogs! One seized him by the rump and tugged, but was soon forced to let go; another stuck to his side, but soon taking a better directed bite of his muzzle than another dog had just done of his tail, coon made him yelp; and pitiful were the cries of luckless Tyke. The Racoon would not let go, but in the mean time the other dogs seized him fast, and worried him to death, yet to the last he held by his antagonist's snout. Knocked on the head by an axe, he lay gasping his last breath, and the heaving of his chest was painful to see. The hunters stood gazing at him in the pool, while all around was by the flare of the torch rendered trebly dark and dismal. It was a good scene for a skilful painter.

We had now two coons, whose furs were worth two quarters of a dollar, and whose bodies, which I must not forget, as Toby informed us, would produce two more. "What now?" I asked— "What now?" quoth the father, "why go after more to be sure." So we did, the dogs ahead, and I far behind. In a short time the curs treed another, and when we came up, we found them seated on their haunches, looking upwards, and barking. The hunters now employed their axes, and sent the chips about at such a rate that one of them coming in contact with my cheek marked it so, that a week after several of my friends asked me where, in the name of wonder, I had got that black eye. At length the tree began to crack, and slowly leaning to one side, the heavy mass swung rustling through the air, and fell to the earth with a crash. It was not one coon that was surprised here, but three—aye three of them, one of which, more crafty than the rest, leaped fairly from the main top while the tree was staggering. The other two stuck to the hollow of a branch, from which they were soon driven by one of the dogs. Tyke and Lion having nosed the cunning old one, scampered after him, not mouthing like the well-trained hounds of our southern fox hunters, but yelling like furies. The hunter's sons attacked those on the tree, while the woodsman and I, preceeded by Toby, made after the other; and busy enough we all were. Our animal was of extraordinary size, and after some parley, a rifle ball was sent through his brain. He reeled once only,—next moment he lay dead. The rest were dispatched by the axe and the club, for a shot in those days was too valuable to be spent when it could be saved. It could procure a deer, and therefore was worth more than a coon's skin.

Now, look at the moon! how full and clear has she risen on the Racoon hunters! Now is the time for sport! Onward we go, one following the long shadow of his precursor. The twigs are no impediment, and we move at a brisker pace, as we return to the hills. What a hue and cry!— here are the dogs. Overhead and all around, on the forks of each tree, the hunter's keen eye searches for something round, which is likely to prove a coiled up Racoon. There's one! Between me and the moon I spied the cunning thing crouched in silence. After taking aim, I raise my barrel ever so little, the trigger is pressed; down falls the Racoon to the ground. Another and another are on the same tree. Off goes a bullet, then a second; and we secure the prey. "Let us go home, stranger," says the woodsman; and contented with our sport, towards his cabin we trudge. On arriving there, we find a cheerful fire. Toby stays without, prepares the game, stretches the skins on a frame of cane, and washes the bodies. The table is already set; the cake and the potatoes are all well done; four bowls of butter-milk are ranged in order; and now the hunters fall to.

The Racoon is a cunning animal, and makes a pleasant pet. Monkey-like, it is quite dexterous in the use of its fore feet, and it will amble after its master, in the manner of a bear, and even follow him into the street. It is fond of eggs, but prefers them raw, and it matters not whether it be morning, noon, or night, when it finds a dozen in the pheasant's nest, or one placed in your pocket to please him. He knows the habits of mussels better than most conchologists. Being an expert climber, he ascends to the hole of the woodpecker, and devours the young birds. He knows, too, how to watch the soft-shelled turtle's crawl, and, better still, how to dig up her eggs. Now by the edge of the pond, grimalkin-like, he lies seemingly asleep, until the summer-duck comes within reach. No Negro knows better when the corn is juicy and pleasant to eat; and although squirrels and woodpeckers know this too, the Racoon is found in the cornfield longer in the season than any of them, the havoc he commits there amounting to a tithe. His fur is good in winter, and many think his flesh good also; but for my part I prefer a live Racoon to a dead one, and should find more pleasure in hunting one than in eating him.

Pitting of the Wolves

THERE seems to be a universal feeling of hostility among men against the Wolf, whose strength, agility, and cunning, which latter is scarcely inferior to that of his relative master Reynard, tend to render him an object of hatred, especially to the husbandman, on whose flocks he is ever apt to commit depredations. In America, where this animal was formerly abundant, and in many parts of which it still occurs in considerable numbers, it is not more mercifully dealt with than in other parts of the world. Traps and snares of all sorts are set for catching it, while dogs and horses are trained for hunting the Fox. The Wolf, however, unless in some way injured, being more powerful and perhaps better winded than the Fox, is rarely pursued with hounds or any other dogs in the open chase; but as his depredations are at times extensive and highly injurious to the farmer, the greatest exertions have been used to exterminate his race. Few instances have occurred among us of any attack made by Wolves on man, and only one has come under my own notice.

Two young Negroes who resided near the banks of the Ohio, in the lower part of the State of Kentucky, about twenty-three years ago, had sweethearts living on a plantation ten miles distant. After the labours of the day were over, they frequently visited the fair ladies of their choice, the nearest way to whose dwelling lay directly across a great cane brake. As to the lover every moment is precious, they usually took this route, to save time. Winter had commenced, cold, dark, and forbidding, and after sunset scarcely a glimpse of light or glow of warmth, one might imagine, could be found in that dreary swamp, excepting in the eyes and bosoms of the ardent youths, or the hungry Wolves that prowled about. The snow covered the earth, and rendered them more easy to be scented from a distance by the famished beasts. Prudent in a certain degree, the young lovers carried their axes on their shoulders, and walked as briskly as the narrow path would allow. Some transient glimpses of light now and then met their eyes, but so faint were they that they believed them to be caused by their faces coming in contact with the slender reeds covered with snow. Suddenly, however, a long and frightful howl burst upon them, and they instantly knew that it proceeded from a troop of hungry, perhaps desperate Wolves. They stopped, and putting themselves in an attitude of defence, awaited the result. All around was dark, save a few feet of snow, and the silence of night was dismal. Nothing could be done to better their situation, and after standing a few minutes in expectation of an attack, they judged it best to resume their march; but no sooner had they replaced their axes on their shoulders, and begun to move, than the foremost found himself assailed by several foes. His legs were held fast as if pressed by a powerful screw, and the torture inflicted by the fangs of the ravenous animal was for a moment excruciating. Several Wolves in the mean time sprung upon the breast of the other Negro, and dragged him to the ground. Both struggled manfully against their foes; but in a short time one of them ceased to move, and the other, reduced in strength, and perhaps despairing of maintaining his ground, still more of aiding his unfortunate companion, sprung to the branch of a tree, and speedily gained a place of safety near the top. The next morning, the mangled remains of his comrade lay scattered around on the snow, which was stained with blood. Three dead wolves lay around, but the rest of the pack had disappeared, and Scipio, sliding to the ground, took up the axes, and made the best of his way home, to relate the sad adventure.

About two years after this occurrence, as I was travelling between Henderson and Vincennes, I chanced to stop for the night at a farmer's house by the side of a road. After putting up my horse and refreshing myself, I entered into conversation with mine host, who asked if I should like to pay a visit to the wolf-pits, which were about half a mile distant. Glad of the opportunity I accompanied him across the fields to the neighbourhood of a deep wood, and soon saw the engines of destruction. He had three pits, within a few hundred yards of each other. They were about eight feet deep, and broader at bottom, so as to render it impossible for the most active animal to escape from them. The aperture was covered with a revolving platform of twigs, attached to a central axis. On either surface of the platform was fastened a large piece of putrid venison, with other matters by no means pleasant to my olfactory nerves, although no doubt attractive to the wolves. My companion wished to visit them that evening, merely as he was in the habit of doing so daily, for the purpose of seeing that all was right. He said that Wolves were very abundant that autumn, and had killed nearly the whole of his sheep and one of his colts, but that he was now "paying them off in full;" and added that if I would tarry a few hours with him next morning, he would beyond a doubt shew me some sport rarely seen in those parts. We retired to rest in due time, and were up with the dawn.

"I think," said my host, "that all's right, for I see the dogs are anxious to get away to the pits, and although they are nothing but curs, their noses are none the worse for that." As he took up his gun, an axe and a large knife, the dogs began to howl and bark, and whisked around us, as if full of joy. When we reached the first pit, we found the bait all gone, and the platform much injured; but the animal that had been entrapped had scraped a subterranean passage for himself and so escaped. On peeping into the next, he assured me that "three famous fellows were safe enough" in it. I also peeped in and saw the Wolves, two black, and the other brindled, all of goodly size, sure enough. They lay flat on the earth, their ears laid close over the head, their eyes indicating fear more than anger. "But how are we to get them out?"— "How sir," said the farmer, "why by going down to be sure, and ham-stringing them." Being a novice in these matters, I begged to be merely a looker-on. "With all my heart," quoth the farmer, "stand here, and look at me through the brush." Whereupon he glided down, taking with him his axe and knife, and leaving his rifle to my care. I was not a little surprised to see the cowardice of the Wolves. He pulled out successively their hind legs, and with a side stroke of the knife cut the principal tendon above the joint, exhibiting as little fear as if he had been marking lambs.

"Lo!" exclaimed the farmer, when he had got out, "we have forgot the rope; I'll go after it." Off he went accordingly, with as much alacrity as any youngster could shew. In a short time he returned out of breath, and wiping his forehead with the back of his hand— "Now for it." I was desired to raise and hold the platform on its central balance, whilst he, with all the dexterity of an Indian, threw a noose over the neck of one of the Wolves. We hauled it up motionless with fright, as if dead, its disabled legs swinging to and fro, its jaws wide open, and the gurgle in its throat alone indicating that it was alive. Letting him drop on the ground, the farmer loosened the rope by means of a stick, and left him to the dogs, all of which set upon him with great fury and soon worried him to death. The second was dealt with in the same manner; but the third, which was probably the oldest, as it was the blackest, shewed some spirit, the moment it was left loose to the mercy of the curs. This Wolf, which we afterwards found to be a female, scuffled along on its fore legs at a surprising rate, giving a snap every now and then to the nearest dog, which went off howling dismally with a mouthful of skin torn from its side. And so well did the furious beast defend itself, that apprehensive of its escape, the farmer levelled his rifle at it, and shot it through the heart, on which the curs rushed upon it, and satiated their vengeance on the destroyer of their master's flock.

Breaking Up of the Ice

WHILE proceeding up the Mississippi above its junction with the Ohio, I found, to my great mortification, that its navigation was obstructed by ice. The chief conductor of my bark, who was a Canadian Frenchman, was therefore desired to take us to a place suitable for winter-quarters, which he accordingly did, bringing us into a great bend of the river called Tawapatee Bottom. The waters were unusually low, the thermometer indicated excessive cold, the earth all around was covered with snow, dark clouds were spread over the heavens, and as all appearances were unfavourable to the hope of a speedy prosecution of our voyage, we quietly set to work. Our bark, which was a large keel-boat, was moored close to the shore, the cargo was conveyed to the woods, large trees were felled over the water, and were so disposed as to keep off the pressure of the floating masses of ice. In less than two days, our stores, baggage, and ammunition, were deposited in a great heap under one of the magnificent trees of which the forest was here composed, our sails were spread over all, and a complete camp was formed in the wilderness. Every thing around us seemed dreary and dismal, and had we not been endowed with the faculty of deriving pleasure from the examination of nature, we should have made up our minds to pass the time in a state similar to that of bears during their hybernation. We soon found employment, however, for the woods were full of game; and deer, turkeys, racoons, and opossums might be seen even around our camp; while on the ice that now covered the broad stream rested flocks of swans, to surprise which the hungry wolves were at times seen to make energetic but unsuccessful efforts. It was curious to see the snow-white birds all lying flat on the ice, but keenly intent on watching the motions of their insidious enemies, until the latter advanced within the distance of a few hundred yards, when the swans, sounding their trumpet-notes of alarm, would all rise, spread out their broad wings, and after running some yards and battering the ice until the noise was echoed like thunder through the woods, rose exultingly into the air, leaving their pursuers to devise other schemes for gratifying their craving appetites.

The nights being extremely cold, we constantly kept up a large fire, formed of the best wood. Fine trees of ash and hickory were felled, cut up into logs of convenient size, and rolled into a pile, on the top of which, with the aid of twigs, a fire was kindled. There were about fifteen of us, some hunters, others trappers, and all more or less accustomed to live in the woods. At night, when all had returned from their hunting-grounds, some successful and others empty handed, they presented a picture in the strong glare of the huge fire that illuminated the forest, which it might prove interesting to you to see, were it copied by a bold hand on canvas. Over a space of thirty yards or more, the snow was scraped away, and piled up into a circular wall, which protected us from the cold blast. Our cooking utensils formed no mean display, and before a week had elapsed, venison, turkeys, and racoons hung on the branches in profusion. Fish, too, and that of excellent quality, often graced our board, having been obtained by breaking holes in the ice of the lakes. It was observed that the opossums issued at night from holes in the banks of the river, to which they returned about day-break; and having thus discovered their retreat, we captured many of them by means of snares.

At the end of a fortnight our bread failed, and two of the party were directed to proceed across the bend, towards a village on the western bank of the Mississippi, in quest of that commodity; for although we had a kind of substitute for it in the dry white flesh of the breast of the wild turkey, bread is bread after all, and more indispensable to civilized man than any other article of food. The expedition left the camp early one morning; one of the party boasted much of his knowledge of woods, while the other said nothing, but followed. They walked on all day, and returned next morning to the camp with empty wallets. The next attempt, however, succeeded, and they brought on a sledge a barrel of flour and some potatoes. After a while, we were joined by many Indians, the observation of whose manners afforded us much amusement.

Six weeks were spent in Tawapatee Bottom. The waters had kept continually sinking, and our boat lay on her side high and dry. On both sides of the stream, the ice had broken into heaps, forming huge walls. Our pilot visited the river daily, to see what prospect there might be of a change. One night, while, excepting himself, all were sound asleep, he suddenly roused us with loud cries of "the ice is breaking! get up, get up, down to the boat lads, bring out your axes, hurry on, or we may lose her, here let us have a torch!" Starting up, as if we had been attacked by a band of savages, we ran pell-mell to the bank. The ice was indeed breaking up; it split with reports like those of heavy artillery, and as the water had suddenly risen from an overflow of the Ohio, the two streams seemed to rush against each other with violence, in consequence of which the congealed mass was broken into large fragments, some of which rose nearly erect here and there, and again fell with thundering crash, as the wounded whale, when in the agonies of death, springs up with furious force, and again plunges into the foaming waters. To our surprise the weather, which in the evening had been calm and frosty, had become wet and blowy. The water gushed from the fissures formed in the ice, and the prospect was extremely dismal. When day dawned, a spectacle strange and fearful presented itself: the whole mass of water was violently agitated, its covering was broken into small fragments, and although not a foot of space was without ice, not a step could the most daring have ventured to make upon it. Our boat was in imminent danger, for the trees which had been placed to guard it from the ice were cut or broken into pieces, and were thrust against her. It was impossible to move her; but our pilot ordered every man to bring down great bunches of cane, which were lashed along her sides; and before these were destroyed by the ice, she was afloat and riding above it. While we were gazing on the scene, a tremendous crash was heard, which seemed to have taken place about a mile below, when suddenly the great dam of ice gave away. The current of the Mississippi had forced its way against that of the Ohio; and in less than four hours, we witnessed the complete breaking up of the ice.

During that winter, the ice was so thick on the Mississippi, that opposite St. Louis, horses and heavy waggons crossed the river. Many boats had been detained in the same manner as our own, so that provisions and other necessary articles had become very scarce, and sold at a high price. This happened about twenty-eight years ago.

The Original Painter

As I was lounging one fair and very warm morning on the *Levee* at New Orleans, I chanced to observe a gentleman, whose dress and other accomplishments greatly attracted my attention. I wheeled about, and followed him for a short space, when, judging by every thing about him that he was a true original, I accosted him.

But here let me give you some idea of his exterior. His head was covered by a straw hat, the brim of which might cope with those worn by the fair sex of 1830; his neck was exposed to the weather; the broad frill of a shirt, then fashionable, flapped about his breast, whilst an extraordinary collar, carefully arranged, fell over the top of his coat. The latter was of a light green colour, harmonizing well with a pair of flowing yellow nankeen trowsers, and a pink waistcoat, from the bosom of which, amidst a large bunch of the splendid flowers of the Magnolia, protruded part of a young alligator, which seemed more anxious to glide through the muddy waters of some retired swamp, than to spend its life swinging to and fro among the folds of the finest lawn. The gentleman held in one hand a cage full of richly-plumed Nonpareils, whilst in the other he sported a silk umbrella, on which I could plainly read *"Stolen from I,"* these words being painted in large white characters. He walked as if conscious of his own importance, that is, with a good deal of pomposity, singing "My love is but a lassie yet," and that with such thorough imitation of the Scotch emphasis, that had not his physiognomy brought to my mind a denial of his being from "within a mile of Edinburgh," I should have put him down in my journal for a true Scot. But no:—his tournure, nay the very shape of his visage, pronounced him an American, from the farthest parts of our eastern Atlantic shores.

All this raised my curiosity to such a height, that I accosted him with "Pray, Sir, will you allow me to examine the birds you have in that cage?" The gentleman stopped, straightened his body, almost closed his left eye, then spread his legs apart, and, with a look altogether quizzical, answered, "Birds, Sir, did you say birds?" I nodded, and he continued, "What the devil do you know about birds, Sir?"

Reader, this answer brought a blush into my face. I felt as if caught in a trap, for I was struck by the force of the gentleman's question; which, by the way, was not much in discordance with a not unusual mode of granting an answer in the United States. Sure enough, thought I, little or perhaps nothing do I know of the nature of those beautiful denizens of the air; but the next moment vanity gave me a pinch, and urged me to conceive that I knew at least as much about birds as the august personage in my presence. "Sir," replied I, "I am a student of nature, and admire her works, from the noblest figure of man to the crawling reptile which you have in your bosom." "Ah!" replied he, "a-a-a naturalist, I presume!" "Just so, my good Sir," was my answer. The gentleman gave me the cage; and I observed from the corner of one of my eyes, that his were cunningly inspecting my face. I examined the pretty finches as long as I wished, returned the cage, made a low bow, and was about to proceed on my walk, when this odd sort of being asked me a question quite accordant with my desire of knowing more of him: "Will you come with me, Sir? If you will, you shall see some more curious birds, some of which are from different parts of the world. I keep quite a collection." I assured him I should feel gratified, and accompanied him to his lodgings.

We entered a long room, where, to my surprise, the first objects that attracted my attention were a large easel, with a full length unfinished portrait upon it, a table with pallets and pencils, and a number of pictures of various sizes placed along the walls. Several cages containing birds were hung near the windows, and two young gentlemen were busily engaged in copying some finished portraits. I was delighted with all I saw. Each picture spoke for itself: the drawing, the colouring, the handling, the composition, and the keeping—all proved, that, whoever was the artist, he certainly was possessed of superior talents.

I did not know that my companion was the painter of the picture, but, as we say in America, I strongly guessed so, and without waiting any longer, paid him the compliments which I thought he fairly deserved. "Aye," said he, "the world is pleased with my work, I wish I were so too, but time and industry are required, as well as talents, to make a good artist. If you will examine the birds, I'll to my labour." So saying, the artist took up his pallet, and was searching for a rest-stick, but not finding the one with which he usually supported his hand, he drew the rod of a gun, and was about to sit, when he suddenly threw down his implements on the table, and, taking the gun, walked to me, and asked if "I had ever seen a percussion-lock." I had not, for that improvement was not yet in

vogue. He not only explained the superiority of the lock in question, but undertook to prove that it was capable of acting effectually under water. The bell was rung, a flat basin of water was produced, the gun was charged with powder, and the lock fairly immersed. The report terrified the birds, causing them to beat against the gilded walls of their prisons. I remarked this to the artist. He replied, "The devil take the birds!— more of them in the market: why, Sir, I wish to show you that I am a markman as well as a painter." The easel was cleared of the large picture, rolled to the farther end of the room, and placed against the wall. The gun was loaded in a trice, and the painter, counting ten steps from the easel, and taking aim at the supporting-pin on the left, fired. The bullet struck the head of the wooden pin fairly, and sent the splinters in all directions, "A bad shot, Sir," said this extraordinary person, "the ball ought to have driven the pin farther into the hole, but it struck on one side; I'll try at the hole itself." After reloading his piece, the artist took aim again, and fired. The bullet this time had accomplished its object, for it had passed through the aperture, and hit the wall behind. "Mr. —
——, ring the bell and close the windows," said the painter, and turning to me, continued, "Sir, I will show you the *ne plus ultra* of shooting." I was quite amazed, and yet so delighted, that I bowed my assent. A servant having appeared, a lighted candle was ordered. When it arrived, the artist placed it in a proper position, and retiring some yards, put out the light with a bullet, in the manner which I have elsewhere, in this volume, described. When light was restored, I observed the uneasiness of the poor little alligator, as it strove to effect its escape from the artist's waistcoat. I mentioned this to him. "True, true," he replied, "I had quite forgot the reptile, he shall have a dram;" and unbuttoning his vest, unclasped a small chain, and placed the alligator in the basin of water on the table.

Perfectly satisfied with the acquaintance which I had formed with this renowned artist, I wished to withdraw, fearing I might inconvenience him by my presence. But my time was not yet come. He bade me sit down, and paying no more attention to the young pupils in the room than if they had been a couple of cabbages, said, "If you have leisure and will stay awhile, I will show you how I paint, and will relate to you an incident of my life, which will prove to you how sadly situated an artist is at times." In full expectation that more eccentricities were to be witnessed, or that the story would prove a valuable one, even to a naturalist, who is seldom a painter, I seated myself at his side, and observed with interest how adroitly he transferred the colours from his glistening pallet to the canvas before him. I was about to compliment him on his facility of touch, when he spoke as follows:

"This is, Sir, or, I ought to say rather, this will be the portrait of one of our best navy officers, a man as brave as Cæsar, and as good a sailor as ever walked the deck of a seventy-four. Do you paint, Sir?" I replied "Not yet." "Not yet! what do you mean?" "I mean what I say: I intend to paint as soon as I can draw better than I do at present." "Good," said he, "you are quite right, to draw is the first object; but, Sir, if you should ever paint, and paint portraits, you will often meet with difficulties. For instance, the brave Commodore, of whom this is the portrait, although an excellent man at every thing else, is the worst sitter I ever saw; and the incident I promised to relate to you, as one curious enough, is connected with his bad mode of sitting. Sir, I forgot to ask if you would take any refreshments—a glass of wine, or———." I assured him I needed nothing more than his agreeable company, and he I proceeded. "Well, Sir, the first morning that the Commodore came to sit, he was in full uniform, and with his sword at his side. After a few moments of conversation, and when all was ready on my part, I bade him ascend the *throne,* place himself in the attitude which I contemplated, and assume an air becoming an officer of the navy." He mounted, placed himself as I had desired, but merely looked at me as if I had been a block of stone. I waited a few minutes, when, observing no change on his placid countenance, I ran the chalk over the canvas to form a rough outline. This done, I looked up to his face again, and opened a conversation which I thought would warm his warlike nature; but in vain. I waited, and waited, talked and talked, until my patience—Sir, you must know I am not overburdened with phlegm—being almost run out, I rose, threw my pallet and brushes on the floor, stamped, walking to and fro about the room, and vociferated such calamities against our navy, that I startled the good Commodore. He still looked at me with a placid countenance, and, as he has told me since, thought I had lost my senses. But I observed him all the while, and, fully as determined to carry my point as he would be to carry off an enemy's ship, I gave my oaths additional emphasis, addressed him as a representative of the navy, and, steering somewhat clear of personal insult, played off my batteries against the craft. The Commodore walked up to me, placed his hand on the hilt of his sword, and told me, in a resolute manner, that if I intended to insult the navy, he would instantly cut off my ears. His features exhibited all the spirit and animation of his noble nature, and as I had now succeeded in rousing the lion, I judged it time to retreat. So, changing my tone, I begged his pardon, and told him he now looked precisely as I wished to represent him. He laughed, and returning to his seat, assumed a bold countenance. And now, Sir, see the picture?"

At some future period, I may present you with other instances of the odd ways in which this admired artist gave animation to his sitters. For the present we shall leave him finishing the Commodore, while we return to our proper studies.

Meadville

THE incidents that occur in the life of a student of nature are not all of the agreeable kind, in proof of which, I will present an extract from one of my journals.

My money was one day stolen from me by a person, who perhaps imagined that to a naturalist it was of little importance. This happened on the shores of Upper Canada. The affair was as unexpected as it well could be, and as adroitly managed as if it had been planned and executed in Cheapside. To have repined when the thing could not be helped, would not have been acting manfully. I therefore told my companion to keep a good heart, for I felt satisfied that Providence had some relief in store for us. The whole amount of cash left with two individuals fifteen hundred miles from home, was just seven dollars and a-half. Our passage across the lake had fortunately been paid for. We embarked and soon got to the entrance of Presque Isle Harbour, but could not pass the bar, on account of a violent gale which came on as we approached it. The anchor was dropped, and we remained on board during the night, feeling at times very disagreeable, under the idea of having taken so little care of our money. How long we might have remained at anchor I cannot tell, had not that Providence, on whom I have never ceased to rely, come to our aid. Through some means to me quite unknown, Captain Judd of the United States Navy, then probably commandant at Presque Isle, sent a gig with six men to our relief. It was on the 29th of August 1824, and never shall I forget that morning. My drawings were put into the boat with the greatest care. We shifted into it, and seated ourselves according to directions politely given us. Our brave fellows pulled hard, and every moment brought us nearer to the American shore. I leaped upon it with elated heart. My drawings were safely landed, and for any thing else I cared little at the moment. I searched in vain for the officer of our navy, to whom I still feel grateful, and gave one of our dollars to the sailors to drink the "freedom of the waters;" after which we betook ourselves to a humble inn to procure bread and milk, and consider how we were to proceed.

Our plans were soon settled, for to proceed was decidedly the best.

Our luggage was rather heavy, so we hired a cart to take it to Meadville, for which we offered five dollars. This sum was accepted, and we set off. The country through which we passed might have proved favourable to our pursuits, had it not rained nearly the whole day. At night we alighted and put up at a house belonging to our conductor's father. It was Sunday night. The good folks had not yet returned from a distant meeting-house, the grandmother of our driver being the only individual about the premises. We found here a cheerful dame, who bestirred herself as actively as age would permit, got up a blazing fire to dry our wet clothes, and put as much bread and milk on the table as might have sufficed for several besides ourselves.

Being fatigued by the jolting of the cart, we asked for a place in which to rest, and were shown into a room in which were several beds. We told the good woman that I should paint her portrait next morning for the sake of her children. My companion and myself were soon in bed, and soon asleep, in which state we should probably have remained till morning, had we not been awakened by a light, which we found to be carried by three young damsels, who having observed where we lay, blew it out, and got into a bed opposite ours. As we had not spoken, it is probable the girls supposed us sound asleep, and we heard them say how delighted they would be to have their portraits taken, as well as that of their grandmother. My heart silently met their desire, and we fell asleep, without farther disturbance. In our back woods it is frequently the case that one room suffices for all the sleepers of a family.

Day dawned, and as we were dressing we discovered that we were alone in the apartment, the good country girls having dressed in silence and left us before we had awakened. We joined the family and were kindly greeted. No sooner had I made known my intentions as to the portraits, than the young folks disappeared, and soon after returned attired in their Sunday clothes. The black chalk was at work in a few minutes, to their great delight, and as the fumes of the breakfast that was meantime preparing reached my sensitive nose, I worked with redoubled ardour. The sketches were soon finished, and soon too was the breakfast over. I played a few airs on my flageolet, while our guide was putting the horses to the cart, and by ten o'clock we were once more under way towards Meadville. Never shall I forget Maxon Randell and his hospitable family. My companion was as pleased as myself, and as the weather was now beautiful, we enjoyed our journey with all that happy thoughtlessness best suited to our character. The country now became covered with heavy timber, principally evergreens, the Pines and the

Cucumber trees loaded with brilliant fruits, and the Spruces throwing a shade over the land in good keeping for a mellow picture. The lateness of the crops was the only disagreeable circumstance that struck us; hay was yet standing, probably, however, a second crop; the peaches were quite small and green, and a few persons here and there, as we passed the different farms, were reaping oats. At length we came in sight of French Creek, and soon after reached Meadville. Here we paid the five dollars promised to our conductor, who instantly faced about, and applying the whip to his nags, bade us adieu and set off.

We had now only a hundred and fifty cents. No time was to be lost. We put our baggage and ourselves under the roof of a tavern-keeper known by the name of J. E. Smith, at the sign of the *Traveller's Rest*, and soon after took a walk to survey the little village that was to be laid under contribution for our further support. Its appearance was rather dull, but thanks to God, I have never despaired while rambling thus for the sole purpose of admiring his grand and beautiful works. I had opened the case that contained my drawings, and putting my portfolio under my arm, and a few good credentials in my pocket, walked up Main Street, looking to the right and left, examining the different *heads* which occurred, until I fixed my eyes on a gentleman in a store who looked as if he might want a sketch. I begged him to allow me to sit down. This granted, I remained purposely silent until he very soon asked me what was *"in that portfolio."* These three words sounded well, and without waiting another instant, I opened it to his view. This was a Hollander, who complimented me much on the execution of the drawings of birds and flowers in my portfolio. Showing him a sketch of the best friend I have in the world at present, I asked him if he would like one in the same style of himself. He not only answered in the affirmative, but assured me that he would exert himself in procuring as many more customers as he could. I thanked him, be assured, kind reader; and having fixed upon the next morning for drawing the sketch, I returned to the *Traveller's Rest,* with a hope that to-morrow might prove propitious. Supper was ready, and as in America we have generally but one sort of *Table d, hôte,* we sat down, when, every individual looking upon me as a Missionary priest, on account of my hair, which in those days flowed loosely on my shoulders, I was asked to say grace, which I did with a fervent spirit.

Daylight returned. I visited the groves and woods around, with my companion, returned, breakfasted, and went to the store, where, notwithstanding my ardent desire to begin my task, it was ten o'clock before the sitter was ready. But, reader, allow me to describe the *artist's room.*

See me ascending a crazy flight of steps, from the back part of a store-room into a large garret extending over the store and counting room, and mark me looking round to see how the light could be stopped from obtruding on me through no less than four windows facing each other at right angles. Then follow me scrutinizing the corners, and finding in one a cat nursing her young, among a heap of rags intended for the paper-mill. Two hogsheads filled with oats, a parcel of Dutch toys carelessly thrown on the floor, a large drum and a bassoon in another part, fur caps hanging along the wall, and the portable bed of the merchant's clerk swinging like a hammock near the centre, together with some rolls of sole leather, made up the picture. I saw all this at a glance, and closing the extra windows with blankets, I soon procured a *painter's light*.

A young gentleman sat, to try my skill. I finished his phiz, which was approved of. The merchant then took the chair, and I had the good fortune to please him also. The room became crowded with the gentry of the village. Some laughed, while others expressed their wonder; but my work went on notwithstanding the observations that were made. My sitter invited me to spend the evening with him, which I did, and joined him in some music on the flute and violin. I returned to my companion with great pleasure; and you may judge how much that pleasure was increased, when I found that he also had made two sketches. Having written a page or two of our journals, we retired to rest.

The following day was spent much in the same manner. I felt highly gratified that from under my grey coat my talents had made their way, and I was pleased to discover that industry and moderate abilities prove at least as valuable as first-rate talents without the former of these qualities. We left Meadville on foot, having forwarded our baggage by wagon. Our hearts were light, our pockets replenished, and we walked in two days to Pittsburg, as happy as circumstances permitted us to be.

The Great Pine Swamp

I LEFT Philadelphia, at four in the morning, by the coach, with no other accoutrements than I knew to be absolutely necessary for the jaunt which I intended to make. These consisted of a wooden box, containing a small stock of linen, drawing paper, my journal, colours and pencils, together with 25 pounds of shot, some flints, the due quantum of cash, my gun *Tear-jacket*, and a heart as true to nature as ever.

Our coaches are none of the best, nor do they move with the velocity of those of some other countries. It was eight, and a dark night, when I reached Mauch Chunk, now so celebrated in the Union for its rich coal mines, and eighty-eight miles distant from Philadelphia. I had passed through a very diversified country, part of which was highly cultivated, while the rest was yet in a state of nature, and consequently much more agreeable to me. On alighting, I was shewn to the traveller's room and on asking for the landlord saw coming towards me a fine-looking young man, to whom I made known my wishes. He spoke kindly, and offered to lodge and board me at a much lower rate than travellers who go there for the very simple pleasure of being dragged on the railway. In a word, I was fixed in four minutes, and that most comfortably.

No sooner had the approach of day been announced by the cocks of the little village, than I marched out with my gun and note-book, to judge for myself of the wealth of the country. After traversing much ground, and crossing many steep hills, I returned, if not wearied, at least much disappointed at the extraordinary scarcity of birds. So I bargained to be carried in a cart to the central parts of the Great Pine Swamp, and, although a heavy storm was rising, ordered my conductor to proceed. We winded round many a mountain, and at last crossed the highest. The weather had become tremendous, and we were thoroughly drenched, but my resolution being fixed, the boy was obliged to continue his driving. Having already travelled about fifteen miles or so, we left the turnpike, and struck up a narrow and bad road, that seemed merely cut out to enable the people of the Swamp to receive the necessary supplies from the village which I had left. Some mistakes were made, and it was almost dark, when a post directed us to the habitation of a Mr. Jediah Irish, to whom I had been recommended. We now rattled down a steep declivity, edged on one side by almost perpendicular rocks, and on the other by a noisy stream, which seemed grumbling at the approach of strangers. The ground was so overgrown by laurels and tall pines of different kinds, that the whole presented only a mass of darkness.

At length we got to the house, the door of which was already opened, the sight of strangers being nothing uncommon in our woods, even in the most remote parts. On entering, I was presented with a chair, while my conductor was shewn the way to the stable, and on expressing a wish that I should be permitted to remain in the house for some weeks, I was gratified by receiving the sanction of the good woman to my proposal, although her husband was then from home. As I immediately fell a-talking about the nature of the country, and inquired if birds were numerous in the neighbourhood, Mrs. Irish, more *au fait* to household affairs than ornithology, sent for a nephew of her husband's, who soon made his appearance, and in whose favour I became at once prepossessed. He conversed like an educated person, saw that I was comfortably disposed of, and finally bade me good-night in such a tone as made me quite happy.

The storm had rolled away before the first beams of the morning sun shone brightly on the wet foliage, displaying all its richness and beauty. My ears were greeted by the notes, always sweet and mellow, of the Wood Thrush and other songsters. Before I had gone many steps, the woods echoed to the report of my gun, and I picked from among the leaves a lovely Sylvia, long sought for, but until then sought for in vain. I needed no more, and standing still for awhile, I was soon convinced that the Great Pine Swamp harboured many other objects as valuable to me.

The young man joined me, bearing his rifle, and offered to accompany me through the woods, all of which he well knew. But I was anxious to transfer to paper the form and beauty of the little bird I had in my hand; and requesting him to break a twig of blooming laurel, we returned to the house, speaking of nothing else than the picturesque beauty of the country around.

A few days passed, during which I became acquainted with my hostess and her sweet children, and made occasional rambles, but spent the greater portion of my time in drawing. One morning, as I stood near the window of my room, I remarked a tall and powerful man alight from his horse, loose the girth of the saddle, raise the latter with one hand, pass the bridle over the head of the animal with the other, and move towards the house, while the horse betook himself to the little brook to drink. I heard some movements in the room below, and again the same tall person walked towards the mills and stores, a few hundred yards from the house. In America, business is the first object in view at all times, and right it is that it should be so. Soon after my hostess entered my room, accompanied by a fine-looking woodsman, to whom, as Mr. Jediah Irish, I was introduced. Reader, to describe to you the qualities of that excellent man were vain; you should know him, as I do, to estimate the value of such men in our sequestered forests. He not only made me welcome, but promised all his assistance in forwarding my views.

The long walks and long talks we have had together I never can forget, or the many beautiful birds which we pursued, shot, and admired. The juicy venison, excellent bear flesh, and delightful trout that daily formed my food, methinks I can still enjoy. And then, what pleasure I had in listening to him as he read his favourite Poems of Burns, while my pencil was occupied in smoothing and softening the drawing of the bird before me! Was not this enough to recall to my mind the early impressions that had been made upon it by the description of the golden age, which I here found realized?

The Lehigh about this place forms numerous short turns between the mountains, and affords frequent falls, as well as below the falls deep pools, which render this stream a most valuable one for mills of any kind. Not many years before this date, my host was chosen by the agent of the Lehigh Coal company, as their mill-wright, and manager for cutting down the fine trees which covered the mountains around. He was young, robust, active, industrious, and persevering. He marched to the spot where his abode now is, with some workmen, and by dint of hard labour first cleared the road mentioned above, and reached the river at the centre of a bend, where he fixed on erecting various mills. The pass here is so narrow that it looks as if formed by the bursting asunder of the mountain, both sides ascending abruptly, so that the place where the settlement was made is in many parts difficult of access, and the road then newly cut was only sufficient to permit men and horses to come to the spot where Jediah and his men were at work. So great, in fact, were the difficulties of access, that, as he told me, pointing to a spot about 150 feet above us, they for many months slipped from it their barrelled provisions, assisted by ropes, to their camp below. But no sooner was the first saw-mill erected, than the axemen began their devastations. Trees one after another were, and are yet, constantly heard falling, during the days; and in calm nights, the greedy mills told the sad tale, that in a century the noble forests around should exist no more. Many mills were erected, many dams raised, in defiance of the impetuous Lehigh. One full third of the trees have already been culled, turned into boards, and floated as far as Philadelphia.

In such an undertaking, the cutting of the trees is not all. They have afterwards to be hauled to the edge of the mountains bordering the river, launched into the stream, and led to the mills over many shallows and difficult places. Whilst I was in the Great Pine Swamp, I frequently visited one of the principal places for the launching of logs. To see them tumbling from such a height, touching here and there the rough angle of a projecting rock, bouncing from it with the elasticity of a foot-ball, and at last falling with awful crash into the river, forms a sight interesting in the highest degree, but impossible for me to describe. Shall I tell you that I have seen masses of these logs heaped above each other to the number of five thousand? I may so tell you, for such I have seen. My friend Irish assured me that at some seasons, these piles consisted of a much greater number, the river becoming in those places completely choked up.

When *freshets* (or floods) take place, then is the time chosen for forwarding the logs to the different mills. This is called a *Frolic*. Jediah Irish, who is generally the leader, proceeds to the upper leap with his men, each provided with a strong wooden handspike, and a short-handled axe. They all take to the water, be it summer or winter, like so many Newfoundland spaniels. The logs are gradually detached, and, after a time, are seen floating down the dancing stream, here striking against a rock and whirling many times round, there suddenly checked in dozens by a shallow, over which they have to be forced with the hand-spikes. Now they arrive at the edge of a dam, and are again pushed over. Certain numbers are left in each dam, and when the party has arrived at the last, which lies just where my friend Irish's camp was first formed, the drenched leader and his men, about sixty in number, make their way home, find there a healthful repast, and spend the evening and a portion of the night in dancing and frolicking, in their own simple manner, in the most perfect amity, seldom troubling themselves with the idea of the labour prepared for them on the morrow.

That morrow now come, one sounds a horn from the door of the store-house, at the call of which each returns to his work. The sawyers, the millers, the rafters and raftsmen are all immediately busy. The mills are all going, and the logs, which a few months before were the supporters of broad and leafy tops, are now in the act of being split asunder.

The boards are then launched into the stream, and rafts are formed of them for market.

During the summer and autumnal months, the Lehigh, a small river of itself, soon becomes extremely shallow, and to float the rafts would prove impossible, had not art managed to provide a supply of water for this express purpose. At the breast of the lower dam is a curiously constructed lock, which is opened at the approach of the rafts. They pass through this lock with the rapidity of lightning, propelled by the water that had been accumulated in the dam, and which is of itself generally sufficient to float them to Mauch Chunk, after which, entering regular canals, they find no other impediments, but are conveyed to their ultimate destination.

Before population had greatly advanced in this part of Pennsylvania, game of all descriptions found within that range was extremely abundant. The Elk itself did not disdain to browse on the shoulders of the mountains, near the Lehigh. Bears and the Common Deer must have been plentiful, as, at the moment when I write, many of both kinds are seen and killed by the resident hunters. The Wild Turkey, the Pheasant and the Grouse, are also tolerably abundant; and as to trout in the streams—Ah, reader, if you are an angler, go there, and try for yourself. For my part, I can only say, that I have been made weary with pulling up from the rivulets the sparkling fish, allured by the struggles of the common grasshopper.

A comical affair happened with the bears, which I will relate. A party of my friend Irish's raftsmen, returning from Mauch Chunk, one afternoon, through sundry short cuts over the mountains, at the season when the huckleberries are ripe and plentiful, were suddenly apprised of the proximity of some of these animals, by their snuffing the air. No sooner was this perceived than, to the astonishment of the party, not fewer than eight bears, I was told, made their appearance. Each man, being provided with his short-handled axe, faced about and willingly came to the scratch; but the assailed soon proved the assailants, and with claw and tooth drove off the men in a twinkling. Down they all rushed from the mountain; the noise spread quickly; rifles were soon procured and shouldered; but when the spot was reached, no bears were to be found; night forced the hunters back to their homes, and a laugh concluded the affair.

I spent six weeks in the Great Pine Forest—Swamp it cannot be called—where I made many a drawing. Wishing to leave Pennsylvania, and to follow the migratory flocks of our birds to the south, I bade adieu to the excellent wife and rosy children of my friend, and to his kind nephew. Jediah Irish, shouldering his heavy rifle, accompanied me, and trudging directly across the mountains, we arrived at Mauch Chunk in good time for dinner. Shall I ever have the pleasure of seeing that good, that generous man again?

At Mauch Chunk, where we both spent the night, Mr. White, the civil engineer, visited me, and looked at the drawings which I had made in the Great Pine Forest. The news he gave me of my sons, then in Kentucky, made me still more anxious to move in their direction, and, long before daybreak, I shook hands with the good man of the forest, and found myself moving towards the capital of Pennsylvania, having as my sole companion a sharp frosty breeze. Left to my thoughts, I felt amazed that such a place as the Great Pine Forest should be so little known to the Philadelphians, scarcely any of whom could direct me towards it. How much is it to be regretted, thought I, that the many young gentlemen who are there so much at a loss how to employ their leisure days should not visit these wild retreats, valuable as they are to the student of nature. How differently would they feel, if, instead of spending weeks in smoothing a useless bow, and walking out in full dress, intent on displaying the make of their legs, to some rendezvous where they may enjoy their wines, they were to occupy themselves in contemplating the rich profusion which nature has poured around them, or even in procuring some desired specimen for their *Peale's Museum*, once so valuable and so finely arranged? But alas! no: they are none of them aware of the richness of the Great Pine Swamp, nor are they likely to share the hospitality to be found there.

Night came on, as I was thinking of such things, and I was turned out of the coach in the streets of the fair city, just as the clock struck ten. I cannot say that my bones were much rested, but not a moment was to be lost. So I desired a porter to take up my little luggage, and leading him towards the nearest wharf, I found myself soon after gliding across the Delaware, towards my former lodgings in the Jerseys. The lights were shining from the parallel streets as I crossed them, all was tranquil and serene, until there came the increasing sound of the Baltimore steamer, which, for some reason unknown to me, was that evening later than usual in its arrival. My luggage was landed, and carried home by means of a bribe. The people had all retired to rest, but my voice was instantly recognised, and an entrance was afforded to me.

St. John's River, in Florida

SOON after landing at St. Augustine, in East Florida, I formed acquaintance with Dr. Simmons, Dr. Pocher, Judge Smith, the Misses Johnson, and other individuals, my intercourse with whom was as agreeable as beneficial to me. Lieutenant Constantine Smith, of the United States Army, I found of a congenial spirit, as was the case with my amiable, but since deceased friend, Dr. Bell, of Dublin. Among the planters who extended their hospitality to me, I must particularly mention General Hernandez, and my esteemed friend John Bulow, Esq. To all these estimable individuals I offer my sincere thanks.

While in this part of the peninsula, I followed my usual avocations, although with little success, it being then winter. I had letters from the Secretaries of the Navy and Treasury of the United States, to the commanding officers of vessels of war of the revenue service, directing them to afford me any assistance in their power; and the schooner Spark having come to St. Augustine, on her way to the St. John's River, I presented my credentials to her commander, Lieutenant Piercy, who readily and with politeness, received me and my assistants on board. We soon after set sail, with a fair breeze. The strict attention to duty on board even this small vessel of war, afforded matter of surprise to me. Every thing went on with the regularity of a chronometer: orders were given, answered, and accomplished, before they ceased to vibrate on the ear. The neatness of the crew equalled the cleanliness of the white planks of the deck; the sails were in perfect condition; and, built as the Spark was, for swift sailing, on she went gambolling from wave to wave.

I thought that, while thus sailing, no feeling but that of pleasure could exist in our breasts; but, alas! how fleeting are our enjoyments. When we were almost at the entrance of the river, the wind changed, the sky became clouded, and, before many minutes had elapsed, the little bark was lying to "like a duck," as her commander expressed himself. It blew a hurricane:—let it blow, reader. At the break of day we were again at anchor within the bar of St. Augustine.

Our next attempt was successful. Not many hours after we had crossed the bar, we perceived the star-like glimmer of the light in the great lantern at the entrance of the St. John's River. This was before daylight; and, as the crossing of the sand-banks or bars, which occur at the mouths of all the streams of this peninsula is difficult, and can be accomplished only when the tide is up, one of the guns was fired as a signal for the government pilot. The good man, it seemed, was unwilling to leave his couch, but a second gun brought him in his canoe alongside. The depth of the channel was barely sufficient. My eyes, however, were not directed towards the waters, but on high, where flew some thousands of snowy Pelicans, which had fled affrighted from their resting grounds. How beautifully they performed their broad gyrations, and how matchless, after a while, was the marshalling of their files, as they flew past us!

On the tide we proceeded apace. Myriads of Cormorants covered the face of the waters, and over it Fish-Crows innumerable were already arriving from their distant roosts. We landed at one place to search for the birds whose charming melodies had engaged our attention, and here and there some young Eagles we shot, to add to our store of fresh provisions! The river did not seem to me equal in beauty to the fair Ohio; the shores were in many places low and swampy, to the great delight of the numberless Herons that moved along in gracefulness, and the grim alligators that swam in sluggish sullenness. In going up a bayou, we caught a great number of the young of the latter for the purpose of making experiments upon them.

After sailing a considerable way, during which our commander and officers took the soundings, as well as the angles and bearings of every nook and crook of the sinuous stream, we anchored one evening at a distance of fully one hundred miles from the mouth of the river. The weather, although it was the 12th of February, was quite warm, the thermometer on board standing at 75°, and on shore at 90°. The fog was so thick that neither of the shores could be seen, and yet the river was not a mile in breadth. The "blind musquitoes" covered every object, even in the cabin, and so wonderfully abundant were these tormentors, that they more than once fairly extinguished the candles whilst I was writing my journal, which I closed in despair, crushing between the leaves more than a hundred of the little wretches. Bad as they are, however, these blind musquitoes do not bite. As if purposely to render our situation doubly uncomfortable, there was an establishment for jerking beef, on the nearer shores to the windward of our vessel, from which the breeze came laden with no sweet odours.

In the morning when I arose, the country was still covered with thick fogs, so that although I could plainly hear the notes of the birds on shore, not an object could I see beyond the bowsprit, and the air was as close and sultry as on the previous evening. Guided by the scent of the jerker's works, we went on shore, where we found the vegetation already far advanced. The blossoms of the jessamine, ever pleasing, lay steeped in dew; the humming bee was collecting her winter's store from the snowy flowers of the native orange; and the little warblers frisked along the twigs of the smilax. Now, amid the tall pines of the forest, the sun's rays began to force their way, and as the dense mists dissolved in the atmosphere, the bright luminary at length shone forth. We explored the woods around, guided by some friendly live-oakers who had pitched their camp in the vicinity. After a while the Spark again displayed her sails, and as she silently glided along, we spied a Seminole Indian approaching us in his canoe. The poor dejected son of the woods, endowed with talents of the highest order, although rarely acknowledged by the proud usurpers of his native soil, has spent the night in fishing, and the morning in procuring the superb-feathered game of the swampy thickets; and with both he comes to offer them for our acceptance. Alas! thou fallen one, descendant of an ancient line of freeborn hunters, would that I could restore to thee thy birthright, thy natural independence, the generous feelings that were once fostered in thy brave bosom. But the irrevocable deed is done, and I can merely admire the perfect symmetry of his frame, as he dexterously throws on our deck the trouts and turkeys which he has captured. He receives a recompense, and without smile or bow, or acknowledgment of any kind, off he starts with the speed of an arrow from his own bow.

Alligators were extremely abundant, and the heads of the fishes which they had snapped off lay floating around on the dark waters. A rifle bullet was now and then sent through the eye of one of the largest, which, with a tremendous splash of its tail expired. One morning we saw a monstrous fellow lying on the shore. I was desirous of obtaining him to make an accurate drawing of his head, and, accompanied by my assistant and two of the sailors, proceeded cautiously towards him. When within a few yards, one of us fired and sent through his side an ounce ball, which tore open a hole large enough to receive a man's hand. He slowly raised his head, bent himself upwards, opened his huge jaws, swung his tail to and fro, rose on his legs, blew in a frightful manner, and fell to the earth. My assistant leaped on shore and, contrary to my injunctions, caught hold of the animal's tail, when the alligator, awakening from its trance, with a last effort crawled slowly towards the water, and plunged heavily into it. Had he thought of once flourishing his tremendous weapon there might have been an end of his assailant's life, but he fortunately went in peace to his grave, where we left him, as the water was too deep. The same morning, another of equal size was observed swimming directly for the bows of our vessel, attracted by the gentle rippling of the water there. One of the officers, who had watched him, fired and scattered his brain through the air, when he tumbled and rolled at a fearful rate, blowing all the while most furiously. The river was bloody for yards around, but although the monster passed close by the vessel, we could not secure him, and after a while he sunk to the bottom.

Early one morning I hired a boat and two men, with the view of returning to St. Augustine by a short cut. Our baggage being placed on board, I bade adieu to the officers, and off we started. About four in the afternoon we arrived at the short cut, forty miles distant from our point of departure, and where we had expected to procure a waggon, but were disappointed. So we laid our things on the bank, and, leaving one of my assistants to look after them, I set out, accompanied by the other, and my Newfoundland dog. We had eighteen miles to go; and as the sun was only two hours high, we struck off at a good rate. Presently we entered a pine barren. The country was as level as a floor; our path, although narrow, was well beaten, having been used by the Seminole Indians for ages, and the weather was calm and beautiful. Now and then a rivulet occurred, from which we quenched our thirst, while the magnolias and other flowering plants on its banks relieved the dull uniformity of the woods. When the path separated into two branches, both seemingly leading the same way, I would follow one, while my companion took the other, and unless we met again in a short time, one of us would go across the intervening forest.

The sun went down behind a cloud, and the south-east breeze that sprung up at this moment, sounded dolefully among the tall pines. Along the eastern horizon lay a bed of black vapour, which gradually rose, and soon covered the heavens. The air felt hot and oppressive, and we knew that a tempest was approaching. Plato was now our guide, the white spots on his skin being the only objects that we could discern amid the darkness, and as if aware of his utility in this respect, he kept a short way before us on the trail. Had we imagined ourselves more than a few miles from the town, we should have made a camp, and remained under its shelter for the night; but conceiving that the distance could not be great, we resolved to trudge along.

Large drops began to fall from the murky mass overhead; thick, impenetrable darkness surrounded us, and to my dismay, the dog refused to proceed. Groping with my hands on the ground, I discovered that several trails branched out at the spot where he lay down; and when I had selected one, he went on. Vivid flashes of lightning streamed across the heavens, the wind increased to a gale, and the rain poured down upon us like a torrent. The water soon rose on the level ground so as almost to cover our feet, and we slowly advanced, fronting the tempest. Here and there a tall pine on fire presented a magnificent spectacle, illumining the trees around it, and surrounded with a halo of dim light, abruptly bordered with the deep black of the night. At one time we passed through a tangled thicket of low trees, at another crossed a stream flushed by the heavy rain, and again proceeded over the open barrens.

How long we thus, half-lost, groped our way is more than I can tell you; but at length the tempest passed over, and suddenly the clear sky became spangled with stars. Soon after we smelt the salt-marshes, and walking directly towards them, like pointers advancing on a covey of partridges, we at last to our great joy descried the light of the beacon near St. Augustine. My dog began to run briskly around, having met with ground on which he had hunted before, and taking a direct course, led us to the great causeway that crosses the marshes at the back of the town. We refreshed ourselves with the produce of the first orange tree that we met with, and in half an hour more arrived at our hotel. Drenched with rain, steaming with perspiration, and covered to the knees with mud, you may imagine what figures we cut in the eyes of the good people whom we found snugly enjoying themselves in the sitting room. Next morning, Major Gates, who had received me with much kindness, sent a waggon with mules and two trusty soldiers for my companion and luggage.

A Ball in Newfoundland

ON our return from the singularly wild and interesting country of Labrador, the "Ripley" sailed close along the northern coast of Newfoundland. The weather was mild and clear; and, while my young companions amused themselves on the deck with the music of various instruments, I gazed on the romantic scenery spread along the bold and often magnificent shores. Portions of the wilds appeared covered with a luxuriance of vegetable growth far surpassing that of the regions which we had just left, and in some of the valleys I thought I saw trees of moderate size. The number of habitations increased apace, and many small vessels and boats danced on the waves of the coves which we passed. Here a precipitous shore looked like the section of a great mountain, of which the lost half had sunk into the depths of the sea, and the dashing of the waters along its base was such as to alarm the most daring seaman. The huge masses of broken rock impressed my mind with awe and reverence, as I thought of the power that still gave support to the gigantic fragments which every where hung, as if by magic, over the sea, awaiting, as it were, the proper moment to fall upon and crush the impious crew of some piratical vessel. There again, gently swelling hills reared their heads towards the sky, as if desirous of existing within the influence of its azure purity; and I thought the bleats of reindeer came on my ear. Dark clouds of Curlews were seen winging their way towards the south, and thousands of Larks and Warblers were flitting through the air. The sight of these birds excited in me a wish that I also had wings to fly back to my country and friends.

Early one morning our vessel doubled the northern cape of the Bay of St. George; and, as the wind was light, the sight of that magnificent expanse of water, which extends inward to the length of eighteen leagues, with a breadth of thirteen, gladdened the hearts of all on board. A long range of bold shores bordered it on one side, throwing a deep shadow over the water, which added greatly to the beauty of the scene. On the other side, the mild beams of the autumnal sun glittered on the water, and whitened the sails of the little barks that were sailing to and fro, like so many silvery gulls. The welcome sight of cattle feeding in cultivated meadows, and of people at their vocations, consoled us for the labours which we had undergone, and the privations which we had suffered; and, as the "Ripley" steered her course into a snug harbour that suddenly opened to our view, the number of vessels that were anchored there, and a pretty village that presented itself, increased our delight.

Although the sun was fast approaching the western horizon when our anchor was dropped, no sooner were the sails furled than we all went ashore. There appeared a kind of curious bustle among the people, as if they were anxious to know who we were, for our appearance, and that of our warlike looking schooner, shewed that we were not fishermen. As we bore our usual arms and hunting accoutrements, which were half Indian and half civilized, the individuals we met on the shore manifested considerable suspicion, which our captain observing, instantly made a signal, when the star-spangled banner glided to the mast-head, and saluted the flags of France and Britain in kindly greeting. We were welcomed and supplied with abundance of fresh provisions. Glad at once more standing on something like soil, we passed through the village, and walked round it, but as night was falling, were quickly obliged to return to our floating home, where, after a hearty supper, we serenaded with repeated glees the peaceful inhabitants of the village.

At early dawn I was on deck admiring the scene of industry that presented itself. The harbour was already covered with fishing-boats, employed in procuring mackerel, some of which we appropriated to ourselves. Signs of cultivation were observed on the slopes of the hills, the trees seemed of goodly size, a river made its way between two ranges of steep rocks, and here and there a group of Mickmack Indians were searching along the shores for lobsters, crabs, and eels, all of which we found abundant and delicious. A canoe laden with rein-deer meat came along-side, paddled by a pair of athletic Indians, who exchanged their cargo for some of our stores. You would have been amused to see the manner in which these men, and their families on shore, cooked the lobsters; they threw them alive into a great wood-fire; and, as soon as they were broiled, devoured them while yet so hot that any of us could not have touched them. When properly cooled, I tasted these roasted lobsters, and found them infinitely better flavoured than boiled ones. The country was represented as abounding in game. The temperature was higher, by twenty degrees than that of Labrador, and yet I was told that the ice of the bay seldom broke up before the middle of May, and that few vessels attempted to go to Labrador before the 10th of June, when the codfishery at once commences.

One afternoon we were visited by a deputation from the inhabitants of the village, inviting our whole party to a ball which was to take place that night, and requesting us to take with us our musical instruments. We unanimously accepted the invitation which had been made from friendly feelings; and finding that the deputies had a relish for "old Jamaica," we helped them pretty freely to some, which soon shewed that it had lost nothing of its energies by having visited Labrador. At ten o'clock, the appointed hour, we landed, and were lighted to the dancing hall by paper lanterns, one of us carrying a flute, another a violin, and I with a flageolet stuck into my waistcoat pocket.

The hall proved nothing less than the ground floor of a fisherman's house. We were presented to his wife, who, like her neighbours, was an adept in the piscatory art. She courtesied, not à la Taglioni, it is true, but with a modest assurance, which to me was quite as pleasing as the airiness with which the admired performer just mentioned might have paid her respects. The good woman was rather unprepared and quite en negligée, as was the apartment, but full of activity, and anxious to arrange things in becoming style. In one hand she held a bunch of candles, in the other a lighted torch, and distributing the former at proper intervals along the walls, she applied the later to them in succession. This done, she emptied the contents of a large tin vessel into a number of glasses which were placed in a tea-tray on the only table in the room. The chimney, black and capacious, was embellished with coffee-pots, milk-jugs, cups and saucers, knives and forks, and all the paraphernalia necessary on so important an occasion. A set of primitive wooden stools and benches was placed around, for the reception of the belles of the village, some of whom now dropped in, flourishing in all the rosy fatness produced by an invigorating northern climate, and in decoration vying with the noblest Indian queen of the west. Their stays seemed ready to burst open, and their shoes were equally pressed, so full of sap were the arctic beauties. Around their necks brilliant beads, mingled with ebony tresses, and their naked arms might have inspired apprehension had they not been constantly employed in arranging flowing ribbons, gaudy flowers, and muslin flounces.

Now arrived one of the beaux, just returned from the fishing, who, knowing all, and being equally known, leaped without ceremony on the loose boards that formed a kind of loft overhead, where he soon exchanged his dripping apparel for a dress suited to the occasion, when he dropped upon the floor, and strutting up and down, bowed and scraped to the ladies, with as much ease, if not elegance, as a Bond Street highly-scented exquisite. Others came in by degrees, ready dressed, and music was called for. My son, by way of overture, played "Hail Columbia, happy land," then went on with "La Marseillaise," and ended with

"God save the King." Being merely a spectator, I ensconsed myself in a corner, by the side of an old European gentleman, whom I found an agreeable and well-informed companion, to admire the decorum of the motley assemblage.

The dancers stood in array, little time having been spent in choosing partners, and a Canadian accompanying my son on his Cremona, mirth and joy soon abounded. Dancing is certainly one of the most healthful and innocent amusements. I have loved it a vast deal more than watching for the nibble of a trout, and I have sometimes thought enjoying it with an agreeable female softened my nature as much as the pale pure light of the moon softens and beautifies a winter night. A maiden lady, who sat at my side, and who was the only daughter of my talkative companion, relished my remarks on the subject so much, that the next set saw her gracing the floor with her tutored feet.

At each pause of the musicians, refreshments were handed round by the hostess and her son, and I was not a little surprised to see all the ladies, maids and matrons, swallow like their sweethearts and husbands, a full glass of pure rum, with evident pleasure. I should perhaps have recollected that, in cold climates, a dose of ardent spirits is not productive of the same effects as in burning latitudes, and that refinement had not yet induced these healthy and robust dames to affect a delicacy foreign to their nature.

It was now late, and knowing how much I had to accomplish next day, I left the party and proceeded towards the shore. My men were sound asleep in the boat, but in a few moments I was on board the "Ripley." My young friends arrived towards daylight, but many of the fishermen's sons and daughters kept up the dance, to this music of the Canadian, until after our breakfast was over.

Although all the females whom I had seen at this ball were perfectly free from *mauvaise honte*, we were much surprised when some of them, which we afterwards met in the course of our rambles in the neighbouring meadows and fields, ran off on seeing us, like gazelles before jackalls. One, bearing a pail of water on her head, dropped it the moment she saw us, and ran into the woods to hide herself. Another, who was in search of a cow, on observing us going towards her, took to the water and waded through an inlet more than waist-deep, after which she made for home with the speed of a frightened hare. On inquiring the reason of this strange conduct, the only answer I received from several was a deep blush!

The Eggers of Labrador

THE distinctive appellation of Eggers is given to certain persons who follow, principally or exclusively, the avocation of procuring the eggs of wild birds, with the view of disposing of them at some distant port. Their great object is to plunder every nest, whenever they can find it, no matter where, or at whatever risk. They are the pest of the feathered tribes, and their brutal propensity to destroy the poor creatures after they have robbed them, is abundantly gratified whenever an opportunity presents itself.

Much had been said to me respecting these destructive pirates before I visited the coast of Labrador, but I could not entirely credit all their cruelties until I had actually witnessed their proceedings, which were such as to inspire no small degree of horror. But you shall judge for yourself.

See yon shallop shyly sailing along;—she sneaks like a thief, wishing as it were to shun the very light of heaven. Under the lee of every rocky isle some one at the tiller steers her course. Were his trade an honest one, he would not think of hiding his back behind the terrific rocks that seem to have been placed there as a resort to the myriads of birds that annually visit this desolate region of the earth, for the purpose of rearing their young, at a distance from all disturbers of their peace. How unlike the open, the bold, the honest mariner, whose face needs no mark, who scorns to skulk under any circumstances! The vessel herself is a shabby thing:—her sails are patched with stolen pieces of better canvas, the owners of which have probably been stranded on some inhospitable coast, and have been plundered, perhaps murdered, by the wretches before us. Look at her again!— Her sides are neither painted, nor even pitched; no—they are daubed over, plastered and patched with strips of seal-skins, laid along the seams. Her deck has never been washed or sanded, her hold—for no cabin has she,—though at present empty sends forth an odour pestilential as that of a charnel-house. The crew, eight in number, lie sleeping at the foot of their tottering mast, regardless of the repairs needed in every part of her rigging. But see! she scuds along, and as I suspect her crew to be bent on the commission of some evil deed, let us follow her to the first harbour.

There rides the filthy thing! The afternoon is half over. Her crew have thrown their boat overboard; they enter and seat themselves, each with a rusty gun. One of them skulls the skiff towards an island for a century past the breeding place of myriads of Guillemots, which are now to be laid under contribution. At the approach of the vile thieves, clouds of birds rise from the rock and fill the air around, wheeling and screaming over their enemies. Yet thousands remain in an erect posture, each covering its single egg, the hope of both parents. The reports of several muskets loaded with heavy shot are now heard while several dead and wounded birds fall heavily on the rock or into the water. Instantly all the sitting birds rise and fly off affrighted to their companions above, and hover in dismay over their assassins who walk forward exultingly, and with their shouts mingling oaths and execrations. Look at them! See how they crush the chick within its shell, how they trample on every egg in their way with their huge and clumsy boots. Onward they go, and when they leave the isle, not an egg that they can find is left entire. The dead birds they collect and carry to their boat. Now they have regained their filthy shallop; they strip the birds by a single jerk of their feathery apparel, while the flesh is yet warm, and throw them on some coals, where in a short time they are broiled. The rum is produced when the guillemots are fit for eating, and after stuffing themselves with this oily fare, and enjoying the pleasure of beastly intoxication, over they tumble on the deck of their crazed craft, where they pass the short hours of night in turbid slumber.

The sun now rises above the snow-clad summit of the eastern mount. "Sweet is the breath of morn" even in this desolate land. The gay Bunting erects his white crest, and gives utterances to the joy he feels in the presence of his brooding mate. The Willow Grous on the rock crows his challenge aloud. Each floweret, chilled by the night air, expands its pure petals; the gentle breeze shakes from the blades of grass the heavy dewdrops. On the Guillemot Isle the birds have again settled, and now renew their loves. Startled by the light of day, one of the Eggers springs on his feet and rouses his companions, who stare around them for a while, endeavouring to recollect their senses. Mark them, as with clumsy fingers they clear their drowsy eyes! Slowly they rise on their feet. See how the filthy lubbers stretch out their arms and yawn; you shrink back, for verily "that throat might frighten a shark."

But the master, soon recollecting that so many eggs are worth a dollar or a crown, casts his eye towards the rock, marks the day in his memory, and gives orders to depart. The light breeze enables them to reach another harbour a few miles distant, one which, like the last, lies concealed from the ocean by some other rock isle. Arrived there, they re-act the scene of yesterday, crushing every egg they can find. For a week each night is passed in drunkenness and brawls, until, having reached the last breeding place on the coast, they return, touch at every isle in succession, shoot as many birds as they need, collect the fresh eggs, and lay in a cargo. At every step each ruffian picks up an egg so beautiful that any man with a feeling heart would pause to consider the motive which could induce him to carry it off. But nothing of this sort occurs to the Egger, who gathers and gathers, until he has swept the rock bare. The dollars alone chink in his sordid mind, and he assiduously plies the trade which no man would ply who had the talents and industry to procure subsistence by honourable means.

With a bark nearly half filled with fresh eggs they proceed to the principal rock, that on which they first landed. But what is their surprise when they find others there helping themselves as industriously as they can! In boiling rage they charge their guns, and ply their oars. Landing on the rock, they run up to the Eggers, who, like themselves, are desperadoes. The first question is a discharge of musketry, the answer another. Now, man to man, they fight like tigers. One is carried to his boat with a fractured skull, another limps with a shot in his leg, and a third feels how many of his teeth have been driven through the hole in his cheek. At last, however, the quarrel is settled; the booty is to be equally divided; and now see them all drinking together. Oaths and curses and filthy jokes are all that you hear; but see, stuffed with food, and reeling with drink, down they drop one by one; groans and execrations from the wounded mingle with the snorings of the heavy sleepers. There let the brutes lie.

Again it is dawn, but no one stirs. The sun is high; one by one they open their heavy eyes, stretch their limbs, yawn, and raise themselves from the deck. But see, here comes a goodly company. A hundred honest fishermen, who for months past have fed on salt meat, have felt a desire to procure some eggs. Gallantly their boats advance, impelled by the regular pull of their long oars. Each buoyant bark displays the flag of its nation. No weapons do they bring, nor any thing that can be used as such save their oars and fists. Cleanly clad in Sunday attire, they arrive at the desired spot, and at once prepare to ascend the rock. The Eggers, now numbering a dozen, all armed with guns and bludgeons, bid defiance to the fishermen. A few angry words pass between the parties. One of the Eggers, still under the influence of drink, pulls his trigger, and an unfortunate sailor is seen to reel in agony. Three loud cheers fill the air. All at once rush on the malefactors; a horrid fight ensues, the result of which is, that every Egger is left on the rock beaten and bruised. Too frequently the fishermen man their boats, row to the shallops, and break every egg in the hold.

The Eggers of Labrador not only rob the birds in this cruel manner, but also the fishermen, whenever they can find an opportunity; and the quarrels they excite are numberless. While we were on the coast, none of our party ever ventured on any of the islands which these wretches call their own, without being well provided with means of defence. On one occasion, when I was present, we found two Eggers at their work of destruction. I spoke to them respecting my visit, and offered them premiums for rare birds and some of their eggs; but although they made fair promises, not one of the gang ever came near the Ripley.

These people gather all the eider down they can find; yet so inconsiderate are they, that they kill every bird that comes in their way. The eggs of Gulls, Guillemots, and Ducks are searched for with care; and the Puffins and some other birds they massacre in vast numbers for the sake of their feathers. So constant and persevering are their depredations, that these species, which, according to the accounts of the few settlers I saw in the country, were exceedingly abundant twenty years ago, have abandoned their ancient breeding places, and removed much farther north in search of peaceful security. Scarcely, in fact, could I procure a young Guillemot before the Eggers had left the coast, nor was it until late in July that I succeeded, after the birds had laid three or four eggs each, instead of one, and when nature having been exhausted, and the season nearly spent, thousands of these birds left the country without having accomplished the purpose for which they had visited it. This war of extermination cannot last many years more. The Eggers themselves will be the first to repent the entire disappearance of the myriads of birds that made the coast of Labrador their summer residence, and unless they follow the persecuted tribes to the northward, they must renounce their trade.

Had not the British Government long since passed strict laws against these ruthless and worthless vagabonds, and laid a heavy penalty on all of them that might be caught in the act of landing their cargoes in Newfoundland or Nova Scotia, I might———

Labrador

WHEN I look back upon the many pleasant hours that I spent with the young gentlemen who composed my party, during our excursions along the coast of sterile and stormy Labrador, I think that a brief account of our employments may prove not altogether uninteresting to my readers.

We had purchased our stores at Boston, with the aid of my generous friend Dr. Parkman of that city; but unfortunately many things necessary on an expedition like ours were omitted. At Eastport in Maine we therefore laid in these requisites. No traveller, let me say, ought to neglect any thing that is calculated to ensure the success of his undertaking, or to contribute to his personal comfort, when about to set out on a long and perhaps hazardous voyage. Very few opportunities of replenishing stores of provisions, clothing or ammunition, occur in such a country as Labrador; and yet, we all placed too much confidence in the zeal and foresight of our purveyors at Eastport. We had abundance of ammunition, excellent bread, meat, and potatoes; but the butter was quite rancid, the oil only fit to grease our guns, the vinegar too liberally diluted with cider, the mustard and pepper deficient in due pungency. All this, however, was not discovered until it was too late to be remedied. Several of the young men were not clothed as hunters should be, and some of the guns were not so good as we could have wished. We were, however, fortunate with respect to our vessel, which was a notable sailer, did not leak, had a good crew, and was directed by a capital seaman.

The hold of the schooner was floored, and an entrance made to it from the cabin, so that in it we had a very good parlour, dining-room, drawing-room, library, &c. all those apartments, however, being united into one. An extravagantly elongated deal table ranged along the centre; one of the party had slung his hammock at one end, and in its vicinity slept the cook and a lad who acted as armourer. The cabin was small; but being fitted in the usual manner with side berths, was used for a dormitory. It contained a small table and a stove, the latter of diminutive size, but smoky enough to discomfit a host. We had adopted in a great measure the clothing worn by the American fisherman on that coast, namely, thick blue cloth trowsers, a comfortable waistcoat, and a pea-jacket of blanket. Our boots were large, round-toed, strong, and well studded with large nails to prevent sliding on the rocks. Worsted comforters, thick mittens, and round broad-brimmed hats, completed our dress, which was more picturesque than fashionable. As soon as we had an opportunity, the boots were exchanged for Esquimau mounted moccasins of sealskin, impermeable to water, light, easy, and fastening at top about the middle of the thigh to straps, which when buckled over the hips secured them well. To complete our equipment, we had several good boats, one of which was extremely light and adapted for shallow water.

No sooner had we reached the coast and got into harbour, than we agreed to follow certain regulations intended for the general benefit. Every morning the cook was called before three o'clock. At half-past three, breakfast was on the table, and every body equipt. The guns, ammunition, botanical boxes, and baskets for eggs or minerals, were all in readiness. Our breakfast consisted of coffee, bread, and various other materials. At four, all except the cook and one seaman, went off in different directions, not forgetting to carry with them a store of cooked provisions. Some betook themselves to the islands, others to the deep bays; the latter landing wandered over the country, until noon, when laying themselves down on the rich moss, or sitting on the granite rock, they would rest for an hour, eat their dinner, and talk of their successes or disappointments. I often regret that I did not take sketches of the curious groups formed by my young friends on such occasions, and when, after returning at night, all were engaged in measuring, weighing, comparing and dissecting the birds we had procured, operations which were carried on with the aid of a number of candles thrust into the necks of bottles. Here one examined the flowers and leaves of a plant, there another explored the recesses of a diver's gullet, while a third skinned a gull or a grouse. Nor was our journal forgotten. Arrangements were made for the morrow, and at twelve we left matters to the management of the cook, and retired to our roosts.

If the wind blew hard, all went on shore, and, excepting on a few remarkably rainy days, we continued our pursuits much in the same manner during our stay in the country. The physical powers of the young men were considered in making our arrangements. Shattuck and Ingals went together; the Captain and Cooledge were fond of each other, the latter having also been an officer; Lincoln and my son being the strongest and most determined hunters, generally marched by themselves; and

I went with one or other of the parties according to circumstances, although it was by no means my custom to do so regularly, as I had abundance of work on hand in the vessel.

The return of my young companions and the sailors was always looked for with anxiety. On getting on board, they opened their budgets, and laid their contents on the deck, amid much merriment, those who had procured most specimens being laughed at by those who had obtained the rarest, and the former joking the latter in return. A substantial meal awaited them, and fortunate we were in having a capital cook, although he was a little too fond of the bottle.

Our "fourth of July" was kept sacred, and every Saturday night the toast of "wives and sweethearts" was the first given, "parents and friends" the last. Never was there a more merry set. Some with the violin and flute accompanied the voices of the rest, and few moments were spent in idleness. Before a month had elapsed, the spoils of many a fine bird hung around the hold; shrubs and flowers were in the press, and I had several drawings finished, some of which you have seen, and of which I hope you will ere long see the remainder. Large jars were filling apace with the bodies of rare birds, fishes, quadrupeds, and reptiles, as well as molluscous animals. We had several pets too, Gulls, Cormorants, Guillemots, Puffins, Hawks, and a Raven. In some of the harbours, curious fishes were hooked in our sight, so clear was the water.

We found that camping out at night was extremely uncomfortable, on account of the annoyance caused by flies and musquitoes, which attacked the hunters in swarms at all times, but more especially when they lay down, unless they enveloped themselves in thick smoke, which is not much more pleasant. Once when camping, the weather became very bad, and the party was twenty miles distant from Whapatiguan as night threw her mantle over the earth. The rain fell in torrents, the north-east wind blew furiously, and the air was extremely cold. The oars of the boats were fixed so as to support some blankets, and a small fire was with difficulty kindled, on the embers of which a scanty meal was cooked. How different from a camp on the shores of the Mississippi, where wood is abundant, and the air generally not lacking heat, where musquitoes, although plentiful enough, are not accompanied by carraboo flies, and where the barkings of a joyful squirrel, or the notes of the Barred Owl, that grave buffoon of our western woods, never fail to gladden the camper as he cuts to the right and left such branches and canes as most easily supply materials for forming a lodging for the night! On the coast of Labrador there are no such things; granite and green moss are spread around, silence like that of the grave envelopes all, and when night has closed the dreary scene from your sight, the wolves, attracted by the scent of the remains of your scanty repast, gather around you. Cowards as they are, they dare not venture on a charge; but their howling effectually banish sleep. You must almost roast your feet to keep them warm, while your head and shoulders are chilled by the blast. When morning comes, she smiles not on you with rosy cheeks, but appears muffled in a grey mantle of cold mist, which shews you that there is no prospect of a fine day. The object of the expedition, which was to procure some Owls that had been observed there by day, was entirely frustrated. At early dawn, the party rose stiffened and dispirited, and glad were they to betake themselves to their boats, and return to their floating home.

Before we left Labrador, several of my young friends began to feel the want of suitable clothing. The sailors' ever-tailoring system was, believe me, fairly put to the test. Patches of various colours ornamented knees and elbows; our boots were worn out; our greasy garments and battered hats were in harmony with our tanned and weather-beaten faces; and, had you met with us, you might have taken us for a squad of wretched vagrants; but we were joyous in the expectation of a speedy return, and exulted at the thoughts of our success.

As the chill blast that precedes the winter's tempest thickened the fogs on the hills and ruffled the dark waters, each successive day saw us more anxious to leave the dreary wilderness of grim rocks and desolate moss-clad valleys. Unfavourable winds prevented us for a while from spreading our white sails; but at last one fair morning smiled on the wintry world, the Ripley was towed from the harbour, her tackle trimmed, and as we bounded over the billows, we turned our eyes toward the wilds of Labrador, and heartily bade them farewell for ever!

Part 🍃 Two

THE ORNITHOLOGICAL BIOGRAPHY

🍃 Work on the five volumes of the Ornithological Biography, which occupied Audubon for a decade, from *1830* until *1839*, frequently led him to wonder in letters and journals why he had ever become a writer. It was an enormous labor. Throughout the project he was aided by William Macgillivray, the Scottish scientist, and by Lucy, who did a good deal of transcribing. But the rich experience, the zestful voice, and the vivid way of seeing are pure Audubon. We are fortunate that he chose to write as well as paint his portraits of birds. I have preserved the original spelling, which reflects British practice—favourite—as well as variants typical of the period—Allabama, teazing. I have also preserved Audubon's own names for the birds. In parentheses below each title I have given the modern scientific name and, where it differs from Audubon's usage, the present common name. I have omitted from each essay the technical notes, for these were the work of Macgillivray. The few cuts I have made in Audubon's text are marked with ellipses.

Wild Turkey

(*Meleagris gallopavo*)

THE great size and beauty of the Wild Turkey, its value as a delicate and highly prized article of food, and the circumstance of its being the origin of the domestic race now generally dispersed over both continents, render it one of the most interesting of the birds indigenous to the United States of America.

The unsettled parts of the States of Ohio, Kentucky, Illinois, and Indiana, an immense extent of country to the north-west of these districts, upon the Mississippi and Missouri, and the vast regions drained by these rivers from their confluence to Louisiana, including the wooded parts of Arkansas, Tennessee, and Alabama, are the most abundantly supplied with this magnificent bird. It is less plentiful in Georgia and the Carolinas, becomes still scarcer in Virginia and Pennsylvania, and is now very rarely seen to the eastward of the last mentioned States. In the course of my rambles through Long Island, the State of New York, and the country around the Lakes, I did not meet with a single individual, although I was informed that some exist in those parts. Turkeys are still to be found along the whole line of the Alleghany Mountains, where they have become so wary as to be approached only with extreme difficulty. While, in the Great Pine Forest, in 1829, I found a single feather that had been dropped from the tail of a female, but saw no bird of the kind. Farther eastward, I do not think they are now to be found. I shall describe the manners of this bird as observed in the countries where it is most abundant, and having resided for many years in Kentucky and Louisiana, may be understood as referring chiefly to them.

The Turkey is irregularly migratory, as well as irregularly gregarious. With reference to the first of these circumstances, I have to state, that whenever the *mast** of one portion of the country happens greatly to exceed that of another, the Turkeys are insensibly led toward that spot, by gradually meeting in their haunts with more fruit the nearer they advance towards the place where it is most plentiful. In this manner flock follows after flock, until one district is entirely deserted, while an-

---

*In America, the term *mast* is not confined to the fruit of the beech, but is used as a general name for all kinds of forest fruits, including even grapes and berries.

other is, as it were, overflowed by them. But as these migrations are irregular, and extend over a vast expanse of country, it is necessary that I should describe the manner in which they take place.

About the beginning of October, when scarcely any of the seeds and fruits have yet fallen from the trees, these birds assemble in flocks, and gradually move towards the rich bottom lands of the Ohio and Mississippi. The males, or, as they are more commonly called, the *gobblers*, associate in parties of from ten to a hundred, and search for food apart from the females; while the latter are seen either advancing singly, each with its brood of young, then about two-thirds grown, or in connexion with other families, forming parties often amounting to seventy or eighty individuals, all intent on shunning the old cocks, which, even when the young birds have attained this size, will fight with, and often destroy them by repeated blows on the head. Old and young, however, all move in the same course, and on foot, unless their progress be interrupted by a river, or the hunter's dog force them to take wing. When they come upon a river, they betake themselves to the highest eminences, and there often remain a whole day, or sometimes two, as if for the purpose of consultation. During this time, the males are heard *gobbling*, calling, and making much ado, and are seen strutting about, as if to raise their courage to a pitch befitting the emergency. Even the females and young assume something of the same pompous demeanour, spread out their tails, and run round each other, *purring* loudly, and performing extravagant leaps. At length, when the weather appears settled, and all around is quiet, the whole party mounts to the tops of the highest trees, whence, at a signal, consisting of a single *cluck*, given by a leader, the flock takes flight for the opposite shore. The old and fat birds easily get over, even should the river be a mile in breadth; but the younger and less robust frequently fall into the water,—not to be drowned, however, as might be imagined. They bring their wings close to their body, spread out their tail as a support, stretch forward their neck, and, striking out their legs with great vigour, proceed rapidly towards the shore; on approaching which, should they find it too steep for landing, they cease their exertions for a few moments, float down the stream until they come to an accessible part, and by a violent effort generally extricate themselves from the water. It is remarkable, that immediately after thus crossing a large stream, they ramble about for some time, as if bewildered. In this state, they fall an easy prey to the hunter.

When the Turkeys arrive in parts where the mast is abundant, they separate into smaller flocks, composed of birds of all ages and both sexes, promiscuously mingled, and devour all before them. This happens about the middle of November. So gentle do they sometimes become after these long journeys, that they have been seen to approach the farm-houses, associate with the domestic fowls, and enter the stables and corncribs in quest of food. In this way, roaming about the forests, and feeding chiefly on mast, they pass the autumn and part of the winter.

As early as the middle of February, they begin to experience the impulse of propagation. The females separate, and fly from the males. The latter strenuously pursue, and begin to gobble or to utter the notes of exultation. The sexes roost apart, but at no great distance from each other. When a female utters a call-note, all the gobblers within hearing return the sound, return rolling note after note with as much rapidity as if they intended to emit the last and the first together, not with spread tail, as when fluttering round the females on the ground, or practising on the branches of the trees on which they have roosted for the night, but much in the manner of the domestic turkey, when an unusual or un-expected noise elicits its singular hubbub. If the call of the female comes from the ground, all the males immediately fly towards the spot, and the moment they reach it, whether the hen be in sight or not, spread out and erect their tail, draw the head back on the shoulders, depress their wings with a quivering motion, and strut pompously about, emitting at the same time a succession of puffs from the lungs, and stopping now and then to listen and look. But whether they spy the female or not, they continue to puff and strut, moving with as much celerity as their ideas of ceremony seem to admit. While thus occupied, the males often en-counter each other, in which case desperate battles take place, ending in bloodshed, and often in the loss of many lives, the weaker falling un-der the repeated blows inflicted upon their head by the stronger.

I have often been much diverted, while watching two males in fierce conflict, by seeing them move alternately backwards and for-wards, as either had obtained a better hold, their wings drooping, their tails partly raised, their body-feathers ruffled, and their heads covered with blood. If, as they thus struggle, and gasp for breath, one of them should lose his hold, his chance is over, for the other, still holding fast, hits him violently with spurs and wings, and in a few minutes brings him to the ground. The moment he is dead, the conqueror treads him under foot, but, what is strange, not with hatred, but with all the motions which he employs in caressing the female.

When the male has discovered and made up to the female (whether such a combat has previously taken place or not), if she be more than one year old, she also struts and gobbles, turns round him as he continues strutting, suddenly opens her wings, throws herself towards him, as if to put a stop to his idle delay, lays herself down, and receives his dilatory caresses. If the cock meet a young hen, he alters his mode of procedure. He struts in a different manner, less pompously and more energetically, moves with rapidity, sometimes rises from the ground, taking a short flight around the hen, as is the manner of some Pigeons, the Red-breasted Thrush, and many other birds, and on alighting, runs with all his might, at the same time rubbing his tail and wings along the ground, for the space of perhaps ten yards. He then draws near the timorous female, allays her fears by purring, and when she at length assents, caresses her.

When a male and a female have thus come together, I believe the connexion continues for that season, although the former by no means confines his attentions to one female, as I have seen a cock caress several hens, when he happened to fall in with them in the same place, for the first time. After this the hens follow their favourite cock, roosting in his immediate neighbourhood, if not on the same tree, until they begin to lay, when they separate themselves, in order to save their eggs from the male, who would break them all, for the purpose of protracting his sexual enjoyments. The females then carefully avoid him, excepting during a short period each day. After this the males become clumsy and slovenly, if one may say so, cease to fight with each other, give up gobbling or calling so frequently, and assume so careless a habit, that the hens are obliged to make all the advances themselves. They *yelp* loudly and almost continually for the cocks, run up to them, caress them, and employ various means to rekindle their expiring ardour.

Turkey-cocks when at roost sometimes strut and gobble, but I have more generally seen them spread out and raise their tail, and emit pulmonic puff, lowering their tail and other feathers immediately after. During clear nights, or when there is moonshine, they perform this action at intervals of a few minutes, for hours together, without moving from the same spot, and indeed sometimes without rising on their legs, especially towards the end of the love season. The males now become greatly emaciated, and cease to gobble, their *breast-sponge* becoming flat. They then separate from the hens, and one might suppose that they had entirely deserted their neighbourhood. At such seasons I have found them lying by the side of a log, in some retired part of the dense woods and cane thickets, and often permitting one to approach within a few feet. They are then unable to fly, but run swiftly, and to a great distance. A slow turkey-hound has led me miles before I could flush the same bird. Chases of this kind I did not undertake for the purpose of killing the bird, it being then unfit for eating, and covered with ticks, but with the view of rendering myself acquainted with its habits. They thus retire to recover flesh and strength, by purging with particular species of grass, and using less exercise. As soon as their condition is improved, the cocks come together again, and recommence their rambles. Let us now return to the females.

About the middle of April, when the season is dry, the hens begin to look out for a place in which to deposit their eggs. This place requires to be as much as possible concealed from the eye of the Crow, as that bird often watches the Turkey when going to her nest, and, waiting in the neighbourhood until she has left it, removes and eats the eggs. The nest, which consists of a few withered leaves, is placed on the ground, in a hollow scooped out by the side of a log, or in the fallen top of a dry leafy tree, a thicket of sumach or briars, or a few feet within the edge of a cane-brake, but always in a dry place. The eggs, which are of a dull cream colour, sprinkled with red dots, sometimes amount to twenty, although the more usual number is from ten to fifteen. When depositing her eggs, the female always approaches the nest with extreme caution, scarcely ever taking the same course twice; and when about to leave them, covers them carefully with leaves, so that it is very difficult for a person who may have seen the bird to discover the nest. Indeed, few Turkeys' nests are found, unless the female has been suddenly started from them, or a cunning Lynx, Fox, or Crow has sucked the eggs and left their shells scattered about.

Turkey hens not unfrequently prefer islands for depositing their eggs and rearing their young, probably because such places are less frequented by hunters, and because the great masses of drifted timber which usually accumulate at their heads, may protect and save them in cases of great emergency. When I have found these birds in such situations, and with young, I have always observed that a single discharge of a gun made them run immediately to the pile of drifted wood, and conceal themselves in it. I have often walked over these masses, which are frequently from ten to twenty feet in height, in search of the game which I knew to be concealed in them.

When an enemy passes within sight of a female, while laying or sitting, she never moves, unless she knows that she has been discovered, but crouches lower until he has passed. I have frequently approached within five or six paces of a nest, of which I was previously aware, on assuming an air of carelessness, and whistling or talking to myself, the female remaining undisturbed; whereas if I went cautiously towards it, she would never suffer me to approach within twenty paces, but would run off, with her tail spread on one side, to a distance of twenty or thirty yards, when assuming a stately gait she would walk about deliberately, uttering every now and then a cluck. They seldom abandon their nest, when it has been discovered by men; but, I believe, never go near it again, when a snake or other animal has sucked any of the eggs. If the eggs have been destroyed or carried off, the female soon yelps again for a male; but, in general, she rears only a single brood each season. Several hens sometimes associate together, I believe for their mutual safety, deposit their eggs in the same nest, and rear their broods together. I once found three sitting, on forty-two eggs. In such cases, the common nest is always watched by one of the females, so that no Crow, Raven, or perhaps even Pole-cat, dares approach it.

The mother will not leave her eggs, when near hatching, under any circumstances, while life remains. She will even allow an enclosure to be made around her, and thus suffer imprisonment, rather than abandon them. I once witnessed the hatching of a brood of Turkeys, which I watched for the purpose of securing them together with the parent. I concealed myself on the ground within a very few feet, and saw her raise herself half the length of her legs, look anxiously upon the eggs, cluck with a sound peculiar to the mother on such occasions, carefully remove each half-empty shell, and with her bill caress and dry the young birds, that already stood tottering and attempting to make their way out of the nest. Yes, I have seen this, and have left mother and young to better care than mine could have proved,—to the care of their Creator and mine. I have seen them all emerge from the shell, and, in a few moments after, tumble, roll, and push each other forward with astonishing and inscrutable instinct.

Before leaving the nest with her young brood, the mother shakes herself in a violent manner, picks and adjusts the feathers about her belly, and assumes quite a different aspect. She alternately inclines her eyes obliquely upwards and sideways, stretching out her neck, to discover hawks or other enemies, spreads her wings a little as she walks, and softly clucks to keep her innocent offspring close to her. They move slowly along, and as the hatching generally takes place in the afternoon, they frequently return to the nest to spend the first night there. After this, they remove to some distance, keeping on the highest undulated grounds, the mother dreading rainy weather, which is extremely dangerous to the young, in this tender state, when they are only covered by a kind of soft hairy down, of surprising delicacy. In very rainy seasons, Turkeys are scarce, for if once completely wetted, the young seldom recover. To prevent the disastrous effects of rainy weather, the mother, like a skillful physician, plucks the buds of the spice-wood bush, and gives them to her young.

In about a fortnight, the young birds, which had previously rested on the ground, leave it and fly, at night, to some very large low branch, where they place themselves under the deeply curved wings of their kind and careful parent, dividing themselves for that purpose into two nearly equal parties. After this, they leave the woods during the day, and approach the natural glades or prairies, in search of strawberries, and subsequently of dewberries, blackberries and grasshoppers, thus obtaining abundant food, and enjoying the beneficial influence of the sun's rays. They roll themselves in deserted ants' nests, to clear their growing feathers of the loose scales, and prevent ticks and other vermin from attacking them, these insects being unable to bear the odour of the earth in which ants have been.

The young Turkeys now advance rapidly in growth, and in the month of August are able to secure themselves from unexpected attacks of Wolves, Foxes, Lynxes, and even Cougars, by rising quickly from the ground, by the help of their powerful legs, and reaching with ease the highest branches of the tallest trees. The young cocks shew the tuft on the breast about this time, and begin to gobble and strut, while the young hens pur and leap, in the manner which I have already described.

The old cocks have also assembled by this time, and it is probable that all the Turkeys now leave the extreme north-western districts, to remove to the Wabash, Illinois, Black River, and the neighbourhood of Lake Erie.

Of the numerous enemies of the Wild Turkey, the most formidable, excepting man, are the Lynx, the Snowy Owl, and the Virginian Owl. The Lynx sucks their eggs, and is extremely expert at seizing both young and old, which he effects in the following manner. When he has discovered a flock of Turkeys, he follows them at a distance for some time, until he ascertains the direction in which they are proceeding. He then makes a rapid circular movement, gets in advance of the flock, and lays himself down in ambush, until the birds come up, when he springs upon one of them by a single bound, and secures it. While once sitting in the woods, on the banks of the Wabash, I observed two large Turkey-cocks on a log, by the river, pluming and picking themselves. I watched their movements for a while, when of a sudden one of them flew across the river, while I perceived the other struggling under the grasp of a lynx. When attacked by the two large species of Owl above mentioned, they often effect their escape in a way which is somewhat remarkable. As Turkeys usually roost in flocks, on naked branches of trees, they are easily discovered by their enemies, the owls, which, on a silent wing, approach and hover around them, for the purpose of reconnoitring. This, however, is rarely done without being discovered, and a single *cluck* from one of the Turkeys announces to the whole party the approach of the murderer. They instantly start upon their legs, and watch the motions of the Owl, which, selecting one as its victim, comes down upon it like an arrow, and would inevitably secure the Turkey, did not the latter at that moment lower its head, stoop, and spread its tail in an inverted manner over its back, by which action the aggressor is met by a smooth inclined plane, along which it glances without hurting the Turkey; immediately after which the latter drops to the ground, and thus escapes, merely with the loss of a few feathers.

The Wild Turkeys cannot be said to confine themselves to any particular kind of food, although they seem to prefer the pecan-nut and winter-grape to any other, and, where these fruits abound, are found in the greatest numbers. They eat grass and herbs of various kinds, corn, berries, and fruit of all descriptions. I have even found beetles, tadpoles, and small lizards in their crops.

Turkeys are now generally extremely shy, and the moment they observe a man, whether of the red or white race, instinctively move from him. Their usual mode of progression is what is termed walking, during which they frequently open each wing partially and successively, replacing them again by folding them over each other, as if their weight were too great. Then, as if to amuse themselves, they will run a few steps, open both wings and fan their sides, in the manner of the common fowl, and often take two or three leaps in the air and shake themselves. Whilst searching for food among the leaves or loose soil, they keep their head up, and are unremittingly on the lookout; but as the legs and feet finish the operation, they are immediately seen to pick up the food, the presence of which, I suspect, is frequently indicated to them through the sense of touch in their feet, during the act of scratching. This habit of scratching and removing the dried leaves in the woods, is pernicious to their safety, as the spots which they thus clear, being about two feet in diameter, are seen at a distance, and, if fresh, shew that the birds are in the vicinity. During the summer months they resort to the paths or roads, as well as the ploughed fields, for the purpose of rolling themselves in the dust, by which means they clear their bodies of the ticks which at that season infest them, as well as free themselves of the mosquitoes, which greatly annoy them, by biting their heads.

When, after a heavy fall of snow, the weather becomes frosty, so as to form a hard crust on the surface, the Turkeys remain on their roosts for three or four days, sometimes much longer, which proves their capability of continued abstinence. When near farms, however, they leave the roosts, and go into the very stables and about the stacks of corn, to procure food. During melting snow-falls, they will travel to an extraordinary distance, and are then followed in vain, it being impossible for hunters of any description to keep up with them. They have then a dangling and straggling way of running, which, awkward as it may seem, enables them to outstrip any other animal. I have often, when on a good horse, been obliged to abandon the attempt to put them up, after following them for several hours. This habit of continued running, in rainy or very damp weather of any kind, is not peculiar to the Wild Turkey, but is common to all gallinaceous birds. In America, the different species of Grouse exhibit the same tendency.

In spring, when the males are much emaciated, in consequence of their attentions to the females, it sometimes happens that, on plain and open ground, they may be overtaken by a swift dog, in which case they squat, and allow themselves to be seized, either by the dog, or the hunter who has followed on a good horse. I have heard of such occurrences, but never had the pleasure of seeing an instance of them.

Good dogs scent the Turkeys, when in large flocks, at extraordinary distances,—I think I may venture to say half a mile. Should the dog be well trained to this sport, he sets off at full speed, and in silence, until he sees the birds, when he instantly barks, and pushing as much as possible into the centre of the flock, forces the whole to take wing in different directions. This is of great advantage to the hunter, for should the Turkeys all go one way, they would soon leave their perches and run again. But when they separate in this manner, and the weather happens to be calm and lowering, a person accustomed to this kind of sport finds the birds with ease, and shoots them at pleasure.

When Turkeys alight on a tree, it is sometimes very difficult to see them, which is owing to their standing perfectly motionless. Should you discover one, when it is down on its legs upon the branch, you may approach it with less care. But if it is standing erect, the greatest precaution is necessary, for should it discover you, it instantly flies off, frequently to such a distance that it would be vain to follow.

When a Turkey is merely winged by a shot, it falls quickly to the ground in a slanting direction. Then, instead of losing time by tumbling and rolling over, as other birds often do when wounded, it runs off at such a rate, that unless the hunter be provided with a swift dog, he may bid farewell to it. I recollect coming on one shot in this manner, more than a mile from the tree where it had been perched, my dog having traced it to this distance, through one of those thick canebrakes that cover many portions of our rich alluvial lands near the banks of our western rivers. Turkeys are easily killed if shot in the head, the neck, or the upper part of the breast; but if hit in the hind parts only, they often fly so far as to be lost to the hunter. During winter many of our *real* hunters shoot them by moonlight, on the roosts, where these birds will frequently stand a repetition of the reports of a rifle, although they would fly from the attack of an owl, or even perhaps from his presence. Thus sometimes nearly a whole flock is secured by men capable of using these guns in such circumstances. They are often destroyed in great numbers when most worthless, that is, early in the fall or autumn, when many are killed in their attempt to cross the rivers, or immediately after they reach the shore.

Whilst speaking of the shooting of Turkeys, I feel no hesitation in relating the following occurrence, which happened to myself. While in search of game, one afternoon late in autumn, when the males go together, and the females are by themselves also, I heard the clucking of one of the latter, and immediately finding her perched on a fence, made towards her. Advancing slowly and cautiously, I heard the yelping notes of some gobblers, when I stopped and listened in order to ascertain the direction in which they came. I then ran to meet the birds, hid myself by the side of a large fallen tree, cocked my gun, and waited with impatience for a good opportunity. The gobblers continued yelping in answer to the female, which all this while remained on the fence. I looked over the log and saw about thirty fine cocks advancing rather cautiously towards the very spot where I lay concealed. They came so near that the light in their eyes could easily be perceived, when I fired one barrel, and killed three. The rest, instead of flying off, fell a strutting around their dead companions, and had I not looked on shooting again as murder without necessity, I might have secured at least another. So I shewed myself, and marching to the place where the dead birds were, drove away the survivors. I may also mention, that a friend of mine shot a fine hen, from his horse, with a pistol, as the poor thing was probably returning to her nest to lay.

Should you, good-natured reader, be a sportsman, and now and then have been fortunate in the exercise of your craft, the following incident, which I shall relate to you as I had it from the mouth of an honest farmer, may prove interesting. Turkeys were very abundant in his neighbourhood, and, resorting to his corn fields, at the period when the maize had just shot up from the ground, destroyed great quantities of it. This induced him to swear vengeance against the species. He cut a long trench in a favourable situation, put a great quantity of corn in it, and having heavily loaded a famous duck gun of his, placed it so as that he could pull the trigger by means of a string, when quite concealed from the birds. The Turkeys soon discovered the corn in the trench, and quickly disposed of it, at the same time continuing their ravages in the fields. He filled the trench again, and one day seeing it quite black with the Turkeys, whistled loudly, on which all the birds raised their heads, when he pulled the trigger by the long string fastened to it. The explosion followed of course, and the Turkeys were seen scampering off in all directions, in utter discomfiture and dismay. On running to the trench, he found nine of them extended in it. The rest did not consider it expedient to visit his corn again for that season.

During spring, Turkeys are *called*, as it is termed, by drawing the air in a particular way through one of the second joint bones of a wing of that bird, which produces a sound resembling the voice of the female, on hearing which the male comes up, and is shot. In managing this, however, no fault must be committed, for Turkeys are quick in distinguishing counterfeit sounds, and when *half civilized* are very wary and cunning. I have known many to answer to this kind of call, without moving a step, and thus entirely defeat the scheme of the hunter, who dared not move from his hiding-place, lest a single glance of the gobbler's eye should frustrate all further attempts to decoy him. Many are shot when at roost, in this season, by answering with a rolling gobble to a sound in imitation of the cry of the Barred Owl.

But the most common method of procuring Wild Turkeys, is by means of *pens*. These are placed in parts of the woods where Turkeys have been frequently observed to roost, and are constructed in the following manner. Young trees of four or five inches diameter are cut down, and divided into pieces of the length of twelve or fourteen feet. Two of these are laid on the ground parallel to each other, at a distance of ten or twelve feet. Two other pieces are laid across the ends of these, at right angles to them; and in this manner successive layers are added, until the fabric is raised to the height of about four feet. It is then covered with similar pieces of wood, placed three or four inches apart, and loaded with one or two heavy logs to render the whole firm. This done, a trench about eighteen inches in depth and width is cut under one side of the cage, into which it opens slantingly and rather abruptly. It is continued on its outside to some distance, so as gradually to attain the level of the surrounding ground. Over the part of this trench within the pen, and close to the wall, some sticks are placed so as to form a kind of bridge about a foot in breadth. The trap being now finished, the owner places a quantity of Indian corn in its centre, as well as in the trench, and as he walks off drops here and there a few grains in the woods, sometimes to the distance of a mile. This is repeated at every visit to the trap, after the Turkeys have found it. Sometimes two trenches are cut, in which case the trenches enter on opposite sides of the trap, and are both strewn with corn. No sooner has a Turkey discovered the train of corn, than it communicates the circumstance to the flock by a cluck, when all of them come up, and searching for the grains scattered about, at length come upon the trench, which they follow, squeezing themselves one after another through the passage under the bridge. In this manner the whole flock sometimes enters, but more commonly six or seven only, as they are alarmed by the least noise, even the cracking of a tree in frosty weather. Those within, having gorged themselves, raise their heads, and try to force their way through the top of sides of the pen, passing and repassing on the bridge, but never for a moment looking down, or attempting to escape through the passage by which they entered. Thus they remain until the owner of the trap arriving, closes the trench, and secures his captives. I have heard of eighteen Turkeys having been caught in this manner at a single visit to the trap. I have had many of these pens myself, but never found more than seven in them at a time. One winter I kept an account of the produce of a pen which I visited daily, and found that seventy-six had been caught in it, in about two months. When these birds are abundant, the owners of the pens sometimes become satiated with their flesh, and neglect to visit the pens for several days, in some cases for weeks. The poor captives thus perish for want of food; for, strange as it may seem, they scarcely ever regain their liberty, by descending into the trench, and retracing their steps. I have, more than once, found four or five, and even ten, dead in a pen, through inattention. Where Wolves or Lynxes are numerous, they are apt to secure the prize before the owner of the trap arrives. One morning, I had the pleasure of securing in one of my pens, a fine Black Wolf, which, on seeing me, squatted, supposing me to be passing in another direction.

Wild Turkeys often approach and associate with tame ones, or fight with them, and drive them off from their food. The cocks sometimes pay their addresses to the domesticated females, and are generally received by them with great pleasure, as well as by their owners, who are well aware of the advantages resulting from such intrusions, the half-breed being much more hardy than the tame, and, consequently, more easily reared.

While at Henderson, on the Ohio, I had, among many other wild birds, a fine male Turkey, which had been reared from its earliest youth under my care, it having been caught by me when probably not more than two or three days old. It became so tame that it would follow any person who called it, and was the favourite of the little village. Yet it would never roost with the tame Turkeys, but regularly betook itself at night to the roof of the house, where it remained until dawn. When two years old, it began to fly to the woods, where it remained for a considerable part of the day, to return to the enclosure as night approached. It continued this practice until the following spring, when I saw it several times fly from its roosting place to the top of a high cotton-tree, on the bank of the Ohio, from which, after resting a little, it would sail to the opposite shore, the river being there nearly half a mile wide, and return towards night. One morning I saw it fly off, at a very early hour, to the woods, in another direction, and took no particular notice of the circumstance. Several days elapsed, but the bird did not return. I was going towards some lakes near Green River to shoot, when, having walked about five miles, I saw a fine large gobbler cross the path before me, moving leisurely along. Turkeys being then in prime condition for the table, I ordered my dog to chase it, and put it up. The animal went off with great rapidity, and as it approached the Turkey, I saw, with great surprise, that the latter paid little attention. Juno was on the point of seizing it, when she suddenly stopped, and turned her head towards me. I hastened to them, but you may easily conceive my surprise when I saw my own favourite bird, and discovered that it had recognised the dog, and would not fly from it; although the sight of a strange dog would have caused it to run off at once. A friend of mine happening to be in search of a wounded deer, took the bird on his saddle before him, and carried it home for me. The following spring it was accidentally shot, having been taken for a wild bird, and brought to me on being recognised by the red ribbon which it had around its neck. Pray, reader, by what word will you designate the recognition made by my favourite Turkey of a dog which had been long associated with it in the yard and grounds? Was it the result of instinct, or of reason, an unconsciously revived impression, or the act of an intelligent mind?

White-Headed Eagle

(Bald Eagle, *Haliaeetus leucocephalus*)

The figure of this noble bird is well known throughout the civilized world, emblazoned as it is on our national standard, which waves in the breeze of every clime, bearing to distant lands the remembrance of a great people living in a state of peaceful freedom. May that peaceful freedom last forever!

The great strength, daring, and cool courage of the White-headed Eagle, joined to his unequalled power of flight, render him highly conspicuous among his brethren. To these qualities did he add a generous disposition towards others, he might be looked up to as a model of nobility. The ferocious, overbearing, and tyrannical temper which is ever and anon displaying itself in his actions, is, nevertheless, best adapted to his state, and was wisely given him by the Creator to enable him to perform the office assigned to him.

To give you, kind reader, some idea of the nature of this bird, permit me to place you on the Mississippi, on which you may float gently along, while approaching winter brings millions of water-fowel on whistling wings, from the countries of the north, to seek a milder climate in which to sojourn for a season. The Eagle is seen perched, in an erect attitude, on the highest summit of the tallest tree by the margin of the broad stream. His glistening but stern eye looks over the vast expanse. He listens attentively to every sound that comes to his quick ear from afar, glancing now and then on the earth beneath, lest even the light tread of the fawn may pass unheard. His mate is perched on the opposite side, and should all be tranquil and silent, warns him by a cry to continue patient. At this well known call, the male partly opens his broad wings, inclines his body a little downwards, and answers to her voice in tones not unlike the laugh of a maniac. The next moment, he resumes his erect attitude, and again all around is silent. Ducks of many species, the Teal, the Wigeon, the Mallard and others, are seen passing with great rapidity, and following the course of the current; but the Eagle heeds them not: they are at that time beneath his attention. The next moment, however, the wild trumpet-like sound of a yet distant but approaching Swan is heard. A shriek from the female Eagle comes across the stream,—for, kind reader, she is fully as alert as her mate. The latter suddenly shakes the whole of his body, and with a few touches of his bill, aided by the action of his cuticular muscles, arranges his plumage in an instant. The snow-white bird is now in sight: her long neck is stretched forward, her eye is on the watch, vigilant as that of her enemy; her large wings seem with difficulty to support the weight of her body, although they flap incessantly. So irksome do her exertions seem, that her very legs are spread beneath her tail, to aid her in her flight. She approaches, however. The Eagle has marked her for his prey. As the Swan is passing the dreaded pair, starts from his perch, in full preparation for the chase, the male bird, with an awful scream, that to the Swan's ear brings more terror than the report of the large duck-gun.

Now is the moment to witness the display of the Eagle's powers. He glides through the air like a falling star, and, like a flash of lightning, comes upon the timorous quarry, which now, in agony and despair, seeks, by various manœuvers, to elude the grasp of his cruel talons. It mounts, doubles, and willingly would plunge into the stream, were it not prevented by the Eagle, which, long possessed of the knowledge that by such a stratagem the Swan might escape him, forces it to remain in the air by attempting to strike it with his talons from beneath. The hope of escape is soon given up by the Swan. It has already become much weakened, and its strength fails at the sight of the courage and swiftness of its antagonist. Its last gasp is about to escape, when the ferocious Eagle strikes with his talons the under side of its wing, and with unresisted power forces the bird to fall in a slanting direction upon the nearest shore.

It is then, reader, that you may see the cruel spirit of this dreaded enemy of the feathered race, whilst, exulting over his prey, he for the first time breathes at ease. He presses down his powerful feet, and drives his sharp claws deeper than ever into the heart of the dying Swan. He shrieks with delight, as he feels the last convulsions of his prey, which has now sunk under his unceasing efforts to render death as painfully felt as it can possibly be. The female has watched every movement of her mate; and if she did not assist him in capturing the Swan, it was not from want of will, but merely that she felt full assurance that the power and courage of her lord were quite sufficent for the deed. She now sails to the spot where he eagerly awaits her, and when she has arrived, they together turn the breast of the luckless Swan upwards, and gorge themselves with gore.

At other times, when these Eagles, sailing in search of prey, discover a Goose, a Duck, or a Swan, that has alighted on the water, they accomplish its destruction in a manner that is worthy of your attention. The Eagles, well aware that water-fowl have it in their power to dive at their approach, and thereby elude their attempts upon them, ascend in the air in opposite directions over the lake or river, on which they have observed the object which they are desirous of possessing. Both Eagles reach a certain height, immediately after which one of them glides with great swiftness towards the prey; the latter, meantime, aware of the Eagle's intention, dives the moment before he reaches the spot. The pursuer then rises in the air, and is met by its mate, which glides toward the waterbird, that has just emerged to breathe, and forces it to plunge again beneath the surface, to escape the talons of this second assailant. The first Eagle is now poising itself in the place where its mate formerly was, and rushes anew to force the quarry to make another plunge. By thus alternately gliding, in rapid and often repeated rushes over the ill-fated bird, they soon fatigue it, when it stretches out its neck, swims deeply, and makes for the shore, in the hope of concealing itself among the rank weeds. But this is of no avail, for the Eagles follow it in all its motions, and the moment it approaches the margin, one of them darts upon it, and kills it in an instant, after which they divide the spoil.

During spring and summer, the White-headed Eagle, to procure sustenance, follows a different course, and one much less suited to a bird apparently so well able to supply itself without interfering with other plunderers. No sooner does the Fish-Hawk make its appearance along our Atlantic shores, or ascend our numerous and large rivers, than the Eagle follows it, and, like a selfish oppressor, robs it of the hard-earned fruits of its labour. Perched on some tall summit, in view of the ocean, or of some water course, he watches every motion of the Osprey while on wing. When the latter rises from the water, with a fish in its grasp, forth rushes the Eagle in pursuit. He mounts above the Fish-Hawk, and threatens it by actions well understood, when the latter, fearing perhaps that its life is in danger, drops its prey. In an instant, the Eagle, accurately estimating the rapid descent of the fish, closes his wings, follows it with the swiftness of thought, and the next moment grasps it. The prize is carried off in silence to the woods, and assists in feeding the ever-hungry brood of the Eagle.

This bird now and then procures fish himself, by pursuing them in the shallows of small creeks. I have witnessed several instances of this in the Perkioming Creek in Pennsylvania, where, in this manner, I saw one of them secure a number of *Red-fins*, by wading briskly through the water, and striking at them with his bill. I have also observed a pair scrambling over the ice of a frozen pond, to get at some fish below, but without success.

It does not confine itself to these kinds of food, but greedily devours young pigs, lambs, fawns, poultry, and the putrid flesh of carcasses of every description, driving off the vultures and carrion-crows, or the dogs, and keeping a whole party at defiance until it is satiated. It frequently gives chase to the vultures, and forces them to disgorge the contents of their stomachs, when it alights and devours the filthy mass. A ludicrous instance of this took place near the city of Natchez, on the Mississippi. Many Vultures were engaged in devouring the body and entrails of a dead horse, when a White-headed Eagle accidentally passing by, the vultures all took to wing, one among the rest with a portion of the entrails partly swallowed, and the remaining part, about a yard in length, dangling in the air. The Eagle instantly marked him, and gave chase. The poor vulture tried in vain to disgorge, when the Eagle, coming up, seized the loose end of the gut and dragged the bird along for twenty or thirty yards, much against its will, until both fell to the ground, when the Eagle struck the vulture, and in a few moments killed it, after which he swallowed the delicious morsel.

I have heard of several attempts made by this bird to destroy children, but have never witnessed any myself, although I have little doubt of its having sufficient daring to do so.

The flight of the White-headed Eagle is strong, generally uniform, and protracted to any distance, at pleasure. Whilst travelling, it is entirely supported by equal easy flappings, without any intermission, in as far as I have observed it, by following it with the eye or the assistance of a glass. When looking for prey, it sails with extended wings, at right angles to its body, now and then allowing its legs to hang at their full length. Whilst sailing, it has the power of ascending in circular sweeps, without a single flap of the wings, or any apparent motion either of them or of the tail; and in this manner it often rises until it disappears from the view, the white tail remaining longer visible than the rest of the body. At other times, it rises only a few hundred feet in the air, and sails off in a direct line, and with rapidity. Again, when thus elevated, it partially closes its wings, and glides downwards for a considerable space, when, as if disappointed, it suddenly checks its career, and reassumes its former steady flight. When at an immense height, and as if observing an object on the ground, it closes its wings, and glides through the air with such rapidity as to cause a loud rustling sound, not unlike that produced by a violent gust of wind passing amongst the branches of trees. Its fall towards the earth can scarcely be followed by the eye on such occasions, the more particularly that these falls or glidings through the air usually take place when they are least expected.

This bird has the power of raising from the surface of the water any floating object not heavier than itself. In this manner it often robs the sportsman of ducks which have been killed by him. Its audacity is quite remarkable. While descending the Upper Mississippi, I observed one of these Eagles in pursuit of a Green-winged Teal. It came so near our boat, although several persons were looking on, that I could perceive the glancings of its eye. The Teal, on the point of being caught, when not more than fifteen or twenty yards from us, was saved from the grasp of its enemy, one of our party having brought the latter down by a shot, which broke one of its wings. When taken on board, it was fastened to the deck of our boat by means of a string, and was fed with pieces of catfish, some of which it began to eat on the third day of its confinement. But, as it became a very disagreeable and dangerous associate, trying on all occasions to strike at some one with its talons, it was killed and thrown overboard.

When these birds are suddenly and unexpectedly approached or surprised, they exhibit a great degree of cowardice. They rise at once and fly off very low, in zig-zag lines, to some distance, uttering a hissing noise, not at all like their usual disagreeable imitation of a laugh. When not carrying a gun, one may easily approach them; but the use of that instrument being to appearance well known to them, they are very cautious in allowing a person having one to get near them. Notwithstanding all their caution, however, many are shot by approaching them under cover of a tree, on horseback, or in a boat They do not possess the power of smelling gunpowder, as the crow and the raven are absurdly supposed to do; nor are they aware of the effects of spring-traps, as I have seen some of them caught by these instruments. Their sight, although probably as perfect as that of any bird, is much affected during a fall of snow, at which time they may be approached without difficulty.

The White-headed Eagle seldom appears in very mountainous districts, but prefers the low lands of the sea-shores, those of our large lakes, and the borders of rivers. It is a constant resident in the United States, in every part of which it is to be seen. The roosts and breeding places of pigeons are resorted to by it, for the purpose of picking up the young birds that happen to fall, or the old ones when wounded. It seldom, however, follows the flocks of these birds when on their migrations.

When shot at and wounded, it tries to escape by long and quickly repeated leaps, and, if not closely pursued, soon conceals itself. Should it happen to fall on the water, it strikes powerfully with expanded wings, and in this manner often reaches the shore, when it is not more than twenty of thirty yards distant. It is capable of supporting life without food for a long period. I have heard of some, which, in a state of confinement, had lived without much apparent distress for twenty days, although I cannot vouch for the truth of such statements, which, however, may be quite correct. They defend themselves in the manner usually followed by other Eagles and Hawks, throwing themselves backwards, and furiously striking with their talons at any object within reach, keeping their bill open, and turning their head with quickness to watch the movements of the enemy, their eyes being apparently more protruded than when unmolested.

It is supposed that Eagles live to a very great age,—some persons have ventured to say even a hundred years. On this subject, I can only observe, that I once found one of these birds, which, on being killed, proved to be a female, and which, judging by its appearance, must have been very old. Its tail and wing-feathers were so worn out, and of such a rusty colour, that I imagined the bird had lost the power of moulting. The legs and feet were covered with large warts, the claws and bill were much blunted, it could scarcely fly more than a hundred yards at a time, and this it did with a heaviness and unsteadiness of motion such as I never witnessed in any other bird of the species. The body was poor and very tough. The eye was the only part which appeared to have sustained no injury. It remained sparkling and full of animation, and even after death seemed to have lost little of its lustre. No wounds were perceivable on its body.

The White-headed Eagle is seldom seen alone, the mutual attachment which two individuals form when they first pair seeming to continue until one of them dies or is destroyed. They hunt for the support of each other, and seldom feed apart, but usually drive off other birds of the same species. They commence their amatory intercourse at an earlier period than any other *land bird* with which I am acquainted, generally in the month of December. At this time, along the Mississippi, or by the margin of some lake not far in the interior of the forest, the male and female birds are observed making a great bustle, flying about and circling in various ways, uttering a loud cackling noise, alighting on the dead branches of the tree on which their nest is already preparing, or in the act of being repaired, and caressing each other. In the beginning of

January incubation commences. I shot a female, on the 17th of that month, as she sat on her eggs, in which the chicks had made considerable progress.

The nest, which in some instances is of great size, is usually placed on a very tall tree, destitute of branches to a considerable height, but by no means always a dead one. It is never seen on the rocks. It is composed of sticks, from three to five feet in length, large pieces of turf, rank weeds, and Spanish moss in abundance, whenever that substance happens to be near. When finished, it measures from five to six feet in diameter, and so great is the accumulation of materials, that it sometimes measures the same in depth, it being occupied for a great number of years in succession, and receiving some augmentation each season. When placed in a naked tree, between the forks of the branches, it is conspicuously seen at a great distance. The eggs, which are from two to four, more commonly two or three, are of a dull white colour, and equally rounded at both ends, some of them being occasionally granulated. Incubation lasts for more than three weeks, but I have not been able to ascertain its precise duration, as I have observed the female on different occasions sit for a few days in the nest, before laying the first egg. Of this I assured myself by climbing to the nest every day in succession, during her temporary absence,—a rather perilous undertaking when the bird is sitting.

I have seen the young birds when not larger than middle-sized pullets. At this time, they are covered with a soft cottony kind of down, their bill and legs appearing disproportionately large. Their first plumage is of a greyish colour, mixed with brown of different depths of tint, and before the parents drive them off from the nest, they are fully fledged. As a figure of the Young White-headed Eagle will appear in the course of the publication of my Illustrations, I shall not here trouble you with a description of its appearance. I once caught three young Eagles of this species, when fully fledged, by having the tree on which their nest was, cut down. It caused great trouble to secure them, as they could fly and scramble much faster than any of our party could run. They, however, gradually became fatigued, and at length were so exhausted as to offer no resistance, when we were securing them with cords. This happened on the border of Lake Pontchartrain, in the month of April. The parents did not think fit to come within gun-shot of the tree while the axe was at work.

The attachment of the parents to the young is very great, when the latter are yet of a small size; and to ascend to the nest at this time would be dangerous. But as the young advance, and, after being able to take wing and provide for themselves, are not disposed to fly off, the old birds turn them out, and beat them away from them. They return to the nest, however, to roost, or sleep on the branches immediately near it, for several weeks after. They are fed most abundantly while under the care of the parents, which procure for them ample supplies of fish, either accidentally cast ashore, or taken from the Fish-Hawk, together with rabbits, squirrels, young lambs, pigs, oppossums, or raccoons. Every thing that comes in the way is relished by the young family, as by the old birds.

The young birds begin to breed the following spring, not always in pairs of the same age, as I have several times observed one of these birds in brown plumage mated with a full-coloured bird, which had the head and tail pure white. I once shot a pair of this kind, when the brown bird (the young one) proved to be the female.

This species requires at least four years before it attains the full beauty of its plumage when kept in confinement. I have known two instances in which the white of the head did not make its appearance until the sixth spring. It is impossible for me to say how much sooner this state of perfection is attained, when the bird is at full liberty, although I should suppose it to be at least one year, as the bird is capable of breeding the first spring after birth.

The weight of Eagles of this species varies considerably. In the males, it is from six to eight pounds, and in the females from eight to twelve. These birds are so attached to particular districts, where they have first made their nest, that they seldom spend a night at any distance from the latter, and often resort to its immediate neighbourhood. Whilst asleep, they emit a loud hissing sort of snore, which is heard at the distance of a hundred yards, when the weather is perfectly calm. Yet, so light is their sleep, that the cracking of a stick under the foot of a person immediately wakens them. When it is attempted to smoke them while thus roosted and asleep, they start up and sail off without uttering any sound, but return next evening to the same spot.

Before steam-navigation commenced on our western rivers, these Eagles were extremely abundant there, particularly in the lower parts of the Ohio, the Mississippi, and the adjoining streams. I have seen hundreds going down from the mouth of the Ohio to New Orleans, when it was not at all difficult to shoot them. Now, however, their number is considerably diminished, the game on which they were in the habit of feeding, having been forced to seek refuge from the persecution of man farther in the wilderness. Many, however, are still observed on these rivers, particularly along the shores of the Mississippi.

In concluding this account of the White-headed Eagle, suffer me, kind reader, to say how much I grieve that it should have been selected as the Emblem of my Country. The opinion of our great Franklin on this subject, as it perfectly coincides with my own, I shall here present to you. "For my part," says he, in one of his letters, "I wish the Bald Eagle had not been chosen as the representative of our country. He is a bird of bad moral character; he does not get his living honestly; you may have seen him perched on some dead tree, where, too lazy to fish for himself, he watches the labour of the Fishing-Hawk; and when that diligent bird has at length taken a fish, and is bearing it to his nest for the support of his mate and young ones, the Bald Eagle pursues him, and takes it from him. With all this injustice, he is never in good case, but, like those among men who live by sharping and robbing, he is generally poor, and often very lousy. Besides, he is a rank coward: the little King Bird, not bigger than a Sparrow, attacks him boldly, and drives him out of the district. He is, therefore, by no means a proper emblem for the brave and honest Cincinnati of America, who have driven all the *King Birds* from our country; though exactly fit for that order of knights which the French call *Chevaliers d'Industrie.*"

It is only necessary for me to add, that the name by which this bird is universally known in America is that of *Bald Eagle*, an erroneous denomination, as its head is as densely feathered as that of any other species, although its whiteness may have suggested the idea of its being bare.

Barred Owl

(*Strix varia*)

SHOULD you, kind reader, find it convenient or agreeable to visit the noble forests existing in the lower parts of the State of Louisiana, about the middle of October, when nature, on the eve of preparing for approaching night, permits useful dews to fall and rest on every plant, with the view of reviving its leaves, its fruits, or its lingering blossoms, ere the return of morn; when every night-insect rises on buzzing wings from the ground, and the fire-fly, amidst thousands of other species, appears as if purposely to guide their motions through the sombre atmosphere; at the moment when numerous reptiles and quadrupeds commence their nocturnal prowlings, and the fair moon, empress of the night, rises peacefully on the distant horizon, shooting her silvery rays over the heavens and the earth, and, like a watchful guardian, moving slowly and majestically along; when the husbandman, just returned to his home, after the labours of the day, is receiving the cheering gratulations of his family, and the wholesome repast is about to be spread out for master and servants alike;—it is at this moment, kind reader, that were you, as I have said, to visit that happy country, your ear would suddenly be struck by the discordant screams of the Barred Owl. Its *whah, whah, whah, whah-aa* is uttered loudly, and in so strange and ludicrous a manner, that I should not be surprised were you, kind reader, when you and I meet, to compare these sounds to the affected bursts of laughter which you may have heard from some of the fashionable members of our own species.

How often, when snugly settled under the boughs of my temporary encampment, and preparing to roast a venison steak or the body of a squirrel, on a wooden spit, have I been saluted with the exulting bursts of this nightly disturber of the peace, that, had it not been for him, would have prevailed around me, as well as in my lonely retreat! How often have I seen this nocturnal marauder alight within a few yards of me, exposing his whole body to the glare of my fire, and eye me in such a curious manner that, had it been reasonable to do so, I would gladly have invited him to walk in and join me in my repast, that I might have enjoyed the pleasure of forming a better acquaintance with him. The liveliness of his motions, joined to their oddness, have often made me think that his society would be at least as agreeable as that of many of the buffoons we meet with in the world. But as such opportunities of forming acquaintance have not existed, be content, kind reader, with the imperfect information which I can give you of the habits of this Sancho Pança of our woods.

Such persons as conclude, when looking upon owls in the glare of day, that they are, as they then appear, extremely dull, are greatly mistaken. Were they to state, like BUFFON, that Woodpeckers are miserable beings, they would be talking as incorrectly; and, to one who might have lived long in the woods, they would seem to have lived only in their libraries.

The Barred Owl is found in all those parts of the United States which I have visited, and is a constant resident. In Louisiana it seems to be more abundant than in any other state. It is almost impossible to travel eight or ten miles in any of the retired woods there, without seeing several of them even in broad day; and, at the approach of night, their cries are heard proceeding from every part of the forest around the plantations. Should the weather be lowering, and indicative of the approach of rain, their cries are so multiplied during the day, and especially in the evening, and they respond to each other in tones so strange, that one might imagine some extraordinary fête about to take place among them. On approaching one of them, its gesticulations are seen to be of a very extraordinary nature. The position of the bird, which is generally erect, is immediately changed. It lowers its head and inclines its body, to watch the motions of the person beneath, throws forward the lateral feathers of its head, which thus has the appearance of being surrounded by a broad ruff, looks towards him as if half blind, and moves its head to and fro in so extraordinary a manner, as almost to induce a person to fancy that part dislocated from the body. It follows all the motions of the intruder with its eyes; and should it suspect any treacherous intentions, flies off to a short distance, alighting with its back to the person, and immediately turning about with a single jump, to recommence its scrutiny. In this manner, the Barred Owl may be followed to a considerable distance, if not shot at, for to halloo after it does not seem to frighten it much. But if shot at and missed, it removes to a considerable distance, after which its *whah-whah-whah* is uttered with considerable pomposity. This owl will answer the imitation of its own sounds, and is frequently decoyed by this means.

The flight of the Barred Owl is smooth, light, noiseless, and capable of being greatly protracted. I have seen them take their departure from a detached grove in a prairie, and pursue a direct course towards the skirts of the main forest, distant more than two miles, in broad daylight. I have thus followed them with the eye until they were lost in the distance, and have reason to suppose that they continued their flight until they reached the woods. Once, whilst descending the Ohio, not far from the well-known *Cave-in-rock*, about two hours before sunset, in the month of November, I saw a Barred Owl teased by several crows, and chased from the tree in which it was. On leaving the tree, it gradually rose in the air, in the manner of a Hawk, and at length attained so great a height that our party lost sight of it. It acted, I thought, as if it had lost itself, now and then describing small circles, and flapping its wings quickly, then flying in zigzag lines. This being so uncommon an occurrence, I noted it down at the time. I felt anxious to see the bird return towards the earth, but it did not make its appearance again. So very lightly do they fly, that I have frequently discovered one passing over me, and only a few yards distant, by first seeing its shadow on the ground, during clear moon-light nights, when not the faintest rustling of its wings could be heard.

Their power of sight during the day seems to be rather of an equivocal character, as I once saw one alight on the back of a cow, which it left so suddenly afterwards, when the cow moved, as to prove to me that it had mistaken the object on which it had perched for something else. At other times, I have observed that the approach of the grey squirrel intimidated them, if one of these animals accidentally jumped on a branch close to them, although the Owl destroys a number of them during the twilight. It is for this reason, kind reader, that I have represented the Barred Owl gazing in amazement at one of the squirrels placed only a few inches from him.

The Barred Owl is a great destroyer of poultry, particularly of chickens when half-grown. It also secures mice, young hares, rabbits, and many species of small birds, but is especially fond of a kind of frog of a brown colour, very common in the woods of Louisiana. I have heard it asserted that this bird catches fish, but never having seen it do so, and never having found any portion of fish in its stomach, I cannot vouch for the truth of the report.

About the middle of March, these Owls begin to lay their eggs. This they usually do in the hollows of trees, on the dust of the decomposed wood. At other times they take possession of the old nest of a Crow or a Red-tailed Hawk. In all these situations I have found their eggs and young. The eggs are of a globular form, pure white, with a smooth shell, and are from four to six in number. So far as I have been able to ascertain, they rear only one brood in a season. The young, like those of all other Owls, are at first covered with a downy substance, some of which is seen intermixed with and protruding from the feathers, some weeks after the bird is nearly fledged. They are fed by the parents for a long time, standing perched, and emitting a hissing noise in lieu of a call. This noise may be heard in a calm night, for fifty or probably a hundred yards, and is by no means musical. To a person lost in a swamp, it is, indeed, extremely dismal.

The plumage of the Barred Owl differs very considerably, in respect to colour, in different individuals, more so among the males. The males are also smaller than the females, but less so than in some other species. During the severe winters of our Middle Districts, those that remain there suffer very much; but the greater number, as in some other species, remove to the Southern States. When kept in captivity, they prove excellent mousers.

The antipathy shewn to Owls by every species of day bird is extreme. They are followed and pursued on all occasions; and although few of the day birds ever prove dangerous enemies, their conduct towards the Barred Owl is evidently productive of great annoyance to them. When the Barred Owl is shot at and wounded, it snaps its bill sharply and frequently, raises all its feathers, looks towards the person in the most uncouth manner, but, on the least chance of escape, moves off in great leaps with considerable rapidity.

The Barred Owl is very often exposed for sale in the New Orleans market. The Creoles make *gumbo* of it, and pronounce the flesh palatable.

Passenger Pigeon

(*Ectopistes migratorius*)

THE Passenger Pigeon, or, as it is usually named in America, the Wild Pigeon, moves with extreme rapidity, propelling itself by quickly repeated flaps of the wings, which it brings more or less near to the body, according to the degree of velocity which is required. Like the Domestic Pigeon, it often flies, during the love season, in a circling manner, supporting itself with both wings angularly elevated, in which position it keeps them until it is about to alight. Now and then, during these circular flights, the tips of the primary quills of each wing are made to strike against each other, producing a smart rap, which may be heard at a distance of thirty or forty yards. Before alighting, the Wild Pigeon, like the Carolina Parrot and a few other species of birds, breaks the force of its flight by repeated flappings, as if apprehensive of receiving injury from coming too suddenly into contact with the branch or the spot of ground on which it intends to settle.

I have commenced my description of this species with the above account of its flight, because the most important facts connected with its habits relate to its migrations. These are entirely owing to the necessity of procuring food, and are not performed with the view of escaping the severity of a northern latitude, or of seeking a southern one for the purpose of breeding. They consequently do not take place at any fixed period or season of the year. Indeed, it sometimes happens that a continuance of a sufficient supply of food in one district will keep these birds absent from another for years. I know, at least, to a certainty, that in Kentucky they remained for several years constantly, and were nowhere else to be found. They all suddenly disappeared one season when the mast was exhausted, and did not return for a long period. Similar facts have been observed in other States.

Their great power of flight enables them to survey and pass over an astonishing extent of country in a very short time. This is proved by facts well known in America. Thus, Pigeons have been killed in the neighbourhood of New York, with their crops full of rice, which they must have collected in the fields of Georgia and Carolina, these districts being the nearest in which they could possibly have procured a supply of that kind of food. As their power of digestion is so great that they will decompose food entirely in twelve hours, they must in this case have travelled between three hundred and four hundred miles in six hours, which shews their speed to be at an average about one mile in a minute. A velocity such as this would enable one of these birds, were it so inclined, to visit the European continent in less than three days.

This great power of flight is seconded by as great a power of vision, which enables them, as they travel at that swift rate, to inspect the country below, discover their food with facility, and thus attain the object for which their journey has been undertaken. This I have also proved to be the case, by having observed them, when passing over a sterile part of the country, or one scantily furnished with food suited to them, keep high in the air, flying with an extended front, so as to enable them to survey hundreds of acres at once. On the contrary, when the land is richly covered with food, or the trees abundantly hung with mast, they fly low, in order to discover the part most plentifully supplied.

Their body is of an elongated oval form, steered by a long well-plumed tail, and propelled by well-set wings, the muscles of which are very large and powerful for the size of the bird. When an individual is seen gliding through the woods and close to the observer, it passes like a thought, and on trying to see it again, the eye searches in vain; the bird is gone.

The multitudes of Wild Pigeons in our woods are astonishing. Indeed, after having viewed them so often, and under so many circumstances, I even now feel inclined to pause, and assure myself that what I am going to relate is fact. Yet I have seen it all, and that too in the company of persons who, like myself, were struck with amazement.

In the autumn of 1813, I left my house at Henderson, on the banks of the Ohio, on my way to Louisville. In passing over the Barrens a few miles beyond Hardensburgh, I observed the pigeons flying from northeast to south-west, in greater numbers than I thought I had ever seen them before, and feeling an inclination to count the flocks that might pass within the reach of my eye in one hour, I dismounted, seated myself on an eminence, and began to mark with my pencil, making a dot for every flock that passed. In a short time finding the task which I had undertaken impracticable, as the birds poured in in countless multitudes, I rose, and counting the dots then put down, found that 163 had been made in twenty-one minutes. I travelled on, and still met more the farther I proceeded. The air was literally filled with Pigeons; the light of noon-day was obscured as by an eclipse; the dung fell in spots, not unlike melting flakes of snow; and the continued buzz of wings had a tendency to lull my senses to repose.

Whilst waiting for dinner at YOUNG's inn, at the confluence of Salt-River with the Ohio, I saw, at my leisure, immense legions still going by, with a front reaching far beyond the Ohio on the west, and the beech-wood forests directly on the east of me. Not a single bird alighted; for not a nut or acorn was that year to be seen in the neighbourhood. They consequently flew so high, that different trials to reach them with a capital rifle proved ineffectual; nor did the reports disturb them in the least. I cannot describe to you the extreme beauty of their aerial evolutions, when a Hawk chanced to press upon the rear of a flock. At once, like a torrent, and with a noise like thunder, they rushed into a compact mass, pressing upon each other towards the centre. In these almost solid masses, they darted forward in undulating and angular lines, descended and swept close over the earth with inconceivable velocity, mounted perpendicularly so as to resemble a vast column, and, when high, were seen wheeling and twisting within their continued lines, which then resembled the coils of a gigantic serpent.

Before sunset I reached Louisville, distant from Hardensburgh fifty-five miles. The Pigeons were still passing in undiminished numbers, and continued to do so for three days in succession. The people were all in arms. The banks of the Ohio were crowded with men and boys, incessantly shooting at the pilgrims, which there flew lower as they passed the river. Multitudes were thus destroyed. For a week or more, the population fed on no other flesh than that of Pigeons, and talked of nothing but Pigeons. The atmosphere, during this time, was strongly impregnated with the peculiar odour which emanates from the species.

It is extremely interesting to see flock after flock performing exactly the same evolutions which had been traced as it were in the air by a preceding flock. Thus, should a Hawk have charged on a group at a certain spot, the angles, curves, and undulations that have been described by the birds, in their efforts to escape from the dreaded talons of the plunderer, are undeviatingly followed by the next group that comes up. Should the bystander happen to witness one of these affrays, and, struck with the rapidity and elegance of the motions exhibited, feel desirous of seeing them repeated, his wishes will be gratified if he only remain in the place until the next group comes up.

It may not, perhaps, be out of place to attempt an estimate of the number of Pigeons contained in one of those mighty flocks, and of the quantity of food daily consumed by its members. The inquiry will tend to shew the astonishing bounty of the great Author of Nature in providing for the wants of his creatures. Let us take a column of one mile in breadth, which is far below the average size, and suppose it passing over us without interruption for three hours, at the rate mentioned above of one mile in the minute. This will give us a parallelogram of 180 miles by 1, covering 180 square miles. Allowing two pigeons to the square yard, we have One billion, one hundred and fifteen millions, one hundred and thirty-six thousand pigeons in one flock. As every pigeon daily consumes fully half a pint of food, the quantity necessary for supplying this vast multitude must be eight millions seven hundred and twelve thousand bushels per day.

As soon as the Pigeons discover a sufficiency of food to entice them to alight, they fly round in circles, reviewing the country below. During their evolutions, on such occasions, the dense mass which they form exhibits a beautiful appearance, as it changes its direction, now displaying a glistening sheet of azure, when the backs of the birds come simultaneously into view, and anon, suddenly presenting a mass of rich deep purple. They then pass lower, over the woods, and for a moment are lost among the foliage, but again emerge, and are seen gliding aloft. They now alight, but the next moment, as if suddenly alarmed, they take to wing, producing by the flappings of their wings a noise like the roar of distant thunder, and sweep through the forests to see if danger is near. Hunger, however, soon brings them to the ground. When alighted, they are seen industriously throwing up the withered leaves in quest of the fallen mast. The rear ranks are continually rising, passing over the main-body, and alighting in front, in such rapid succession, that the whole flock seems still on wing. The quantity of ground thus swept is astonishing, and so completely has it been cleared, that the gleaner who might follow in their rear would find his labour completely lost. Whilst feeding, their avidity is at times so great that in attempting to swallow a large acorn or nut, they are seen gasping for a long while, as if in the agonies of suffocation.

On such occasions, when the woods are filled with these Pigeons, they are killed in immense numbers, although no apparent diminution ensues. About the middle of the day, after their repast is finished, they settle on the trees, to enjoy rest, and digest their food. On the ground they walk with ease, as well as on the branches, frequently jerking their beautiful tail, and moving the neck backwards and forwards in the most graceful manner. As the sun begins to sink beneath the horizon, they depart *en masse* for the roosting-place, which not unfrequently is hundreds of miles distant, as has been ascertained by persons who have kept an account of their arrivals and departures.

Let us now, kind reader, inspect their place of nightly rendezvous. One of these curious roosting-places, on the banks of the Green River in Kentucky, I repeatedly visited. It was, as is always the case, in a portion of the forest where the trees were of great magnitude, and where there was little underwood. I rode through it upwards of forty miles, and, crossing it in different parts, found its average breadth to be rather more than three miles. My first view of it was about a fortnight subsequent to the period when they had made choice of it, and I arrived there nearly two hours before sunset. Few Pigeons were then to be seen, but a great number of persons, with horses and waggons, guns and ammunition, had already established encampments on the borders. Two farmers from the vicinity of Russelsville, distant more than a hundred miles, had driven upwards of three hundred hogs to be fattened on the pigeons which were to be slaughtered. Here and there, the people employed in plucking and salting what had already been procured, were seen sitting in the midst of large piles of these birds. The dung lay several inches deep, covering the whole extent of the roosting-place, like a bed of snow. Many trees two feet in diameter, I observed, were broken off at no great distance from the ground; and the branches of many of the largest and tallest had given way, as if the forest had been swept by a tornado. Every thing proved to me that the number of birds resorting to this part of the forest must be immense beyond conception. As the period of their arrival approached, their foes anxiously prepared to receive them. Some were furnished with iron-pots containing sulphur, others with torches of pine-knots, many with poles, and the rest with guns. The sun was lost to our view, yet not a Pigeon had arrived. Every thing was ready, and all eyes were gazing on the clear sky, which appeared in glimpses amidst the tall trees. Suddenly there burst forth a general cry of "Here they come!" The noise which they made, though yet distant, reminded me of a hard gale at sea, passing through the rigging of a close-reefed vessel. As the birds arrived and passed over me, I felt a current of air that surprised me. Thousands were soon knocked down by the pole-men. The birds continued to pour in. The fires were lighted, and a magnificent, as well as wonderful and almost terrifying, sight presented itself. The Pigeons, arriving by thousands, alighted everywhere, one above another, until solid masses as large as hogsheads were formed on the branches all round. Here and there the perches gave way under the weight with a crash, and falling to the ground, destroyed hundreds of the birds beneath, forcing down the dense groups with which every stick was loaded. It was a scene of uproar and confusion. I found it quite useless to speak, or even to shout to those persons who were nearest to me. Even the reports of the guns were seldom heard, and I was made aware of the firing only by seeing the shooters reloading.

No one dared venture within the line of devastation. The hogs had been penned up in due time, the picking up of the dead and wounded being left for the next morning's employment. The Pigeons were constantly coming, and it was past midnight before I perceived a decrease in the number of those that arrived. The uproar continued the whole night; and as I was anxious to know to what distance the sound reached, I sent off a man, accustomed to perambulate the forest, who, returning two hours afterwards, informed me he had heard it distinctly when three miles distant from the spot. Towards the approach of the day, the noise in some measure subsided, long before objects were distinguishable, the Pigeons began to move off in a direction quite different from that in which they had arrived the evening before, and at sunrise all that were able to fly had disappeared. The howlings of the wolves now reached our ears, and the foxes, lynxes, cougars, bears, raccoons, oppossums and pole-cats were seen sneaking off, whilst eagles and hawks of different species, accompanied by a crowd of vultures, came to supplant them, and enjoy their share of the spoil.

It was then that the authors of all this devastation began their entry amongst the dead, the dying, and the mangled. The pigeons were picked up and piled in heaps, until each had as many as he could possibly dispose of, when the hogs were let loose to feed on the remainder.

Persons unacquainted with these birds might naturally conclude that such dreadful havock would soon put an end to the species. But I have satisfied myself, by long observation, that nothing but the gradual diminution of our forests can accomplish their decrease, as they not unfrequently quadruple their numbers yearly, and always at least double it. In 1805 I saw schooners loaded in bulk with Pigeons caught up the Hudson River, coming in to the wharf at New York, when the birds sold for a cent a piece. I knew a man in Pennsylvania, who caught and killed upwards of 500 dozens in a clap-net in one day, sweeping sometimes twenty dozens or more at a single haul. In the month of March 1830, they were so abundant in the markets of New York, that piles of them met the eye in every direction. I have seen the Negroes at the United States' Salines or Saltworks of Shawanee Town, wearied with killing Pigeons, as they alighted to drink the water issuing from the leading pipes, for weeks at a time; and yet in 1826, in Louisiana, I saw congregated flocks of these birds as numerous as ever I had seen them before, during a residence of nearly thirty years in the United States.

The breeding of the Wild Pigeons, and the places chosen for that purpose, are points of great interest. The time is not much influenced by season, and the place selected is where food is most plentiful and most attainable, and always at a convenient distance from water. Forest-trees of great height are those in which the Pigeons form their nests. Thither the countless myriads resort, and prepare to fulfil one of the great laws of nature. At this period the note of the Pigeon is a soft *coo-coo-coo-coo*, much shorter than that of the domestic species. The common notes resemble the monosyllables *kee-kee-kee-kee*, the first being the loudest, the others gradually diminishing in power. The male assumes a pompous demeanour, and follows the female whether on the ground or on the branches, with spread tail and drooping wings, which it rubs against the part over which it is moving. The body is elevated, the throat swells, the eyes sparkle. He continues his notes, and now and then rises on the wing, and flies a few yards to approach the fugitive and timorous female. Like the domestic Pigeon and other species, they caress each other by billing, in which action, the bill of the one is introduced transversely into that of the other, and both parties alternately disgorge the contents of their crop by repeated efforts. These preliminary affairs are soon settled, and the Pigeons commence their nests in general peace and harmony. They are composed of a few dry twigs, crossing each other, and are supported by forks of the branches. On the same tree from fifty to a hundred nests may frequently be seen:—I might say a much greater number, were I not anxious, kind reader, that however wonderful my account of the Wild Pigeon is, you may not feel disposed to refer it to the marvellous. The eggs are two in number, of a broadly elliptical form, and pure white. During incubation, the male supplies the female with food. Indeed, the tenderness and affection displayed by these birds towards their mates, are in the highest degree striking. It is a remarkable fact, that each brood generally consists of a male and a female.

Here again, the tyrant of the creation, man, interferes, disturbing the harmony of this peaceful scene. As the young birds grow up, their enemies, armed with axes, reach the spot, to seize and destroy all they can. The trees are felled, and made to fall in such a way that the cutting of one causes the overthrow of another, or shakes the neighbouring trees so much, that the young Pigeons, or *squabs*, as they are named, are violently hurried to the ground. In this manner also, immense quantities are destroyed.

The young are fed by the parents in the manner described above; in other words, the old bird introduces its bill into the mouth of the young one in a transverse manner, or with the back of each mandible opposite the separations of the mandibles of the young bird, and disgorges the contents of its crop. As soon as the young birds are able to shift for themselves, they leave their parents, and continue separate until they attain maturity. By the end of six months they are capable of reproducing their species.

The flesh of the Wild Pigeon is of a dark colour, but affords tolerable eating. That of young birds from the nest is much esteemed. The skin is covered with small white filmy scales. The feathers fall off at the least touch, as has been remarked to be the case in the Carolina Turtle. I have only to add, that this species, like others of the same genus, immerses its head up to the eyes while drinking.

In March 1830, I bought about 350 of these birds in the market of New York, at four cents a piece. Most of these I carried alive to England, and distributed amongst several noblemen, presenting some at the same time to the Zoological Society.

Ivory-Billed Woodpecker

(*Campephilus principalis*)

I HAVE always imagined, that in the plumage of the beautiful Ivory-billed Woodpecker, there is something very closely allied to the style of colouring of the great VANDYKE. The broad extent of its dark glossy body and tail, the large and well-defined white markings of its wings, neck, and bill, relieved by the rich carmine of the pendent crest of the male, and the brilliant yellow of its eye, have never failed to remind me of some of the boldest and noblest productions of that inimitable artist's pencil. So strongly indeed have these thoughts become ingrafted in my mind, as I gradually obtained a more intimate acquaintance with the Ivory-billed Woodpecker, that whenever I have observed one of these birds flying from one tree to another, I have mentally exclaimed, "There goes a Vandyke!" This notion may seem strange, perhaps ludicrous, to you, good reader, but I relate it as a fact, and whether or not it may be found in accordance with your own ideas, after you have inspected the plate in which is represented this great chieftain of the Woodpecker tribe, is perhaps of little consequence.

The Ivory-billed Woodpecker confines its rambles to a comparatively very small portion of the United States, it never having been observed in the Middle States within the memory of any person now living there. In fact, in no portion of these districts does the nature of the woods appear suitable to its remarkable habits.

Descending the Ohio, we meet with this splendid bird for the first time near the confluence of that beautiful river and the Mississippi; after which, following the windings of the latter, either downwards toward the sea, or upwards in the direction of the Missouri, we frequently observe it. On the Atlantic coast, North Carolina may be taken as the limit of its distribution, although now and then an individual of the species may be accidentally seen in Maryland. To the westward of the Mississippi, it is found in all the dense forests bordering the streams which empty their waters into that majestic river, from the very declivities of the Rocky Mountains. The lower parts of the Carolinas, Georgia, Alabama, Louisiana, and Mississippi, are, however, the most favourite resorts of this bird, and in those States it constantly resides, breeds, and passes a life of peaceful enjoyment, finding a profusion of food in all the deep, dark, and gloomy swamps dispersed throughout them.

I wish, kind reader, it were in my power to present to your mind's eye the favourite resort of the Ivory-billed Woodpecker. Would that I could describe the extent of those deep morasses, overshadowed by millions of gigantic dark cypresses, spreading their sturdy moss-covered branches, as if to admonish intruding man to pause and reflect on the many difficulties which he must encounter, should he persist in venturing farther into their almost inaccessible recesses, extending for miles before him, where he should be interrupted by huge projecting branches, here and there the massy trunk of a fallen and decaying tree, and thousands of creeping and twining plants of numberless species! Would that I could represent to you the dangerous nature of the ground, its oozing, spongy, and miry disposition, although covered with a beautiful but treacherous carpeting, composed of the richest mosses, flags, and water-lillies, no sooner receiving the pressure of the foot than its yields and endangers the very life of the adventurer, whilst here and there, as he approaches an opening, that proves merely a lake of black muddy water, his ear is assailed by the dismal croaking of innumerable frogs, the hissing of serpents, or the bellowing of alligators! Would that I could give you an idea of the sultry pestiferous atmosphere that nearly suffocates the intruder during the meridian heat of our dogdays, in those gloomy and horrible swamps! But the attempt to picture these scenes would be vain. Nothing short of ocular demonstration can impress any adequate idea of them.

How often, kind reader, have I thought of the difference of the tasks imposed on different minds, when, travelling in countries far distant from those where birds of this species and others as difficult to be procured are now and then offered for sale in the form of dried skins, I have heard the amateur or closet-naturalist express his astonishment that half-a-crown was asked by the person who had perhaps followed the bird when alive over miles of such swamps, and after procuring it, had prepared its skin in the best manner, and carried it to a market thousands of miles distant from the spot where he had obtained it. I must say, that it has at least grieved me as much as when I have heard some idle fop complain of the poverty of the Gallery of the Louvre, where he had paid nothing, or when I have listened to the same infatuated idler lamenting the loss of his shilling, as he sauntered through the Exhibition Rooms of the Royal Academy of London, or any equally valuable repository of art. But, let us return to the biography of the famed Ivory-billed Woodpecker.

The flight of this bird is graceful in the extreme, although seldom prolonged to more than a few hundred yards at a time, unless when it has to cross a large river, which it does in deep undulations, opening its wings at first to their full extent, and nearly closing them to renew the propelling impulse. The transit from one tree to another, even should the distance be as much as a hundred yards, is performed by a single sweep, and the bird appears as if merely swinging itself from the top of the one tree to that of the other, forming an elegantly curved line. At this moment all the beauty of the plumage is exhibited, and strikes the beholder with pleasure. It never utters any sound whilst on wing, unless during the love season; but at all other times, no sooner has this bird alighted than its remarkable voice is heard, at almost every leap which it makes, whilst ascending against the upper parts of the trunk of a tree, or its highest branches. It notes are clear, loud, and yet rather plaintive. They are heard at a considerable distance, perhaps half a mile, and resemble the false high note of a clarionet. They are usually repeated three times in succession, and may be represented by the monosyllable *pait, pait, pait*. These are heard so frequently as to induce me to say that the bird spends few minutes of the day without uttering them, and this circumstance leads to its destruction, which is aimed at, not because (as is supposed by some) this species is a destroyer of trees, but more because it is a beautiful bird, and its rich scalp attached to the upper mandible forms an ornament for the war-dress of most of our Indians, or for the shot-pouch of our squatters and hunters, by all of whom the bird is shot merely for that purpose.

Travellers of all nations are also fond of possessing the upper part of the head and the bill of the male, and I have frequently remarked, that on a steam-boat's reaching what we call a *wooding-place*, the *strangers* were very apt to pay a quarter of a dollar for two or three heads of this Woodpecker. I have seen entire belts of Indian chiefs closely ornamented with the tufts and bills of this species, and have observed that a great value is frequently put upon them.

The Ivory-billed Woodpecker nestles earlier in spring than any other species of its tribe. I have observed it boring a hole for that purpose in the beginning of March. The hole is, I believe, always made in the trunk of a live tree, generally an ash or a hagberry, and is at a great height. The birds pay great regard to the particular situation of the tree, and the inclination of its trunk; first, because they prefer retirement, and again, because they are anxious to secure the aperture against the access of water during beating rains. To prevent such a calamity, the hole is generally dug immediately under the junction of a large branch with the trunk. It is first bored horizontally for a few inches, then directly downwards, and not in a spiral manner, as some people have imagined. According to circumstances, this cavity is more or less deep, being sometimes not more than ten inches, whilst at other times it reaches nearly three feet downwards into the core of the tree. I have been led to think that these differences result from the more or less immediate necessity under which the female may be of depositing her eggs, and again have thought that the older the Woodpecker is, the deeper does it make its hole. The average diameter of the different nests which I have examined was about seven inches within, although the entrance, which is perfectly round, is only just large enough to admit the bird.

Both birds work most assiduously at this excavation, one waiting outside to encourage the other, whilst it is engaged in digging, and when the latter is fatigued, taking its place. I have approached trees whilst these Woodpeckers were thus busily employed in forming their nest, and by resting my head against the bark, could easily distinguish every blow given by the bird. I observed that in two instances, when the Woodpeckers saw me thus at the foot of the tree in which they were digging their nest, they abandoned it for ever. For the first brood there are generally six eggs. They are deposited on a few chips at the bottom of the hole, and are of a pure white colour. The young are seen creeping out of the hole about a fortnight before they venture to fly to any other tree. The second brood makes its appearance about the 15th of August.

In Kentucky and Indiana, the Ivory-bills seldom raise more than one brood in the season. The young are at first of the colour of the female, only that they want the crest, which, however, grows rapidly, and towards autumn, particularly in birds of the first breed, is nearly equal to that of the mother. The males have then a slight line of red on the head, and do not attain their richness of plumage until spring, or their full size until the second year. Indeed, even then, a difference is easily observed between them and individuals which are much older.

The food of this species consists principally of beetles, larvæ, and large grubs. No sooner, however, are the grapes of our forests ripe than they are eaten by the Ivory-billed Woodpecker with great avidity. I have seen this bird hang by its claws to the vines, in the position so often assumed by a Titmouse, and, reaching downwards, help itself to a bunch of grapes with much apparent pleasure. Persimons are also sought for by them, as soon as the fruit becomes quite mellow, as are hagberries.

The Ivory-bill is never seen attacking the corn, or the fruit of the orchards, although it is sometimes observed working upon and chipping off the bark from the belted trees of the newly-cleared plantations. It seldom comes near the ground, but prefers at all times the tops of the tallest trees. Should it, however, discover the half-standing broken shaft of a large dead and rotten tree, it attacks it in such a manner as nearly to demolish it in the course of a few days. I have seen the remains of some of these ancient monarchs of our forests so excavated, and that so singularly, that the tottering fragments of the trunk appeared to be merely supported by the great pile of chips by which its base was surrounded. The strength of this Woodpecker is such, that I have seen it detach pieces of bark seven or eight inches in length at a single blow of its powerful bill, and by beginning at the top branch of a dead tree, tear off the bark, to an extent of twenty or thirty feet, in the course of a few hours, leaping downwards with its body in an upward position, tossing its head to the right and left, or leaning it against the bark to ascertain the precise spot where the grubs were concealed, and immediately after renewing its blows with fresh vigour, all the while sounding its loud notes, as if highly delighted.

This species generally moves in pairs, after the young have left their parents. The female is always the most clamorous and the least shy. Their mutual attachment is, I believe, continued through life. Excepting when digging a hole for the reception of their eggs, these birds seldom, if ever, attack living trees, for any other purpose than that of procuring food, in doing which they destroy the insects that would otherwise prove injurious to the trees.

I have frequently observed the male and female retire to rest for the night, into the same hole in which they had long before reared their young. This generally happens a short time after sunset.

When wounded and brought to the ground, the Ivory-bill immediately makes for the nearest tree, and ascends it with great rapidity and perseverance, until it reaches the top branches, when it squats and hides, generally with great effect. Whilst ascending, it moves spirally round the tree, utters its loud *pait, pait, pait*, at almost every hop, but becomes silent the moment it reaches a place where it conceives itself secure. They sometimes cling to the bark with their claws so firmly, as to remain cramped to the spot for several hours after death. When taken by the hand, which is rather a hazardous undertaking, they strike with great violence, and inflict very severe wounds with their bill as well as claws, which are extremely sharp and strong. On such occasions, this bird utters a mournful and very piteous cry.

Broad-Winged Hawk

(*Buteo platypterus*)

ONE fine May morning, when nature seemed to be enchanted at the sight of her own great works, when the pearly dew-drops were yet hanging at the point of each leaf, or lay nursed in the blossoms, gently rocked, as it were by the soft breeze of early summer, I took my gun, and, accompanied by my excellent brother-in-law, WILLIAM G. BAKEWELL, Esq. at that time a youth, walked towards some lovely groves, where many songsters attracted our attention by their joyous melodies. The woods were all alive with the richest variety, and, divided in choice, we kept going on without shooting at any thing, so great was our admiration of every bird that presented itself to our view. As we crossed a narrow skirt of wood, my young companion spied a nest on a tree of moderate height, and, as my eye reached it, we both perceived that the parent bird was sitting in it. Some little consultation took place, as neither of us could determine whether it was a Crow's or a Hawk's nest, and it was resolved that my young friend should climb the tree, and bring down one of the eggs. On reaching the nest, he said the bird, which still remained quiet, was a Hawk and unable to fly. I desired him to cover it with his handkerchief, try to secure it, and bring it down, together with the eggs. All this was accomplished without the least difficulty. I looked at it with indescribable pleasure, as I saw it was new to me, and then felt vexed that it was not of a more spirited nature, as it had neither defended its eggs nor itself. It lay quietly in the handkerchief, and I carried it home to my father-in-law's, shewed it to the family, and went to my room, where I instantly began drawing it. The drawing which I then made is at this moment before me, and is dated "Fatland Ford, Pennsylvania, May 27, 1812."

I put the bird on a stick made fast to my table. It merely moved its feet to grasp the stick, and stood erect, but raised its feathers, and drew in its neck on its shoulders. I passed my hand over it, to smooth the feathers by gentle pressure. It moved not. The plumage remained as I wished it. Its eye, directed towards mine, appeared truly sorrowful, with a degree of pensiveness, which rendered me at that moment quite uneasy. I measured the length of its bill with the compass, began my outlines, continued measuring part after part as I went on, and finished the drawing, without the bird ever moving once. My wife sat at my side, reading to me at intervals, but our conversation had frequent reference to the singularity of the incident. The drawing being finished, I raised the window, laid hold of the poor bird, and launched it into the air, where it sailed off until out of my sight, without uttering a single cry, or deviating from its course. The drawing from which the plate is taken, was subsequently made, as I had to wait until I should procure a male, to render it complete.

The above incident you will doubtless consider as extraordinary as I myself did, and perhaps some may feel disposed to look upon it as a specimen of travellers' tales; but as I have resolved to present you with the incidents as they occured, I have felt no hesitation in relating this. . . .

White-Crowned Sparrow

(*Zonotrichia leucophrys*)

IT is to the wild regions of Labrador that you must go, kind reader, if you wish to form a personal acquaintance with the White-crowned Sparrow. There in every secluded glen opening upon the boisterous Gulf of St Lawrence, while amazed you glance over the wilderness that extends around you, so dreary and desolate that the blood almost congeals in your veins, you meet with this interesting bird. Your body is sinking under the fatigue occasioned by your wading through beds of moss, as extraordinary for their depth, as for the brilliancy of their tints, and by the difficulties which you have encountered in forcing your way through the tangled creeping pines, so dwarfish and so stubborn, that you often find it easier to trample down their branches than to separate them so as to allow you a passage. In such a place, when you are far away from all that is dear to you, how cheering is it to hear the mellow notes of a bird, that seems as if it had been sent expressly for the purpose of relieving your mind from the heavy melancholy that bears it down! The sounds are so sweet, so refreshing, so soothing, so hope inspiring, that as they come upon the soul in all their gentleness and joy, the tears begin to flow from your eyes, the burden on your mind becomes lighter, your heart expands, and you experience a pure delight, produced by the invitation thus made to offer your humblest and most sincere thanks to that all-wondrous Being, who has caused you to be there no doubt for the purpose of becoming better acquainted with the operations of his mighty power.

Thus it was with me, when, some time after I had been landed on the dreary coast of Labrador, I for the first time heard the song of the White-crowned Sparrow. I could not refrain from indulging in the thought that, notwithstanding the many difficulties attending my attempts—my mission I must call it—to study God's works in this wild region, I was highly favoured. At every step, new objects presented themselves, and whenever I rested, I enjoyed a delight never before experienced. Humbly and fervently did I pray for a continuation of those blessings, through which I now hoped to see my undertaking completed, and again to join my ever-dear family.

I first became acquainted with the White-crowned Sparrow at Henderson, in the autumn of 1817. I then thought it the handsomest bird of its kind, and my opinion still is that none other known to me as a visitor or inhabitant of the United States, exceeds it in beauty. I procured five individuals, three of which were in full plumage and proved to be males. The sex of the other two could not be ascertained; but I have since become convinced that these birds lose the white stripes on the head in the winter season, when they might be supposed to be of a different species. During spring and summer the male and the female are of equal beauty, the former being only a little larger than the latter. The young which I procured in Labrador, shewed the white stripes on the head as they were fully fledged, and I think they retain those marks in autumn longer than the old birds, of which the feathers have become much worn at that season. In the winter of 1833, I procured at Charleston in South Carolina, one in its brown livery.

One day, while near American Harbour, in Labrador, I observed a pair of these birds frequently resorting to a small hummock of firs, where I concluded they must have had a nest. After searching in vain, I intimated my suspicion to my young friends, when we all crept through the tangled branches, and examined the place, but without success. Determined, however, to obtain our object, we returned with hatchets, cut down every tree to its roots, removed each from the spot, pulled up all the mosses between them, and completely cleared the place; yet no nest did we find. Our disappointment was the greater that we saw the male bird frequently flying about with food in its bill, no doubt intended for its mate. In a short while, the pair came near us, and both were shot. In the female we found an egg, which was pure white, but with the shell yet soft and thin. On the 6th July, while my son was creeping among some low bushes, to get a shot at some Red-throated Divers, he accidentally started a female from her nest. It made much complaint. The nest was placed in the moss, near the foot of a low fir, and was formed externally of beautiful dry green moss, matted in bunches like the coarse hair of some quadruped, internally of very fine dry grass, arranged with great neatness, to the thickness of nearly half an inch, with a full lining of delicate fibrous roots of a rich transparent yellow. . . .

Pewee Flycatcher

(Eastern Phoebe, *Sayornis phoebe*)

CONNECTED with the biography of this bird are so many incidents relative to my own, that could I with propriety deviate from my proposed method, the present volume would contain less of the habits of birds than of those of the youthful days of an American woodsman. While young, I had a plantation that lay on the sloping declivities of a creek, the name of which I have already given, but as it will ever be dear to my recollection, you will, I hope, allow me to repeat it—the Perkioming. I was extremely fond of rambling along its rocky banks, for it would have been difficult to do so either without meeting with a sweet flower, spreading open its beauties to the sun, or observing the watchful King's-fisher perched on some projecting stone over the clear water of the stream. Nay, now and then, the Fish Hawk itself, followed by a White-headed Eagle, would make his appearance, and by his graceful aerial motions, raise my thoughts far above them into the heavens, silently leading me to the admiration of the sublime Creator of all. These impressive, and always delightful, reveries often accompanied my steps to the entrance of a small cave scooped out of the solid rock by the hand of nature. It was, I then thought, quite large enough for my study. My paper and pencils, with now and then a volume of EDGEWORTH'S natural and fascinating Tales or LAFONTAINE'S Fables, afforded me ample pleasures. It was in that place, kind reader, that I first saw with advantage the force of parental affection in birds. There it was that I studied the habits of the Pewee; and there I was taught most forcibly that to destroy the nest of a bird, or to deprive it of its eggs or young, is an act of great cruelty.

I had observed the nest of this plain-coloured Flycatcher fastened, as it were, to the rock immediately over the arched entrance of this calm retreat. I had peeped into it: although empty, it was yet clean, as if the absent owner intended to revisit it with the return of spring. The buds were already much swelled, and some of the trees were ornamented with blossoms, yet the ground was still partially covered with snow, and the air retained the piercing chill of winter. I chanced one morning early to go to my retreat. The sun's glowing rays gave a rich colouring to every object around. As I entered the cave, a rustling sound over my head attracted my attention, and, on turning, I saw two birds fly off, and alight on a tree close by:—the Pewees had arrived! I felt delighted, and fearing that my sudden appearance might disturb the gentle pair, I walked off, not, however, without frequently looking at them. I concluded that they must have just come, for they seemed fatigued:—their plaintive note was not heard, their crests were not erected, and the vibration of the tail, so very conspicuous in this species, appeared to be wanting in power. Insects were yet few, and the return of the birds looked to me as prompted more by their affection to the place, than by any other motive. No sooner had I gone a few steps than the Pewees, with one accord glided down from their perches and entered the cave. I did not return to it any more that day, and as I saw none about it, or in the neighbourhood, I supposed that they must have spent the day within it. I concluded also that these birds must have reached this haven, either during the night, or at the very dawn of that morn. Hundreds of observations have since proved to me that this species always migrates by night.

Filled with the thoughts of the little pilgrims, I went early next morning to their retreat, yet not early enough to surprise them in it. Long before I reached the spot, my ears were agreeably saluted by their well-known note, and I saw them darting about through the air, giving chase to some insects close over the water. They were full of gaiety, frequently flew into and out of the cave, and while alighted on a favourite tree near it, seemed engaged in the most interesting converse. The light fluttering or tremulous motions of their wings, the jetting of their tail, the erection of their crest, and the neatness of their attitudes, all indicated that they were no longer fatigued, but on the contrary refreshed and happy. On my going into the cave, the male flew violently towards the entrance, snapped his bill sharply and repeatedly, accompanying this action with a tremulous rolling note, the import of which I soon guessed. Presently he flew into the cave and out of it again, with a swiftness scarcely credible: it was like the passing of a shadow.

Several days in succession I went to the spot, and saw with pleasure that as my visits increased in frequency, the birds became more familiarized to me, and, before a week had elapsed, the Pewees and myself were quite on terms of intimacy. It was now the 10th of April; the spring was forward that season, no more snow was to be seen, Redwings and Grakles were to be found here and there. The Pewees, I observed, began working at their old nest. Desirous of judging for myself, and anxious to enjoy the company of this friendly pair, I determined to spend the greater part of each day in the cave. My presence no longer alarmed either of them. They brought a few fresh materials, lined the nest anew, and rendered it warm by adding a few large soft feathers of the common goose, which they found strewn along the edge of the water in the creek. There was a remarkable and curious twittering in their note while both sat on the edge of the nest at those meetings, and which is never heard on any other occasion. It was the soft, tender expression, I thought, of the pleasure they both appeared to anticipate of the future. Their mutual caresses, simple as they might have seemed to another, and the delicate manner used by the male to please his mate, rivetted my eyes on these birds, and excited sensations which I can never forget.

The female one day spent the greater part of the time in her nest; she frequently changed her position; her mate exhibited much uneasiness, he would alight by her sometimes, sit by her side for a moment, and suddenly flying out, would return with an insect, which she took from his bill with apparent gratification. About three o'clock in the afternoon, I saw the uneasiness of the female increase; the male showed an unusual appearance of despondence, when, of a sudden, the female rose on her feet, looked sidewise under her, and flying out, followed by her attentive consort, left the cave, rose high in the air, performing evolutions more curious to me than any I had seen before. They flew about over the water, the female leading her mate, as it were, through her own meanderings. Leaving the Pewees to their avocations, I peeped into their nest, and saw there their first egg, so white and so transparent— for I believe, reader, that eggs soon loose this peculiar transparency after being laid—that to me the sight was more pleasant than if I had met with a diamond of the same size. The knowledge that in an enclosure so frail, life already existed, and that ere many weeks would elapse, a weak, delicate, and helpless creature, but perfect in all its parts, would burst the shell, and immediately call for the most tender care and attention of its anxious parents, filled my mind with as much wonder as when, looking towards the heavens, I searched, alas! in vain, for the true import of all that I saw.

In six days, six eggs were deposited; but I observed that as they increased in number, the bird remained a shorter time in the nest. The last she deposited in a few minutes after alighting. Perhaps, thought I, this is a law of nature, intended for keeping the eggs fresh to the last. Kind reader, what are your thoughts on the subject? About an hour after laying the last egg, the female Pewee returned, settled in her nest, and, after arranging the eggs, as I thought, several times under her body, expanded her wings a little, and fairly commenced the arduous task of incubation.

Day after day passed by. I gave strict-orders that no one should go near the cave, much less enter it, or indeed destroy any bird's nest on the plantation. Whenever I visited the Pewees, one or other of them was on the nest, while its mate was either searching for food, or perched in the vicinity, filling the air with its loudest notes. I not unfrequently reached out my hand near the sitting bird; and so gentle had they both become, or rather so well acquainted were we, that neither moved on such occasions, even when my hand was quite close to it. Now and then the female would shrink back into the nest, but the male frequently snapped at my fingers, and once left the nest as if in great anger, flew round the cave a few times, emitting his querulous whining notes, and alighted again to resume his labours.

At this very time, a Pewee's nest was attached to one of the rafters of my mill, and there was another under a shed in the cattle-yard. Each pair, any one would have felt assured, had laid out the limits of its own domain, and it was seldom that one trespassed on the grounds of its neighbour. The Pewee of the cave generally fed or spent its time so far above the mill on the creek, that he of the mill never came in contact with it. The Pewee of the cattle-yard confined himself to the orchard, and never disturbed the rest. Yet I sometimes could hear distinctly the notes of the three at the same moment. I had at that period an idea that the whole of these birds were descended from the same stock. If not correct in this supposition, I had ample proof afterwards that the brood of young Pewees, raised in the cave, returned the following spring, and established themselves farther up on the creek, and among the outhouses in the neighbourhood.

On some other occasion, I will give you such instances of the return of birds, accompanied by their progeny, to the place of their nativity, that perhaps you will become convinced, as I am at this moment, that to this propensity every country owes the augmentation of new species, whether of birds or of quadrupeds, attracted by the many benefits met with, as countries become more-open and better cultivated: but now I will, with your leave, return to the Pewees of the cave.

On the thirteenth day, the little ones were hatched. One egg was unproductive, and the female, on the second day after the birth of her brood, very deliberately pushed it out of the nest. On examining this egg, I found it containing the embryo of a bird partly dried up, with its vertebræ quite fast to the shell, which had probably occasioned its death. Never have I since so closely witnessed the attention of birds to their young. Their entrance with insects was so frequently repeated, that I thought I saw the little ones grow as I gazed upon them. The old birds no longer looked upon me as an enemy, and would often come in close by me, as if I had been a post. I now took upon me to handle the young frequently; nay, several times I took the whole family out, and blew off the exuviæ of the feathers from the nest. I attached light threads to their legs: these they invariably removed, either with their bills, or with the assistance of their parents. I renewed them, however, until I found the little fellows habituated to them; and at last, when they were about to leave the nest, I fixed a light silver thread to the leg of each, loose enough not to hurt the part, but so fastened that no exertions of theirs could remove it.

Sixteen days had passed, when the brood took to wing: and the old birds, dividing the time with caution, began to arrange the nest anew. A second set of eggs were laid, and in the beginning of August a new brood made its appearance.

The young birds took much to the woods, as if feeling themselves more secure there than in the open fields; but before they departed, they all appeared strong, and minded not making long sorties into the open air, over the whole creek, and the fields around it. On the 8th of October, not a Pewee could I find on the plantation: my little companions had all set off on their travels. For weeks afterwards, however, I saw Pewees arriving from the north, and lingering a short time, as if to rest, when they also moved southward.

At the season when the Pewee returns to Pennsylvania, I had the satisfaction to observe those of the cave in and about it. There again, in the very same nest, two broods were raised. I found several Pewees nests at some distance up the creek, particularly under a bridge, and several others in the adjoining meadows, attached to the inner part of sheds erected for the protection of hay and grain. Having caught several of these birds on the nest, I had the pleasure of finding that two of them had the little ring on the leg.

I was now obliged to go to France, where I remained two years. On my return, which happened early in August, I had the satisfaction of finding three young Pewees in the nest of the cave; but it was not the nest which I had left in it. The old one had been torn off from the roof, and the one which I found there was placed above where it stood. I observed at once that one of the parent birds was as shy as possible, while the other allowed me to approach within a few yards. This was the male bird, and I felt confident that the old female had paid the debt of nature. Having inquired of the miller's son, I found that he had killed the old Pewee and four young ones, to make bait for the purpose of catching fish. Then the male Pewee had brought another female to the cave! As long as the plantation of Mill Grove belonged to me, there continued to be a Pewee's nest in my favourite retreat; but after I had sold it, the cave was destroyed, as were nearly all the beautiful rocks along the shores of the creek, to build a new dam across the Perkioming.

This species is so peculiarly fond of attaching its nest to rocky caves, that, were it called the Rock Flycatcher, it would be appropriately named. Indeed I seldom have passed near such a place, particularly during the breeding season, without seeing the Pewee, or hearing its notes. I recollect that, while travelling in Virginia with a friend, he desired that I would go somewhat out of our intended route, to visit the renowned Rock Bridge of that State. My companion, who had passed over this natural bridge before, proposed a wager that he could lead me across it before I should be aware of its existence. It was early in April; and, from the descriptions of this place which I had read, I felt confident that the Pewee Flycatcher must be about it. I accepted the proposal of my friend and trotted on, intent on proving to myself that, by constantly attending to one subject, a person must sooner or later become acquainted with it. I listened to the notes of the different birds, which at intervals came to my ear, and at last had the satisfaction to distinguish those of the Pewee. I stopped my horse, to judge of the distance at which the bird might be, and a moment after told my friend that the bridge was short of a hundred yards from us, although it was impossible for us to see the spot itself. The surprise of my companion was great. "How do you know this?" he asked, "for," continued he, "you are correct."—"Simply," answered I, "because I hear the notes of the Pewee, and know that a cave, or a deep rocky creek, is at hand." We moved on; the Pewees rose from under the bridge in numbers; I pointed to the spot and won the wager.

This rule of observation I have almost always found to work, as arithmeticians say, both ways. Thus the nature of the woods or place in which the observer may be, whether high or low, moist or dry, sloping north or south, with whatever kind of vegetation, tall trees of particular species, or low shrubs, will generally disclose the nature of their inhabitants. . . .

American Crow

(Common Crow, *Corvus brachyrhynchos*)

THE Crow is an extremely shy bird, having found familiarity with man no way to his advantage. He is also cunning—at least he is so called, because he takes care of himself and his brood. The state of anxiety, I may say of terror, in which he is constantly kept, would be enough to spoil the temper of any creature. Almost every person has an antipathy to him, and scarcely one of his race would be left in the land, did he not employ all his ingenuity, and take advantage of all his experience, in counteracting the evil machinations of his enemies. I think I see him perched on the highest branch of a tree, watching every object around. He observes a man on horseback travelling towards him; he marks his movements in silence. No gun does the rider carry,—no, that is clear; but perhaps he has pistols in the holsters of his saddle!—of that the Crow is not quite sure, as he cannot either see them or "smell powder." He beats the points of his wings, jerks his tail once or twice, bows his head, and merrily sounds the joy which he feels at the moment. Another man he spies walking across the field towards his stand, but he has only a stick. Yonder comes a boy shouldering a musket loaded with large shot for the express purpose of killing crows! The bird immediately sounds an alarm; he repeats his cries, increasing their vehemence the nearer his enemy advances. All the crows within half a mile round are seen flying off, each repeating the well known notes of the trusty watchman, who, just as the young gunner is about to take aim, betakes himself to flight. But alas, he chances unwittingly to pass over a sportsman, whose dexterity is greater; the mischievous prowler aims his piece, fires;—down towards the earth broken-winged, falls the luckless bird in an instant. "It is nothing but a crow," quoth the sportsman, who proceeds in search of game, and leaves the poor creature to die in the most excruciating agonies.

Wherever within the Union the laws encourage the destruction of this species, it is shot in great numbers for the sake of the premium offered for each crow's head. You will perhaps be surprised, reader, when I tell you that in one single State, in the course of a season, 40,000 were shot, besides the multitudes of young birds killed in their nests. Must I add to this slaughter other thousands destroyed by the base artifice of laying poisoned grain along the fields to tempt these poor birds? Yes, I will tell you of all this too. The natural feelings of every one who admires the bounty of Nature in providing abundantly for the subsistence of all her creatures, prompt me to do so. Like yourself, I admire all her wonderful works, and respect her wise intentions, even when her laws are far beyond our limited comprehension.

The Crow devours myriads of grubs every day of the year, that might lay waste the farmer's fields; it destroys quadrupeds innumerable, every one of which is an enemy to his poultry and his flocks. Why then should the farmer be so ungrateful, when he sees such services rendered to him by a providential friend, as to persecute that friend even to the death? Unless he plead ignorance, surely he ought to be found guilty at the bar of common sense. Were the soil of the United States, like that of some other countries, nearly exhausted by long continued cultivation, human selfishness in such a matter might be excused, and our people might look on our Crows, as other people look on theirs; but every individual in the land is aware of the superabundance of food that exists among us, and of which a portion may well be spared for the feathered beings, that tend to enhance our pleasures by the sweetness of their song, the innocence of their lives, or their curious habits. Did not every American open his door and his heart to the wearied traveller, and afford him food, comfort and rest, I would at once give up the argument; but when I know by experience the generosity of the people, I cannot but wish that they would reflect a little, and become more indulgent toward our poor, humble, harmless, and even most serviceable bird, the Crow. . . .

The most remarkable feat of the Crow, is the nicety with which it, like the Jay, pierces an egg with its bill, in order to carry it off, and eat it with security. In this manner I have seen it steal, one after another, all the eggs of a wild Turkey's nest. You will perceive, reader, that I endeavour to speak of the Crow with all due impartiality, not wishing by any means to conceal its faults, nor withholding my testimony to its merits, which are such as I can well assure the farmer, that were it not for its race, thousands of corn stalks would every year fall prostrate, in consequence of being cut over close to the ground by the destructive grubs which are called "cut-worms."

I never saw a pet Crow in the United States, and therefore cannot say with how much accuracy they may imitate the human voice, or, indeed, if they possess the power of imitating it at all, which I very much doubt, as in their natural state they never evince any talents for mimicry. I cannot say if it possess the thieving propensities attributed by authors to the European Crow.

Its gait, while on the ground, is elevated and graceful, its ordinary mode of progression being a sedate walk, although it occasionally hops when under excitement. It not unfrequently alights on the backs of cattle, to pick out the worms lurking in their skin, in the same manner as the Magpie, Fish-Crow, and Cow-bird. Its note or cry may be imitated by the syllables *cāw, cāw, cāw*, being different from the cry of the European Carrion Crow, and resembling the distant bark of a small dog.

At Pittsburgh in Pennsylvania I saw a pair of Crows perfectly white, in the possession of Mr LAMPDIN, the owner of the museum there, who assured me that five which were found in the nest were of the same colour.

I have placed the pensive oppressed Crow of our country on a beautiful branch of the Black Walnut tree, loaded with nuts, on the lower twig of which I have represented the delicate nest of our Common Humming Bird, to fulfil the promise which I made when writing the history of that species for my first volume.

In conclusion, I would again address our farmers, and tell them that if they persist in killing Crows, the best season for doing so is when their corn begins to ripen.

Chimney Swallow or American Swift

(Chimney Swift, *Chaetura pelagica*)

SINCE our country has furnished thousands of convenient places for this Swallow to breed in, free from storms, snakes, or quadrupeds, it has abandoned, with a judgement worthy of remark, its former abodes in the hollows of trees, and taken possession of the chimneys, which emit no smoke in the summer season. For this reason, no doubt, it has obtained the name by which it is generally known. I well remember the time when, in Lower Kentucky, Indiana, and Illinois, many resorted to excavated branches and trunks, for the purpose of breeding; nay, so strong is the influence of original habit, that not a few still betake themselves to such places, not only to roost, but also to breed, especially in those wild portions of our country that can scarcely be said to be inhabited. In such instances, they appear to be as nice in the choice of a tree, as they generally are in our cities in the choice of a chimney, wherein to roost, before they leave us. Sycamores of gigantic growth, and having a mere shell of bark and wood to support them, seem to suit them best, and wherever I have met with one of those patriarchs of the forest rendered habitable by decay, there I have found the Swallows breeding in spring and summer, and afterwards roosting until the time of their departure. I had a tree of this kind cut down, which contained about thirty of their nests in its trunk, and one in each of the hollow branches.

The nest, whether placed in a tree or chimney, consists of small dry twigs, which are procured by the birds in a singular manner. While on wing, the Chimney Swallows are seen in great numbers whirling round the tops of some decayed or dead tree, as if in pursuit of their insect prey. Their movements at this time are extremely rapid; they throw their body, suddenly against the twig, grapple it with their feet, and by an instantaneous jerk, snap it off short, and proceed with it to the place intended for the nest. The Frigate Pelican sometimes employs the same method for a similar purpose, carrying away the stick in its bill, in place of holding it with its feet.

The Swallow fixes the first sticks on the wood, the rock, or the chimney wall, by means of its saliva, arranging them in a semicircular form, crossing and interweaving them, so as to extend the framework outwards. The whole is afterwards glued together with saliva, which is spread around it for an inch or more, to fasten it securely. When the nest is in a chimney, it is generally placed on the east side, and is from five to eight feet from the entrance; but in the hollow of a tree, where only they breed in communities, it is placed high or low according to convenience. The fabric, which is very frail, now and then gives way, either under the pressure of the parents and young, or during sudden bursts of heavy rain, when the whole is dashed to the ground. The eggs are from four to six, and of a pure white colour. Two broods are raised in the season.

The flight of this species is performed somewhat in the manner of the European Swift, but in a more hurried although continued style, and generally by repeated flappings, unless when courtship is going on, on which occasion it is frequently seen sailing with its wings fixed as it were, both sexes as they glide through the air issuing a shrill rattling twitter, and the female receiving the caresses of the male. At other times it is seen ranging far and wide at a considerable elevation over the forests and cities; again, in wet weather, it flies close over the ground; and anon it skims the water, to drink and bathe. When about to descend into a hollow tree or a chimney, its flight, always rapid, is suddenly interrupted as if by magic, for down it goes in an instant, whirling in a peculiar manner, and whirring with its wings, so as to produce a sound in the chimney like the rumbling of very distant thunder. They never alight on trees or on the ground. If one is caught and placed on the latter, it can only move in a very awkward fashion. I believe that the old birds sometimes fly at night, and have reason to think that the young are fed at such times, as I have heard the whirring sound of the former, and the acknowledging cries of the latter, during calm and clear nights.

When the young accidentally fall, which sometimes happens, although the nest should remain, they scramble up again, by means of their sharp claws, lifting one foot after another, in the manner of young Wood Ducks, and supporting themselves with their tail. Some days before the young are able to fly, they scramble up the walls to near the mouth of the chimney, where they are fed. Any observer may discover this, as he sees the parents passing close over them, without entering the funnel. The same occurrence takes place when they are bred in a tree.

In the cities, these birds make choice of a particular chimney for their roosting place, where, early in spring, before they have begun building, both sexes resort in multitudes, from an hour or more before sunset, until long after dark. Before entering the aperture, they fly round and over it many times, but finally go in one at a time, until hurried by the lateness of the hour, several drop in together. They cling to the wall with their claws, supporting themselves also by their sharp tail, until the dawn, when, with a roaring sound, the whole pass out almost at once. Whilst at St Francisville in Louisiana, I took the trouble of counting how many entered one chimney before dark. I sat at a window not far from the spot, and reckoned upwards of a thousand, having missed a considerable number. The place at that time contained about a hundred houses, and no doubt existed in my mind that the greater number of these birds were on their way southward, and had merely stopped there for the night.

Immediately after my arrival at Louisville, in the State of Kentucky, I became acquainted with the hospitable and amiable Major WILLIAM CROGHAN and his family. While talking one day about birds, he asked me if I had seen the trees in which the Swallows were supposed to spend the winter, but which they only entered, he said, for the purpose of roosting. Answering in the affirmative, I was informed that on my way back to town, there was a tree remarkable on account of the immense numbers that resorted to it, and the place in which it stood was described to me. I found it to be a sycamore, nearly destitute of branches, sixty or seventy feet high, between seven and eight feet in diameter at the base, and about five for the distance of forty feet up, where the stump of a broken hollowed branch, about two feet in diameter, made out from the main stem. This was the place at which the Swallows entered. On closely examining the tree, I found it hard, but hollow to near the roots. It was now about four o'clock after noon, in the month of July. Swallows were flying over Jeffersonville, Louisville, and the woods around, but there were none near the tree. I proceeded home, and shortly after returned on foot. The sun was going down behind the Silver Hills; the evening was beautiful; thousands of Swallows were flying closely above me, and three or four at a time were pitching into the hole, like bees hurrying into their hive. I remained, my head leaning on the tree, listening to the roaring noise made within by the birds as they settled and arranged themselves, until it was quite dark, when I left the place, although I was convinced that many more had to enter. I did not pretend to count them, for the number was too great, and the birds rushed to the entrance so thick as to baffle the attempt. I had scarcely returned to Louisville, when a violent thunderstorm passed suddenly over the town, and its appearance made me think that the hurry of the Swallows to enter the tree was caused by their anxiety to avoid it. I thought of the Swallows almost the whole night, so anxious had I become to ascertain their number, before the time of their departure should arrive.

Next morning I rose early enough to reach the place long before the least appearance of daylight, and placed my head against the tree. All was silent within. I remained in that posture probably twenty minutes, when suddenly I thought the great tree was giving way, and coming down upon me. Instinctively I sprung from it, but when I looked up to it again, what was my astonishment to see it standing as firm as ever. The Swallows were now pouring out in a black continued stream. I ran back to my post, and listened in amazement to the noise within, which I could compare to nothing else than the sound of a large wheel revolving under a powerful stream. It was yet dusky, so that I could hardly see the hour on my watch, but I estimated the time which they took in getting out at more than thirty minutes. After their departure, no noise was heard within, and they dispersed in every direction with the quickness of thought.

I immediately formed the project of examining the interior of the tree, which, as my kind friend, Major CROGHAN, had told me, proved the most remarkable I had ever met with. This I did, in company with a hunting associate. We went provided with a strong line and a rope, the first of which we, after several trials, succeeded in throwing across the broken branch. Fastening the rope to the line we drew it up, and pulled it over until it reached the ground again. Provided with the longest cane we could find, I mounted the tree by the rope, without accident, and at length seated myself at ease on the broken branch; but my labour was fruitless, for I could see nothing through the hole, and the cane, which was about fifteen feet long, touched nothing on the sides of the tree within that could give any information. I came down fatigued and disappointed.

The next day I hired a man, who cut a hole at the base of the tree. The shell was only eight or nine inches thick, and the axe soon brought the inside to view, disclosing a matted mass of exuviæ, with rotten feathers reduced to a kind of mould, in which, however, I could perceive fragments of insects and quills. I had a passage cleared, or rather bored through this mass, for nearly six feet. This operation took up a good deal of time, and knowing by experience that if the birds should notice the hole below, they would abandon the tree, I had it carefully closed. The Swallows came as usual that night, and I did not disturb them for several days. At last, provided with a dark lantern, I went with my companion about nine in the evening, determined to have a full view of the interior of the tree. The hole was opened with caution. I scrambled up the sides of the mass of exuviæ, and my friend followed. All was perfectly silent. Slowly and gradually I brought the light of the lantern to bear on the sides of the hole above us, when we saw the Swallows clinging side by side, covering the whole surface of the excavation. In no instance did I see one above another. Satisfied with the sight, I closed the lantern. We then caught and killed with as much care as possible more than a hundred, stowing them away in our pockets and bosoms, and slid down into the open air. We observed that, while on this visit, not a bird had dropped its dung upon us. Closing the entrance, we marched towards Louisville perfectly elated. On examining the birds which we had procured, a hundred and fifteen in number, we found only six females. Eighty-seven were adult males; of the remaining twenty-two the sex could not be ascertained, and I had no doubt that they were young of that year's first brood, the flesh and quill-feathers being tender and soft.

Let us now make a rough calculation of the number that clung to the tree. The space beginning at the pile of feathers and moulded exuviæ, and ending at the entrance of the hole above, might be fully 25 feet in height, with a breadth of 15 feet, supposing the tree to be 5 in diameter at an average. There would thus be 375 feet square of surface. Each square foot, allowing a bird to cover a space of 3 inches by 1½, which is more than enough, judging from the manner in which they were packed, would contain 32 birds. The number of Swallows, therefore, that roosted in this single tree was 9000.

I watched the motions of the Swallows, and when the young birds that had been reared in the chimneys of Louisville, Jeffersonville, and the houses of the neighbourhood, or the trees suited for the purpose, had left their native recesses, I visited the tree on the 2d day of August. I concluded that the numbers resorting to it had not increased; but I found many more females and young than males, among upwards of fifty, which were caught and opened. Day after day I watched the tree. On the 13th of August, not more than two or three hundred came there to roost. On the 18th of the same month, not one did I see near it, and only a few scattered individuals were passing, as if moving southward. In September I entered the tree at night, but not a bird was in it. Once more I went to it in February, when the weather was very cold; and perfectly satisfied that all these Swallows had left our country, I finally closed the entrance, and left off visiting it.

May arrived, bringing with its vernal warmth the wanderers of the air, and I saw their number daily augmenting, as they resorted to the tree to roost. About the beginning of June, I took it in my head to close the aperture above, with a bundle of straw, which with a string I could draw off whenever I might chuse. The result was curious enough; the birds as usual came to the tree towards night; they assembled, passed and repassed, with apparent discomfort, until I perceived many flying off to a great distance, on which I removed the straw, when many entered the hole, and continued to do so until I could no longer see from the ground.

I left Louisville, having removed my residence to Henderson, and did not see the tree until five years after, when I still found the Swallows resorting to it. The pieces of wood with which I had closed the entrance had rotted, or had been carried off, and the hole was again completely filled with exuviæ and mould. During a severe storm, their ancient tenement at length gave way, and came to the ground.

General WILLIAM CLARK assured me that he saw this species on the whole of his route to the Pacific, and there can be no doubt that in those wilds it still breeds in trees or rocky caverns.

Its food consists entirely of insects, the pellets composed of the indigestible parts of which it disgorges. It is furnished with glands which supply the unctuous matter with which it fastens its nest.

This species does not appear to extend its migrations farther east than the British provinces of New Brunswick and Nova Scotia. It is unknown in Newfoundland and Labrador; nor was it until the 29th of May that I saw some at Eastport in Maine, where a few breed.

Golden Eagle

(*Aquila chrysaetos*)

IN the early part of February 1833, while at Boston in Massachusetts, I chanced to call on Mr GREENWOOD, the proprietor of the Museum of that city, who informed me that he had purchased a very fine Eagle, the name of which he was desirous of knowing. The bird was produced, and as I directed my eye towards its own deep, bold and stern one, I recognised it at once as belonging to the species whose habits I have here to describe, and I determined to obtain possession of it. Mr GREENWOOD, who is a very kind as well as talented person, being asked if he would part with the noble bird, readily answered in the affirmative, and left to me to determine its value, which I accordingly did, and carried off my purchase. His report of the manner in which the royal prisoner had been secured, was as follows:—"The man from which I bought it had it in the same cage it is now in, on the top of his market-waggon, and when I asked its price, said that the Eagle had been caught in a spring-trap set for foxes on the white mountains of New Hampshire. One morning the trap was missing, but on searching for it, it was at last discovered more than a mile from its original place, and held the bird by one of its toes only. The eagle flew about through the woods for several hundred yards, but was at last with difficulty secured. This took place a few days ago."

The Eagle was immediately conveyed to my place of residence, covered by a blanket, to save him, in his adversity, from the gaze of the people. I placed the cage so as to afford me a good view of the captive, and I must acknowledge that as I watched his eye, and observed his looks of proud disdain, I felt towards him not so generously as I ought to have done. At times I was half inclined to restore to him his freedom, that he might return to his native mountains; nay, I several times thought how pleasing it would be to see him spread out his broad wings and sail away towards the rocks of his wild haunts; but then, reader, some one seemed to whisper that I ought to take the portrait of the magnificent bird, and I abandoned the more generous design of setting him at liberty, for the express purpose of shewing you his semblance.

I occupied myself a whole day in watching his movements; on the next I came to a determination as to the position in which I might best represent him; and on the third thought of how I could take away his life with the least pain to him. I consulted several persons on the subject, and among others my most worthy and generous friend, GEORGE PARK-MAN, Esq. M. D., who kindly visited my family every day. He spoke of suffocating him by means of burning charcoal, of killing him by electricity, &c. and we both concluded that the first method would probably be the easiest for ourselves, and the least painful to him. Accordingly the bird was removed in his prison into a very small room, and closely covered with blankets, into which was introduced a pan of lighted charcoal, when the windows and door were fastened, and the blankets tucked in beneath the cage. I waited, expecting every moment to hear him fall down from his perch; but after listening for *hours*, I opened the door, raised the blankets, and peeped under them amidst a mass of suffocating fumes. There stood the Eagle on his perch, with his bright unflinching eye turned towards me, and as lively and vigorous as ever! Instantly reclosing every aperture, I resumed my station at the door, and towards midnight, not having heard the least noise, I again took a peep at my victim. He was still uninjured, although the air of the closet was insupportable to my son and myself, and that of the adjoining apartment began to feel unpleasant. I persevered, however, for ten hours in all, when finding that the charcoal fumes would not produce the desired effect, I retired to rest wearied and disappointed.

Early next morning I tried the charcoal anew, adding to it a quantity of sulphur, but we were nearly driven from our home in a few hours by the stifling vapours, while the noble bird continued to stand erect, and to look defiance at us whenever we approached his post of martyrdom. His fierce demeanour precluded all internal application, and at last I was compelled to resort to a method always used as the last expedient, and a most effectual one. I thrust a long pointed piece of steel through his heart, when my proud prisoner instantly fell dead, without even ruffling a feather.

I sat up nearly the whole of another night to outline him, and worked so constantly at the drawing, that it nearly cost me my life. I was suddenly seized with a spasmodic affection, that much alarmed my family, and completely prostrated me for some days; but, thanks to my heavenly Preserver, and the immediate and unremitting attention of my most worthy friends Drs PARKMAN, SHATTUCK, and WARREN, I was soon restored to health, and enabled to pursue my labours. The drawing of this Eagle took me fourteen days, and I had never before laboured so incessantly excepting at that of the Wild Turkey. . . .

Canada Goose

(*Branta canadensis*)

ALTHOUGH the Canada Goose is considered as a northern species, the number of individuals that remain at all seasons in the milder latitudes, and in different portions of the United States, fully entitles this bird to be looked upon as a permanent resident there. It is found to breed sparingly at the present day, by many of the lakes, lagoons, and large streams of our Western Districts, on the Missouri, the Mississippi, the lower parts of the Ohio, on Lake Erie, the lakes farther north, and in several large pools situated in the interior of the eastern parts of the States of Massachusetts and Maine. As you advance farther toward the east and north, you find it breeding more abundantly. While on my way to Labrador, I found it in the Magdeleine Islands, early in June, sitting on its eggs. In the Island of Anticosti there is a considerable stream, near the borders of which great numbers are said to be annually reared; and in Labrador these birds breed in every suitable marshy plain. The greater number of those which visit us from still more northern regions, return in the vernal season, like many other species, to the dismal countries which gave them birth.

Few if any of these birds spend the winter in Nova Scotia, my friend Mr THOMAS M'CULLOCH having informed me that he never saw one about Pictou at that period. In spring, as they proceed northward, thousands are now and then seen passing high in the air; but in autumn, the flocks are considerably smaller, and fly much lower. During their spring movements, the principal places at which they stop to wait for milder days are Bay Chaleur, the Magdeleine Islands, Newfoundland, and Labrador, at all of which some remain to breed and spend the summer.

The general spring migration of the Canada Goose, may be stated to commence with the first melting of the snows in our Middle and Western Districts, or from the 20th of March to the end of April; but the precise time of its departure is always determined by the advance of the season, and the vast flocks that winter in the great savannahs or swampy prairies south-west of the Mississippi, such as exist in Opellousas, on the borders of the Arkansas River, or in the dismal "Ever Glades" of the Floridas, are often seen to take their flight, and steer their course northward, a month earlier than the first of the above mentioned periods. It is indeed probable that the individuals of a species most remote from the point at which the greater number ultimately assemble, commence their flight earlier than those which have passed the winter in stations nearer to it.

It is my opinion that all the birds of this species, which leave our States and territories each spring for the distant north, pair before they depart. This, no doubt, necessarily results from the nature of their place of summer residence, where the genial season is so short as scarcely to afford them sufficient time for bringing up their young and renewing their plumage, before the rigours of advancing winter force them to commence their flight towards milder countries. This opinion is founded on the following facts:—I have frequently observed large flocks of Geese, in ponds, on marshy grounds, or even on dry sand bars, the mated birds renewing their courtship as early as the month of January, while the other individuals would be contending or coquetting for hours every day, until all seemed satisfied with the choice they had made, after which, although they remained together, any person could easily perceive that they were careful to keep in pairs. I have observed also that the older the birds, the shorter were the preliminaries of their courtship, and that the barren individuals were altogether insensible to the manifestations of love and mutual affection that were displayed around them. The bachelors and old maids, whether in regret, or not caring to be disturbed by the bustle, quietly moved aside, and lay down on the grass or sand at some distance from the rest; and whenever the flocks rose on wing, or betook themselves to the water, these forlorn birds always kept behind. This mode of preparing for the breeding season has appeared to me the more remarkable, that, on reaching the place appointed for their summer residence, the birds of a flock separate in pairs, which form their nests and rear their young at a considerable distance from each other.

It is extremely amusing to witness the courtship of the Canada Goose in all its stages; and let me assure you, reader, that although a Gander does not strut before his beloved with the pomposity of a Turkey, or the grace of a Dove, his ways are quite as agreeable to the female of his choice. I can imagine before me one who has just accomplished the defeat of another male after a struggle of half an hour or more. He advances gallantly towards the object of contention, his head scarcely raised an inch from the ground, his bill open to its full stretch, his fleshy tongue elevated, his eyes darting fiery glances, and as he moves he hisses loudly, while the emotion which he experiences, causes his quills to shake, and his feathers to rustle. Now he is close to her who in his eyes is all loveliness; his neck bending gracefully in all directions, passes all round her, and occasionally touches her body; and as she congratulates him on his victory, and acknowledges his affection, they move their necks in a hundred curious ways. At this moment fierce jealousy urges the defeated gander to renew his efforts to obtain his love; he advances apace, his eye glowing with the fire of rage; he shakes his broad wings, ruffles up his whole plumage, and as he rushes on the foe, hisses with the intensity of anger. The whole flock seems to stand amazed, and opening up a space, the birds gather round to view the combat. The bold bird who has been caressing his mate, scarcely deigns to take notice of his foe, but seems to send a scornful glance towards him. He of the mortified feelings, however, raises his body, half opens his sinewy wings, and with a powerful blow, sends forth his defiance. The affront cannot be borne in the presence of so large a company, nor indeed is there much disposition to bear it in any circumstances; the blow is returned with vigour, the aggressor reels for a moment, but he soon recovers, and now the combat rages. Were the weapons more deadly, feats of chivalry would now be performed; as it is, thrust and blow succeed each other like the strokes of hammers driven by sturdy forgers. But now, the mated gander has caught hold of his antagonist's head with his bill; no bull-dog could cling faster to his victim; he squeezes him with all the energy of rage, lashes him with his powerful wings, and at length drives him away, spreads out his pinions, runs with joy to his mate, and fills the air with cries of exultation.

But now, see yonder, not a couple, but half a dozen of ganders are engaged in battle! Some desperado, it seems, has fallen upon a mated bird, and several bystanders, as if sensible of the impropriety of such conduct, rush to the assistance of the wronged one. How they strive and tug, biting, and striking with their wings! and how their feathers fly about! Exhausted, abashed, and mortified, the presumptuous intruder retreats in disgrace;—there he lies almost breathless on the sand!

Such are the conflicts of these ardent lovers, and so full of courage and of affection towards their females are they, that the approach of a male invariably ruffles their tempers as well as their feathers. No sooner has the goose laid her first egg, than her bold mate stands almost erect by her side, watching even the rustling sound of the breeze. The least noise brings from him a sound of anger. Should he spy a raccoon making its way among the grass, he walks up to him undauntedly, hurls a vigorous blow at him, and drives him instantly away. Nay I doubt if man himself, if unarmed, would come off unscathed in such an encounter. The brave gander does more; for, if imminent danger excite him, he urges his mate to fly off, and resolutely remains near the nest until he is assured of her safety, when he also betakes himself to flight, mocking as it were by his notes his disappointed enemy.

Suppose all to be peace and quiet around the fond pair, and the female to be sitting in security upon her eggs. The nest is placed near the bank of a noble stream or lake; the clear sky is spread over the scene, the bright beams glitter on the waters, and a thousand odorous flowers give beauty to the swamp which of late was so dismal. The gander passes to and fro over the liquid element, moving as if lord of the waters; now he inclines his head with a graceful curve, now sips to quench his thirst; and, as noontide has arrived, he paddles his way towards the shore, to relieve for a while his affectionate and patient consort. The lisping sounds of their offspring are heard through the shell; their little bills have formed a breach in the inclosing walls; full of life, and bedecked with beauty, they come forth, with tottering steps and downy covering. Toward the water they now follow their careful parent, they reach the border of the stream, their mother already floats on the loved element, one after another launches forth, and now the flock glides gently along. What a beautiful sight! Close by the grassy margin, the mother slowly leads her innocent younglings; to one she shews the seed of the floating grass, to another points out the crawling slug. Her careful eye watches the cruel turtle, the garfish, and the pike, that are lurking for their prey, and, with head inclined, she glances upwards to the eagle or the gull that are hovering over the water in search of food. A ferocious bird dashes at her young ones; she instantly plunges beneath the surface, and, in the twinkling of an eye, her brood disappear after her; now they are among the thick rushes, with nothing above water but their little bills. The mother is marching towards the land, having lisped to her brood in accents so gentle that none but they and her mate can understand their import, and all are safely lodged under cover until the disappointed eagle or gull bears away.

More than six weeks have now elapsed. The down of the goslings, which was at first soft and tufty, has become coarse and hairlike. Their wings are edged with quills, and their bodies bristled with feathers. They have increased in size, and, living in the midst of abundance, they have become fat, so that on shore they make their way with difficulty, and as they are yet unable to fly, the greatest care is required to save them from their numerous enemies. They grow apace, and now the burning days of

August are over. They are able to fly with ease from one shore to another, and as each successive night the hoarfrosts cover the country, and the streams are closed over by the ice, the family joins that in their neighbourhood, which is also joined by others. At length they spy the advance of a snow-storm, when the ganders with one accord sound the order for their departure.

After many wide circlings, the flock has risen high in the thin air, and an hour or more is spent in teaching the young the order in which they are to move. But now, the host has been marshalled, and off it starts, shewing, as it proceeds, at one time an extended front, at another a single lengthened file, and now arraying itself in an angular form. The old males advance in front, the females follow, the young come in succession according to their strength, the weakest forming the rear. Should one feel fatigued, his position is changed in the ranks, and he assumes a place in the wake of another, who cleave the air before him; perhaps the parent bird flies for a while by his side to encourage him. Two, three, or more days elapse before they reach a secure resting place. The fat with which they were loaded at their departure has rapidly wasted; they are fatigued, and experience the keen gnawings of hunger; but now they spy a wide estuary, towards which they direct their course. Alighting on the water, they swim to the beach, stand, and gaze around them; the young full of joy, the old full of fear, for well are they aware that many foes have been waiting their arrival. Silent all night remains the flock, but not inactive; with care they betake themselves to the grassy shores, where they allay the cravings of appetite, and recruit their wasted strength. Soon as the early dawn lightens the surface of the deep they rise into the air, extend their lines, and proceed southward, until arriving in some place where they think they may be enabled to rest in security, they remain during the winter. At length, after many annoyances, they joyfully perceive the return of spring, and prepare to fly away from their greatest enemy man.

The Canada Goose often arrives in our Western and Middle Districts as early as the beginning of September, and does not by any means confine itself to the seashore. Indeed, my opinion is, that for every hundred seen during the winter along our large bays and estuaries, as many thousands may be found in the interior of the country, where they frequent the large ponds, rivers, and wet savannahs. During my residence in the State of Kentucky, I never spent a winter without observing immense flocks of these birds, especially in the neighbourhood of Henderson, where I have killed many hundreds of them, as well as on the

Falls of the Ohio at Louisville, and in the neighbouring country, which abounds in ponds overgrown with grasses and various species of Nympheæ, on the seeds of which they greedily feed. Indeed all the lakes situated within a few miles of the Missouri and Mississippi, or their tributaries, are still amply supplied with them from the middle of autumn to the beginning of spring. In these places, too, I have found them breeding, although sparingly. It seems to me more than probable, that the species bred abundantly in the temperate parts of North America before the white population extended over them. This opinion is founded on the relations of many old and respectable citizens of our country, and in particular of General GEORGE CLARK, one of the first settlers on the banks of the Ohio, who, at a very advanced age, assured me that, fifty years before the period when our conversation took place (about seventy-five years from the present time), wild geese were so plentiful at all seasons of the year, that he was in the habit of having them shot to feed his soldiers, then garrisoned near Vincennes, in the present State of Indiana. My father, who travelled down the Ohio shortly after BRADOCK's defeat, related the same to me; and I, as well as many persons now residing at Louisville in Kentucky, well remember that, twenty-five or thirty years ago, it was quite easy to procure young Canada Geese in the ponds around. So late as 1819, I have met with the nests, eggs, and young of this species near Henderson. However, as I have already said, the greater number remove far north to breed. I have never heard of an instance of their breeding in the Southern States. Indeed, so uncongenial to their constitution seems the extreme heat of these parts to be, that the attempts made to rear them in a state of domestication very rarely succeed.

The Canada Goose, when it remains with us to breed, begins to form its nest in March, making choice of some retired place not far from the water, generally among the rankest grass, and not unfrequently under a bush. It is carefully formed of dry plants of various kinds, and is of a large size, flat, and raised to the height of several inches. Once only did I find a nest elevated above the ground. It was placed on the stump of a large tree, standing in the centre of a small pond, about twenty feet high, and contained five eggs. As the spot was very secluded, I did not disturb the birds, anxious as I was to see in what manner they should convey the young to the water. But in this I was disappointed, for, on going to the nest, near the time at which I expected the process of incubation to terminate, I had the mortification to find that a racoon, or some other animal, had destroyed the whole of the eggs, and that the birds had abandoned the place. The greatest number of eggs which I have found in the nest of this species was nine, which I think is more by three than these birds usually lay in a wild state. In the nests of those which I have had in a domesticated state, I have sometimes counted as many as eleven, several of them, however, usually proving unproductive. The eggs measure, on an average, 3½ inches by 2½, are thick shelled, rather smooth, and of a very dull yellowish green colour. The period of incubation is twenty-eight days. They never have more than one brood in a season, unless their eggs are removed or broken at an early period.

The young follow their parents to the water a day or two after they have issued from the egg, but generally return to land to repose in the sunshine in the evening, and pass the night there under their mother, who employs all imaginable care to ensure their comfort and safety, as does her mate, who never leaves her during incubation for a longer time than is necessary for procuring food, and takes her place at intervals. Both remain with their brood until the following spring. It is during the breeding-season that the gander displays his courage and strength to the greatest advantage. I knew one that appeared larger than usual, and of which all the lower parts were of a rich cream colour. It returned three years in succession to a large pond a few miles from the mouth of Green River in Kentucky, and whenever I visited the nest, it seemed to look upon me with utter contempt. It would stand in a stately attitude, until I reached within a few yards of the nest, when suddenly lowering its head, and shaking it as if it were dislocated from the neck, it would open its wings, and launch into the air, flying directly at me. So daring was this fine fellow, that in two instances he struck me a blow with one of his wings on the right arm, which, for an instant, I thought, was broken. I observed that immediately after such an effort to defend his nest and mate, he would run swiftly towards them, pass his head and neck several times over and around the female, and again assume his attitude of defiance.

Always intent on making experiments, I thought of endeavouring to conciliate this bold son of the waters. For this purpose I always afterwards took with me several ears of corn, which I shelled, and threw towards him. It remained untouched for several days; but I succeeded at last, and before the end of a week both birds fed freely on the grain even in my sight! I felt much pleasure on this occasion, and repeating my visit daily, found, that before the eggs were hatched, they would allow me to approach within a few feet of them, although they never suffered me to touch them. Whenever I attempted this the male met my fingers with his bill, and bit me so severely that I gave it up. The great beauty and courage of the male rendered me desirous of obtaining possession of him. I had marked the time at which the young were likely to appear, and on the preceding day I baited with corn a large coop made of twine, and waited until he should enter. He walked in, I drew the string, and he was my prisoner. The next morning the female was about to lead her off-spring to the river, which was distant nearly half a mile, when I caught the whole of the young birds, and with them the mother too, who came within reach in attempting to rescue one of her brood, and had them taken home. There I took a cruel method of preventing their escape, for with a knife I pinioned each of them on the same side, and turned them loose in my garden, where I had a small but convenient artificial pond. For more than a fortnight, both the old birds appeared completely cowed. Indeed, for some days I felt apprehensive that they would abandon the care of the young ones. However, with much attention, I succeeded in rearing the latter by feeding them abundantly with the larvae of locusts, which they ate greedily, as well as with corn-meal moistened with water, and the whole flock, consisting of eleven individuals, went on prosperously. In December the weather became intensely cold, and I observed that now and then the gander would spread his wings, and sound a loud note, to which the female first, and then all the young ones in succession, would respond, when they would all run as far as the ground allowed them in a southerly direction, and attempt to fly off. I kept the whole flock three years. The old pair never bred while in my possession, but two pairs of the young ones did, one of them raising three, the other seven. They all bore a special enmity to dogs, and shewed dislike to cats; but they manifested a still greater animosity towards an old swan and a wild turkey-cock which I had. I found them useful in clearing the garden of slugs and snails; and although they now and then nipped the vegetables, I liked their company. When I left Henderson, my flock of geese was given away, and I have not since heard how it has fared with them.

On one of my shooting excursions in the same neighbourhood, I chanced one day to kill a wild Canada Goose, which, on my return, was sent to the kitchen. The cook, while dressing it, found in it an egg ready for being laid, and brought it to me. It was placed under a common hen, and in due time hatched. Two years afterwards the bird thus raised, mated with a male of the same species, and produced a brood. This goose was so gentle that she would suffer any person to caress her, and would readily feed from the hand. She was smaller than usual, but in every other respect as perfect as any I have ever seen. At the period of migration she shewed by her movements less desire to fly off than any other I have known; but her mate, who had once been free, did not participate in this apathy.

I have not been able to discover why many of those birds which I have known to have been reared from the egg, or to have been found when very young and brought up in captivity, were so averse to reproduce, unless they were naturally sterile. I have seen several that had been kept for more than eight years, without ever mating during that period, while other individuals had young the second spring after their birth. I have also observed that an impatient male would sometimes abandon the females of his species, and pay his addresses to a common tame goose, by which a brood would in due time be brought up, and would thrive. That this tardiness is not the case in the wild state I feel pretty confident, for I have observed having broods of their own many individuals which, by their size, the dullness of their plumage, and such other marks as are known to the practical ornithologist, I judged to be not more than fifteen or sixteen months old. I have therefore thought that in this, as in many other species, a long series of years is necessary for counteracting the original wild and free nature which has been given them; and indeed it seems probable that our attempts to domesticate many species of wild fowls, which would prove useful to mankind, have often been abandoned in despair, when a few years more of constant care might have produced the desired effect.

The Canada Goose, although immediately after the full development of its young it becomes gregarious, does not seem to be fond of the company of any other species. Thus, whenever the White-fronted Goose, the Snow Goose, the Brent Goose, or others, alight in the same ponds, it forces them to keep at a respectful distance; and during its migrations I have never observed a single bird of any other kind in its ranks.

The flight of this species of Goose is firm, rather rapid, and capable of being protracted to a great extent. When once high in the air, they advance with extreme steadiness and regularity of motion. In rising from the water or from the ground, they usually run a few feet with out-spread wings; but when suddenly surprised and in full plumage, a single spring on their broad webbed feet is sufficient to enable them to get on wing. While travelling to some considerable distance, they pass through the air at the height of about a mile, steadily following a direct course towards the point to which they are bound. Their notes are distinctly heard, and the various changes made in the disposition of their ranks are easily seen. But although on these occasions they move with the greatest regularity, yet when they are slowly advancing from south to north at an early period of the season, they fly much lower, alight more frequently, and are more likely to be bewildered by suddenly formed banks of fog, or by passing over cities or arms of the sea where much shipping may be in sight. On such occasions great consternation prevails among them, they crowd together in a confused manner, wheel irregularly, and utter a constant cackling resembling the sounds from a disconcerted mob. Sometimes the flock separates, some individuals leave the rest, proceed in a direction contrary to that in which they came, and after a while, as if quite confused, sail towards the ground, once alighted on which they appear to become almost stupified, so as to suffer themselves to be shot with ease, or even knocked down with sticks. This I have known to take place on many occasions, besides those of which I have myself been a witness. Heavy snow-storms also cause them great distress, and in the midst of them some have been known to fly against beacons and light-houses, dashing their heads against the walls in the middle of the day. In the night they are attracted by the lights of these buildings, and now and then a whole flock is caught on such occasions. At other times their migrations northward are suddenly checked by a change of weather, the approach of which seems to be well known to them, for they will suddenly wheel and fly back in a southern direction several hundred miles. In this manner I have known flocks to return to the places which they had left a fortnight before. Nay even during the winter months, they are keenly sensible to changes of temperature, flying north or south in search of feeding-grounds, with so much knowledge of the future state of the weather, that one may be assured when he sees them proceeding southward in the evening, that the next morning will be cold, and *vice versa*.

The Canada Goose is less shy when met with far inland, than when on the sea-coast, and the smaller the ponds or lakes to which they resort, the more easy it is to approach them. They usually feed in the manner of Swans and fresh-water Ducks, that is, by plunging their heads towards the bottom of shallow ponds or the borders of lakes and rivers, immersing their fore parts, and frequently exhibiting their legs and feet with the posterior portion of their body elevated in the air. They never dive on such occasions. If feeding in the fields or meadows, they nip the blades of grass sidewise, in the manner of the Domestic Goose, and after rainy weather, they are frequently seen rapidly patting the earth with both feet, as if to force the earth-worms from their burrows. If they dabble at times with their bills in muddy water, in search of food, this action is by no means so common with them as it is with Ducks, the Mallard for example. They are extremely fond of alighting in corn-fields covered with tender blades, where they often remain through the night and commit great havoc. Wherever you find them, and however remote from the haunts of man the place may be, they are at all times so vigilant and suspicious, that it is extremely rare to surprise them. In keenness of sight and acuteness of hearing, they are perhaps surpassed by no bird whatever. They act as sentinels towards each other, and during the hours at which the flock reposes, one or more ganders stand on the watch. At the sight of cattle, horses, or animals of the deer kind, they are seldom alarmed, but a bear or a cougar is instantly announced, and if on such occasions the flock is on the ground near water, the birds immediately betake themselves in silence to the latter, swim to the middle of the pond or river, and there remain until danger is over. Should their enemies pursue them in the water, the males utter loud cries, and the birds arrange themselves in close ranks, rise simultaneously in a few seconds, and fly off in a compact body, seldom at such times forming lines or angles, it being in fact only when the distance they have to travel is great that they dispose themselves in those forms. So acute is their sense of hearing, that they are able to distinguish the different sounds or footsteps of their foes with astonishing accuracy. Thus the breaking of a dry stick by a deer is at once distinguished from the same accident occasioned by a man. If a dozen of large turtles drop into the water, making a great noise in their fall, or if the same effect is produced by an alligator, the Wild Goose pays no regard to it; but however faint and distant may be the sound of an Indian's paddle, that may by accident have struck the side of his canoe, it is at once marked, every individual raises its head and looks intently towards the place from which the noise has proceeded, and in silence all watch the movements of their enemy.

These birds are extremely cunning also, and should they conceive themselves unseen, they silently move into the tall grasses by the margin of the water, lower their heads, and lie perfectly quiet until the boat has passed by. I have seen them walk off from a large frozen pond into the woods, to elude the sight of the hunter, and return as soon as he had crossed the pond. But should there be snow on the ice or in the woods, they prefer watching the intruder, and take to wing long before he is within shooting distance, as if aware of the ease with which they could be followed by their tracks over the treacherous surface.

The Canada Geese are fond of returning regularly to the place which they have chosen for resting in, and this they continue to do until they find themselves greatly molested while there. In parts of the country where they are little disturbed, they seldom go farther than the nearest sandbank or the dry shore of the places in which they feed; but in other parts they retire many miles to spots of greater security, and of such extent as will enable them to discover danger long before it can reach them. When such a place is found, and proves secure, many flocks resort to it, but alight apart in separate groups. Thus, on some of the great sandbars of the Ohio, the Mississippi, and other large streams, congregated flocks, often amounting to a thousand individuals, may be seen at the approach of night, which they spend there, lying on the sand within a few feet of each other, every flock having its own sentinel. In the dawn of next morning they rise on their feet, arrange and clean their feathers, perhaps walk to the water to drink, and then depart for their feeding grounds.

When I first went to the Falls of the Ohio, the rocky shelvings of which are often bare for fully half a mile, thousands of wild geese of this species rested there at night. The breadth of the various channels that separate the rocky islands from either shore, and the rapidity of the currents which sweep along them, render this place of resort more secure than most others. The wild geese still betake themselves to these islands during winter for the same purpose, but their number has become very small; and so shy are these birds at present in the neighbourhood of Louisville, that the moment they are disturbed at the ponds where they go to feed each morning, were it but by the report of a single gun, they immediately return to their rocky asylums. Even there, however, they are by no means secure, for it not unfrequently happens that a flock alights within half gunshot of a person concealed in a pile of drifted wood, whose aim generally proves too true for their peace. Nay, I knew a gentleman, who had a large mill opposite Rock Island, and who used to kill the poor geese at the distance of about a quarter of a mile, by means of a small cannon heavily charged with rifle bullets; and, if I recollect truly, Mr TARASCON in this manner not unfrequently obtained a dozen or more geese at a shot. This was done at dawn, when the birds were busily engaged in trimming their plumage with the view of flying off in a few minutes to their feeding grounds. This war of extermination could not last long: the geese deserted the fatal rock, and the great gun of the mighty miller was used only for a few weeks.

While on the water, the Canada Goose moves with considerable grace, and in its general deportment resembles the wild Swan, to which I think it is nearly allied. If wounded in the wing, they sometimes dive to a small depth, and make off with astonishing address, always in the direction of the shore, the moment they reach which, you see them sneaking through the grass or bushes, their necks extended an inch or so above the ground, and in this manner proceeding so silently, that, unless closely watched, they are pretty sure to escape. If shot at and wounded while on the ice, they immediately walk off in a dignified manner, as if anxious to make you believe that they have not been injured, emitting a loud note all the while; but the instant they reach the shore they become silent, and make off in the manner described. I was much surprised one day, while on the coast of Labrador, to see how cunningly one of these birds, which, in consequence of the moult, was quite unable to fly, managed for a while to elude our pursuit. It was first perceived at some distance from the shore, when the boat was swiftly rowed towards it, and it swam before us with a great speed, making directly towards the land; but when we came within a few yards of it, it dived, and nothing could be seen of it for a long time. Every one of the party stood on tiptoe to mark the spot at which it should rise, but all in vain, when the man at the rudder accidentally looked down over the stern and there saw the goose, its body immersed, the point of its bill alone above water, and its feet busily engaged in propelling it so as to keep pace with the movements of the boat. The sailor attempted to catch it while within a foot or two of him, but with the swiftness of thought it shifted from side to side, fore and aft, until delighted at having witnessed so much sagacity in a *goose*, I begged the party to suffer the poor bird to escape.

The crossing of the Canada Goose with the common domestic species has proved as advantageous as that of the wild with the tame Turkey, the cross breed being much larger than the original one, more easily raised, and more speedily fattened. This process is at present carried on to a considerable extent in our Western and Eastern States, where the hybrids are regularly offered for sale during autumn and winter, and where they bring a higher price than either of the species from which they are derived.

The Canada Goose makes its first appearance in the western country, as well as along our Atlantic coast, from the middle of September to that of October, arriving in flocks composed of a few families. The young birds procured at this early season soon get into good order, become tender and juicy, and therefore afford excellent eating. If a sportsman is expert and manages to shoot the old birds first, he is pretty sure to capture the less wily young ones afterwards, as they will be very apt to return to the same feeding places to which their parents had led them at their first arrival. To await their coming to a pond where they are known to feed is generally effectual, but to me this mode of proceeding never afforded much pleasure, more especially because the appearance of any other bird which I wished to obtain would at once induce me to go after it, and thus frighten the game, so that I rarely procured any on such occasions. But yet, as I have witnessed the killing of many a fine goose, I hope you will suffer me to relate one or two anecdotes connected with the shooting of this kind of game.

Reader, I am well acquainted with one of the best sportsmen now living in the whole of the western country, one possessed of strength, activity, courage, and patience,—qualities of great importance in a gunner. I have frequently seen him mount a capital horse of speed and bottom at midnight, when the mercury in the thermometer was about the freezing point, and the ground was covered with snow and ice, the latter of which so encased the trees that you might imagine them converted into glass. Well, off he goes at a round gallop, his steed rough shod, but nobody knows whither, save myself, who am always by his side. He has a wallet containing our breakfast, and abundance of ammunition, together with such implements as are necessary on occasions like the present. The night is pitch-dark, and dismal enough; but who cares! *He* knows the woods as well as any Kentucky hunter, and in this respect I am not much behind him. A long interval has passed, and now the first glimpse of day appears in the east. We know quite well where we are, and that we have travelled just twenty miles. The Barred Owl alone interrupts the melancholy silence of the hour. Our horses we secure, and on foot we move cautiously towards a "long pond," the feeding place of several flocks of geese, none of which have yet arrived, although the whole surface of open water is covered with Mallards, Widgeons, Pintail Ducks, Blue-winged and Green-winged Teals. My friend's gun, like mine, is a long and trusty one, and the opportunity is too tempting. On all fours we cautiously creep to the very edge of the pond; we now raise ourselves on our knees, level our pieces, and let fly. The woods resound with repeated echoes, the air is filled with Ducks of all sorts, our dogs dash into the half frozen water, and in a few minutes a small heap of game lies at our feet. Now, we retire, separate, and betake ourselves to different sides of the pond. If I may judge of my companion's fingers by the state of my own, I may feel certain that it would be difficult for him to fasten a button. There we are shivering, with contracted feet and chattering teeth; but the geese are coming, and their well known cry, *hauk, hauk, awhawk, awhawk*, resounds through the air. They wheel and wheel for a while, but at length gracefully alight on the water, and now they play and wash themselves, and begin to look about for food. There must be at least twenty of them. Twenty more soon arrive, and in less than half an hour we have before us a flock of a hundred individuals. My experienced friend has put a snow-white shirt over his apparel, and although I am greatly intent on observing his motions, I see that it is impossible even for the keen eye of the sentinel goose to follow them. Bang, bang, quoth his long gun, and the birds in dismay instantly start, and fly towards the spot where I am. When they approach I spring up on my feet, the geese shuffle, and instantaneously rise upright; I touch my triggers singly, and broken-winged and dead two birds come heavily to the ground at my feet. Oh that we had more guns! But the business at this pond has been transacted. We collect our game, return to our horses, fasten the necks of the geese and ducks together, and throwing them across our saddles, proceed towards another pond. In this manner we continue to shoot until the number of geese obtained would seem to you so very large that I shall not specify it.

At another time my friend proceeds alone to the Falls of the Ohio, and, as usual, reaches the margins of the stream long before day. His well-trained steed plunges into the whirls of the rapid current, and, with some difficulty, carries his bold rider to an island, where he lands drenched and cold. The horse knows what he has to do as well as his master, and while the former ranges about and nips the frozen herbage, the latter carefully approaches a well-known pile of drifted wood, and conceals himself in it. His famous dog Nep is close at his heels. Now the dull grey dawn gives him a dim view of the geese; he fires, several fall on the spot, and one severely wounded rises and alights in the Indian Chute. Neptune dashes after it, but as the current is powerful, the gunner whistles to his horse, who, with pricked ears, gallops up. He instantly vaults into the saddle, and now see them plunge into the treacherous stream. The wounded game is overtaken, the dog is dragged along, and at length on the Indiana shore the horse and his rider have effected a landing. Any other man than he of whose exploits I am the faithful recorder, would have perished long ago. But it is not half so much for the sake of the plunder that he undergoes all this labour and danger, as for the gratification it affords his kind heart to distribute the game among his numerous friends in Louisville.

On our eastern shores matters are differently managed. The gunners there shoot geese with the prospect of pecuniary gain, and go to work in another way. Some attract them with wooden geese, others with actual birds; they lie in ambush for many hours at a time, and destroy an immense number of them, by using extremely long guns; but as there is little sport in this sort of shooting, I shall say no more about it. Here the Canada Goose feeds much on a species of long slender grass, the *Zostera marina*, along with marine insects, crustacea, and small shell-fish, all of which have a tendency to destroy the agreeable flavour which their flesh has when their food consists of fresh-water plants, corn, and grass. They spend much of their time at some distance from the shores, become more shy, diminish in bulk, and are much inferior as food to those which visit the interior of the country. None of these, however, are at all to be compared with the goslings bred in the inland districts, and procured in September, when, in my opinion, they far surpass the renowned Canvass-backed Duck.

A curious mode of shooting the Canada Goose I have practised with much success. I have sunk in the sand of the bars to which these birds resort at night, a tight hogshead, to within an inch of its upper edges, and placing myself within it at the approach of evening, have drawn over me a quantity of brushwood, placing my gun on the sand, and covering it in like manner with twigs and leaves. The birds would sometimes alight very near me, and in this concealment I have killed several at a shot; but the stratagem answers for only a few nights in the season. During severe winters these birds are able to keep certain portions of the deepest parts of a pond quite open and free from ice, by their continued movements in the water; at all events, such open spaces occasionally occur in ponds and lakes, and are resorted to by the geese, among which great havoc is made.

It is alleged in the State of Maine that a distinct species of Canada Goose resides there, which is said to be much smaller than the one now under your notice, and is described as resembling it in all other particulars. Like the true Canada Goose, it builds a large nest, which it lines with its own down. Sometimes it is placed on the sea-shore, at other times by the margin of a fresh-water lake or pond. That species is distinguished there by the name of *Flight Goose*, and is said to be entirely migratory, whereas the Canada Goose is resident. But, notwithstanding all my exertions, I did not succeed in procuring so much as a feather of this alleged species.

While we were at Newfoundland, on our return from Labrador, on the 15th August 1833, small flocks of the Canada Goose were already observed flying southward. In that country their appearance is hailed with delight, and great numbers of them are shot. They breed rather abundantly by the lakes of the interior of that interesting country. In the harbour of Great Macatina in Labrador, I saw a large pile of young Canada Geese, that had been procured a few days before, and were already salted for winter use. The pile consisted of several hundred individuals, all of which had been killed before they were able to fly. I was told there that this species fed much on the leaves of the dwarf firs, and, on examining their gizzards, found the statement to be correct.

The young dive very expertly, soon after their reaching the water, at the least appearance of danger. In the Southern and Western States, the enemies of the Canada Goose are, by water, the Alligator, the Garfish, and the Turtle; and on land, the Cougar, the Lynx, and the Racoon. While in the air, they are liable to be attacked by the White-headed Eagle. It is a very hardy bird, and individuals have been in a state of captivity or domestication for upwards of forty years. Every portion of it is useful to man, for besides the value of the flesh as an article of food, the feathers, the quills, and the fat, are held in request. The eggs also afford very good eating.

Whooping Crane

(*Grus americana*)

THE variegated foliage of the woods indicates that the latter days of October have arrived; gloomy clouds spread over the heavens; the fierce blasts of the north, as if glad to escape from the dreary regions of their nativity, sport in dreadful revelry among the forests and glades. Showers of sleet and snow descend at intervals, and the careful husbandman gathers his flocks, to drive them to a place of shelter. The traveller gladly accepts the welcome of the forester, and as he seats himself by the blazing fire, looks with pleasure on the spinning wheels of the industrious inmates. The lumberer prepares to set out on his long voyage, the trapper seeks the retreats of the industrious beaver, and the red Indian is making arrangements for his winter hunts. The Ducks and Geese have already reached the waters of the western ponds; here a Swan or two is seen following in their train, and as the observer of nature stands watching the appearances and events of this season of change, he hears from on high the notes of the swiftly travelling but unseen Whooping Crane. Suddenly the turbid atmosphere clears, and now he can perceive the passing birds. Gradually they descend, dress their extended lines, and prepare to alight on the earth. With necks outstretched, and long bony legs extended behind, they proceed supported by wings white as the snow but tipped with jet, until arriving over the great savannah they wheel their circling flight, and slowly approach the ground, on which with half-closed wings, and outstretched feet they alight, running along for a few steps to break the force of their descent.

Reader, see the majestic bird shake its feathers, and again arrange them in order. Proud of its beautiful form, and prouder still of its power of flight, it stalks over the withering grasses with all the majesty of a gallant chief. With long and measured steps he moves along, his head erect, his eye glistening with delight. His great journey is accomplished, and being well acquainted with a country which has often been visited by him, he at once commences his winter avocations.

The Whooping Crane reaches the Western Country about the middle of October, or the beginning of November, in flocks of twenty or thirty individuals, sometimes of twice or thrice that number, the young by themselves, but closely followed by their parents. They spread from Illinois over Kentucky, and all the intermediate States, until they reach the Carolinas on the southern coast, the Floridas, Louisiana, and the countries bordering on Mexico, in all of which they spend the winter, seldom returning northward until about the middle of April, or towards the beginning of May. They are seen on the edges of large ponds supplied with rank herbage, on fields or savannahs, now in swampy woods, and again on extensive marshes. The interior of the country, and the neighbourhood of the sea shores, suit them equally well, so long as the temperature is sufficiently high. In the Middle States, it is very seldom indeed that they are seen; and to the eastward of these countries they are unknown; for all their migrations are performed far inland, and thus they leave and return to the northern retreats where, it is said, they breed and spend the summer. While migrating they appear to travel both by night and by day, and I have frequently heard them at the former, and seen them at the latter time, as they were proceeding towards their destination. Whether the weather be calm or tempestuous, it makes no difference to them, their power of flight being such as to render them regardless of the winds. Nay I have observed them urging their way during very heavy gales, shifting from high to low in the air with remarkable dexterity. The members of a flock sometimes arrange themselves in the form of an acute-angled triangle; sometimes they move in a long line; again they mingle together without order, or form an extended front; but in whatever manner they advance, each bird sounds his loud note in succession, and on all occasions of alarm these birds manifest the same habit. While with us they are also always met with in flocks. But now, Reader, allow me to refer to my journals, whence I shall extract some circumstances relative to this majestic bird, which I hope you will find not uninteresting.

Louisville, State of Kentucky, March 1810.—I had the gratification of taking ALEXANDER WILSON to some ponds within a few miles of town, and of shewing him many birds of this species, of which he had not previously seen any other than stuffed specimens. I told him that the white birds were the adults, and that the grey ones were the young. WILSON, in his article on the Whooping Crane, has alluded to this, but, as on other occasions, has not informed his readers whence the information came.

Henderson, November 1810.—The Sand Hill Crane arrived at the Long Pond on the 28th of last month. I saw two flocks of young ones there, and one of adults on the Slim Pond. Both old and young immediately set to digging through the mud, the rains having scarcely begun to cover those places with water, for during summer they become almost dry. The birds work very assiduously with their bills, and succeed in uncovering the large roots of the great water-lily, which often run to a depth of two or three feet. Several cranes are seen in the same hole, tugging at roots and other substances, until they reach the object of their desire, which they greedily devour. While thus engaged, they are easily approached; for if their heads are bent down they cannot see you, and until they raise themselves again, to take notice of what may be going on around the place, you may advance so as to get within shot. While I watched them at this work, they were perfectly silent; and as I lay concealed behind a large cypress tree, within thirty paces of a flock, thus buried, as it were, in the great holes they had formed, so as to put me in mind of a parcel of hogs or bears at their wallowing spots, I could plainly see the colour of their eyes, which is brown in the young, and yellow in the adult. After observing them as long as I wished, I whistled, on which they all at once raised their heads to see what the matter might be. I had so fair an opportunity that I could not resist the temptation, especially as several of the birds had their necks so close together that I felt confident I must kill more than one of them. Accordingly, just as their last croaking notes were heard, and I saw them preparing to set to work again, I fired. Only two flew up, to my surprise. They came down the pond towards me and my next shot brought them to the ground. On walking to the hole, I found that I had disabled seven in all. Those which were in different holes farther off, all flew away, uttering loud cries, and did not return that afternoon. In the course of a week these birds turned up the earth, and dug holes all over the dry parts of the ponds. As soon as heavy rains fill the pools, the Cranes abandon them, and resort to other places.

   Natchez, November 1821.—The Sand-hill Cranes now resort to the fields, in which corn, pease, and sweet potatoes have been planted, as well as to the cotton plantations. They feed on the grains and pease, dig up the potatoes, which they devour with remarkable greediness; and in the wet fields seize on water insects, toads and frogs, but never, I believe, on fishes.

   Bayou Sara, April 12, 1822.—The Sand-hill Cranes have left all the fields, and removed to the swamps and inner lakes. I saw some catching young bull-frogs, water-lizards, and water-snakes, as well as very small alligators. One struck at a young snapping turtle, which, however, escaped. The Wood Ibises and these birds do not agree together; the latter chase the former up to their bellies in the water.

April 16.—I saw nine beautiful adult birds apparently in perfect plumage. They were round a fallen log, about twenty yards from the water, all very busily occupied in killing a band of young alligators, which had probably endeavored to save themselves from the attacks of the Cranes by crawling beneath the sides of the log. I shot at them without much effect, for, although I believe I wounded two of them, they all flew off. On going up to the log, I found several young alligators, measuring from seven to eight inches in length, apparently dead, with their heads sadly bruised as if by a powerful blow. This led me to think that they kill a number of animals before they feed upon them, as the Wood Ibis is wont to do. This afternoon I saw four of these young Cranes tearing up the ground in search of cray-fish. One caught a butterfly as it was fluttering near, and instantly swallowed it.

This species feeds only during the day. Besides the objects which I have already mentioned, it now and then swallows a mole or a meadow-mouse, and not unfrequently, I think, snakes of considerable length. I opened one that had a garter-snake, more than fifteen inches long, in its stomach.

The wariness of this species is so remarkable, that it takes all the cunning and care of an Indian hunter to approach it at times, especially in the case of an old bird. The acuteness of their sight and hearing is quite wonderful. If they perceive a man approaching, even at the distance of a quarter of a mile, they are sure to take to wing. Should you accidentally tread on a stick and break it, or suddenly cock your gun, all the birds in the flock raise their heads and emit a cry. Shut the gate of a field after you, and from that moment they all watch your motions. To attempt to crawl towards them, even among long grass, after such an intimation, would be useless; and unless you lie in wait for them, and be careful to maintain a perfect silence, or may have the cover of some large trees, heaps of brushwood, or fallen logs, you may as well stay at home. They generally see you long before you perceive them, and so long as they are aware that you have not observed them, they remain silent; but the moment that, by some inadvertency, you disclose to them your sense of their presence, some of them sound an alarm. For my part, Reader, I would as soon undertake to catch a deer by fair running, as to shoot a Sand-hill Crane that had observed me. Sometimes, indeed, towards the approach of spring, when they are ready to depart for their breeding grounds, the voice of one will startle and urge to flight all within a mile of the spot. When this happens, all the birds around join into a great flock, gradually rise in a spiral manner, ascend to a vast height, and sail off in a straight course.

When wounded, these birds cannot be approached without caution, as their powerful bill is capable of inflicting a severe wound. Knowing this as I do, I would counsel any sportsman not to leave his gun behind, while pursuing a wounded Crane. One afternoon in winter, as I was descending the Mississippi, on my way to Natchez, I saw several Cranes standing on a large sand-bar. The sight of these beautiful birds excited in me a desire to procure some of them. Accordingly, taking a rifle and some ammunition, I left the flat-bottomed boat in a canoe, and told the men to watch for me, as the current was rapid at that place, the river being there narrowed by the sand-bar. I soon paddled myself to the shore, and having observed, that, by good management, I might approach the Cranes under cover of a huge stranded tree, I landed opposite to it, drew up my canoe, and laying myself flat on the sand, crawled the best way I could, pushing my gun before me. On reaching the log, I cautiously raised my head opposite to a large branch, and saw the birds at a distance somewhat short of a hundred yards. I took, as I thought, an excellent aim, although my anxiety to shew the boatmen how good a marksman I was rendered it less sure than it might otherwise have been. I fired, when all the birds instantly flew off greatly alarmed, excepting one which leaped into the air, but immediately came down again, and walked leisurely away with a drooping pinion. As I rose on my feet, it saw me, I believe, for the first time, cried out lustily, and ran off with the speed of an ostrich. I left my rifle unloaded, and in great haste pursued the wounded bird, which doubtless would have escaped had it not made towards a pile of driftwood, where I overtook it. As I approached it, panting and almost exhausted, it immediately raised itself to the full stretch of its body, legs, and neck, ruffled its feathers, shook them, and advanced towards me with open bill, and eyes glancing with anger. I cannot tell you whether it was from feeling almost exhausted with the fatigue of the chase; but, however it was, I felt unwilling to encounter my antagonist, and keeping my eye on him, moved backwards. The farther I removed, the more he advanced, until at length I fairly turned my back to him, and took to my heels, retreating with fully more speed than I had pursued. He followed, and I was glad to reach the river, into which I plunged up to the neck, calling out to my boatmen, who came up as fast as they could. The Crane stood looking angrily on me all the while, immersed up to his belly in the water, and only a few yards distant, now and then making thrusts at me with his bill. There he stood until the people came up; and highly delighted they were with my situation. However, the battle was soon over, for, on landing, some of them struck the winged warrior on the neck with an oar, and we carried him on board.

While in the Floridas, I saw only a few of these birds alive, but many which had been shot by the Spaniards and Indians, for the sake of their flesh and beautiful feathers, of which latter they make fans and fly-brushes. None of these birds remain there during summer; and WILLIAM BARTRAM, when speaking of this species, must have mistaken the Wood Ibis for it.

The young are considerably more numerous than the old white birds; and this circumstance has probably led to the belief among natu-ralists that the former constitute a distinct species, to which the name of Canada Crane, *Grus canadensis*, has been given. This, however, I hope, I shall be able to clear up to your satisfaction. In the mean time, I shall continue my remarks.

According to circumstances, this species roosts either on the ground or on high trees. In the latter case, they leave their feeding-ground about an hour before sun-set, and going off in silence, proceed towards the interior of high land forests, where they alight on the largest branches of lofty trees, six or seven settling on the same branch. For half an hour or so, they usually dress their plumage, standing erect: but af-terwards they crouch in the manner of Wild Turkeys. In this situation they are sometimes shot by moonlight. Those which resort to planta-tions, situated in the vicinity of large marshes, covered with tall grasses, cat's tails, and other plants, spend the night on some hillock, standing on one leg, the other being drawn under the body, whilst the head is thrust beneath the broad feathers of the shoulder. In returning towards the feeding grounds, they all emit their usual note, but in a very low undertone, leaving their roost at an earlier or later hour, according to the state of the weather. When it is cold and clear, they start very early; but when warm and rainy, not until late in the morning. Their motions toward night are determined by the same circumstances. They rise easily from the ground after running a few steps, fly low for thirty or forty yards, then rise in circles, crossing each other in their windings, like Vultures, Ibises, and some other birds. If startled or shot at, they utter loud and piercing cries. These cries, which I cannot compare to the sounds of any instrument known to me, I have heard at the distance of three miles, at the approach of spring, when the males were paying their addresses to the females, or fighting among themselves. They may be in some degree represented by the syllables *kewrr, kewrr, kewrooh;* and strange and un-couth as they are, they have always sounded delightful in my ear.

In December 1833, I sent my son to Spring Island, on the coast of Georgia, to which these birds are in the habit of resorting every winter. Mr HAMMOND, the proprietor of this island, treated him with all the hospitality for which the southern planters are celebrated. The Cranes, which were plentiful, resorted to the sweet potato fields, digging up their produce as expertly as a troop of negroes. They walked carefully over the little heaps, probed them in various parts in the manner of Woodcocks or Snipes, and whenever they hit upon a potato, removed the soil, took out the root, and devoured it in rather small pieces. In this manner they would search over the whole field, which was two miles in length, and rather more than a quarter of a mile in breadth, gleaning all the potatoes that had escaped the gatherers. They were so shy, however, that notwithstanding all the endeavors of my son, who is a good hand at getting in upon game, as well as a good shot, he only killed a young one, which was evidently of that year's brood, it being yet almost reddish-brown, the long feathers of the rump just beginning to shew, and the head yet covered with hairlike feathers to the mandible, and merely shewing between them the wrinkled skins so conspicuous in the old birds. The specimen procured on Spring Island was carefully examined and described, and the skin is now in the British Museum in London. Its flesh was tender and juicy, of a colour resembling that of young venison, and afforded excellent eating. This I have always found to be the case with young birds of this species, so long as they are in their brown livery, and even when they have begun to be patched with white; but in old birds the flesh becomes very dark, tough and unfit for the table, although the Seminole Indians shoot them on all occasions for food.

In captivity the Whooping Crane becomes extremely gentle, and feeds freely on grain and other vegetable substances. A Mr MAGWOOD, residing near Charleston, in South Carolina, kept one for some time feeding it on maize. It accidentally wounded one of its feet on the shell of an oyster, and, although the greatest care was taken of it, died after lingering some weeks. Having myself kept one alive, I will give you an account of its habits.

It was nearly full-grown when I obtained it, and its plumage was changing from greyish-brown to white. Its figure you will see in the plate to which this article refers. I received it as a present from Captain CLACK of the United States Navy, commander of the Erie sloop of war. It had been wounded in the wing, on the coast of Florida, but the fractured limb had been amputated and soon healed. During a voyage of three months, it became very gentle, and was a great favourite with the sailors. I placed it in a yard, in company with a beautiful Snow Goose. This was at Boston. It was so gentle as to suffer me to caress it with the hand, and was extremely fond of searching for worms and grubs about the wood pile, probing every hole it saw with as much care and dexterity as an Ivory-billed Woodpecker. It also watched with all the patience of a cat the motions of some mice which had burrows near the same spot, killed them with a single blow, and swallowed them entire, one after another, until they were extirpated. I fed it on corn and garbage from the kitchen, to which were added bits of bread and cheese, as well as some apples. It would pick up the straws intended to keep its feet from being soiled, and arrange them round its body, as if intent on forming a nest. For hours at a time, it would stand resting on one foot in a very graceful posture; but what appeared to me very curious was, that it had a favourite leg for this purpose; and in fact none of my family ever found it standing on the other, although it is probable that this happened in consequence of the mutilation of the wing, the leg employed being that of the injured side. The stump of its amputated wing appeared to be a constant source of trouble, particularly at the approach of the winter: it would dress the feathers about it, and cover it with so much care, that I really felt for the poor fellow. When the weather became intensely cold, it regularly re-tired at the approach of night under a covered passage, where it spent the hours of darkness; but it always repaired to this place with marked reluctance, and never until all was quiet and nearly dark, and it came out, even when the snow lay deep on the ground, at the first appearance of day. Now and then it would take a run, extend its only wing, and, uttering a loud cry, leap several times in the air, as if anxious to return to its haunts. At other times it would look upwards, cry aloud as if calling to some acquaintance passing high in the air, and again use its ordinary note whenever its companion the Snow Goose sent forth her own sig-nals. It seldom swallowed its food without first carrying it to the water, and dipping it several times, and now and then it would walk many yards for that express purpose. Although the winter was severe, the thermometer some mornings standing as low as 10°, the bird fattened and looked extremely well. So strong was the natural suspicion of this bird, that I frequently saw it approach some cabbage leaves with mea-sured steps, look at each sideways before it would touch one of them, and after all, if it by accident tossed the leaf into the air when attempting to break it to pieces, it would run off as if some dreaded enemy were at hand. . . .

Great White Heron

(*Ardea occidentalis*)

I AM now about to present you with an account of the habits of the largest species of the Heron tribe hitherto found in the United States, and which is indeed remarkable not only for its great size, but also for the pure white of its plumage at every period of its life. Writers who have subdivided the family, and stated that none of the True Herons are white, will doubtless be startled when they, for the first time, look at my plate of this bird. I think, however, that our endeavours to discover the natural arrangement of things cannot be uniformly successful, and it is clear that he only who has studied *all* can have much chance of disposing all according to their relations.

On the 24th of April 1832, I landed on Indian Key in Florida, and immediately after formed an acquaintance with Mr EGAN, of whom I have already several times spoken. He it was who first gave me notice of the species which forms the subject of this article, and of which I cannot find any description. The next day after that of my arrival, when I was prevented from accompanying him by my anxiety to finish a drawing, he came in with two young birds alive, and another lying dead in a nest, which he had cut off from a mangrove. You may imagine how delighted I was, when at the very first glance I felt assured that they were different from any that I had previously seen. The two living birds were of a beautiful white, slightly tinged with cream-colour, remarkably fat and strong for their age, which the worthy Pilot said could not be more than three weeks. The dead bird was quite putrid and much smaller. It looked as if it had accidentally been trampled to death by the parent birds ten or twelve days before, the body being almost flat and covered with filth. The nest with the two live birds was placed in the yard. The young Herons seemed quite unconcerned when a person approached them, although on displaying one's hand to them, they at once endeavoured to strike it with their bill. My Newfoundland dog, a well-trained and most sagacious animal, was whistled for and came up; on which the birds rose partially on their legs, ruffled all their feathers, spread their wings, opened their bills, and clicked their mandibles in great anger, but without attempting to leave the nest. I ordered the dog to go near them, but not to hurt them. They waited until he went within striking distance, when the largest suddenly hit him with its bill, and hung to his nose. Plato, however, took it all in good part, and merely brought the bird towards me, when I seized it by the wings, which made it let go its hold. It walked off as proudly as any of its tribe, and I was delighted to find it possessed of so much courage. These birds were left under the charge of Mrs EGAN, until I returned from my various excursions to the different islands along the coast.

On the 26th of the same month, Mr THRUSTON took me and my companions in his beautiful barge to some keys on which the Florida Cormorants were breeding in great numbers. As we were on the way we observed two tall white Herons standing on their nests; but although I was anxious to procure them alive, an unfortunate shot from one of the party brought them to the water. They were, I was told, able to fly, but probably had never seen a man before. While searching that day for nests of the Zenaida Dove, we observed a young Heron of this species stalking among the mangroves that bordered the key on which we were, and immediately pursued it. Had you been looking on, good Reader, you might have enjoyed a hearty laugh, although few of us could have joined you. Seven or eight persons were engaged in the pursuit of this single bird, which, with extended neck, wings, and legs, made off among the tangled trees at such a rate, that, anxious as I was to obtain it alive, I several times thought of shooting it. At length, however, it was caught, its bill was securely tied, its legs were drawn up, and fastened by a strong cord, and the poor thing was thus conveyed to Indian Key, and placed along with its kinsfolk. On seeing it, the latter immediately ran towards it with open bills, and greeted it with a most friendly welcome, passing their heads over and under its own in the most curious and indeed ludicrous manner. A bucketful of fish was thrown to them, which they swallowed in a few minutes. After a few days, they also ate pieces of pork-rhind, cheese, and other substances.

While sailing along the numerous islands that occur between Indian Key and Key West, I saw many birds of this species, some in pairs, some single, and others in flocks; but on no occasion did I succeed in getting within shot of one. Mr EGAN consoled me by saying that he knew some places beyond Key West where I certainly should obtain several, were we to spend a day and a night there for the purpose. Dr BENJAMIN STROBEL afterwards gave me a similar assurance. In the course of a week after reaching Key West, I in fact procured more than a dozen birds of different ages, as well as nests and eggs, and their habits were carefully examined by several of my party.

At three o'clock one morning, you might have seen Mr EGAN and myself, about eight miles from our harbour, paddling as silently as possible over some narrow and tortuous inlets, formed by the tides through a large flat and partially submersed key. There we expected to find many White Herons; but our labour was for a long time almost hopeless, for, although other birds occurred, we had determined to shoot nothing but the Great White Heron, and none of that species came near us. At length, after six or seven hours of hard labour, a Heron flew right over our heads, and to make sure of it, we both fired at once. The bird came down dead. It proved to be a female, which had either been sitting on her eggs or had lately hatched her young, her belly being bare, and her plumage considerably worn. We now rested a while, and breakfasted on some biscuit soaked in molasses and water, reposing under the shade of the mangroves, where the mosquitoes had a good opportunity of breaking their fast also. We went about from one key to another, saw a great number of White Herons, and at length, towards night, reached the Marion, rather exhausted, and having a solitary bird. Mr EGAN and I had been most of the time devising schemes for procuring others with less trouble, a task which might easily have been accomplished a month before, when, as he said, the birds were "sitting hard." He asked if I would return that night at twelve o'clock to the last key which we had visited. I mentioned the proposal to our worthy Captain, who, ever willing to do all in his power to oblige me, when the service did not require constant attendance on board, said that if I would go, he would accompany us in the gig. Our guns were soon cleaned, provisions and ammunition placed in the boats, and after supping we talked and laughed until the appointed time.

"Eight Bells" made us bound on our feet, and off we pushed for the islands. The moon shone bright in the clear sky; but as the breeze had died away, we betook ourselves to our oars. The state of the tide was against us, and we had to drag our boats several miles over the soapy shallows; but at last we found ourselves in a deep channel beneath the hanging mangroves of a large key, where we had observed the Herons retiring to roost the previous evening. There we lay quietly until daybreak. But the mosquitoes and sandflies! Reader, if you have not been in such a place, you cannot easily conceive the torments we endured for a whole hour, when it was absolutely necessary for us to remain perfectly motionless. At length day dawned, and the boats parted, to meet on the other side of the key. Slowly and silently each advanced. A Heron sprung from its perch almost directly over our heads. Three barrels were discharged,—in vain; the bird flew on unscathed; the pilot and I had probably been too anxious. As the bird sped away, it croaked loudly, and the noise, together with the report of our guns, roused some hundreds of these Herons, which flew from the mangroves, and in the grey light appeared to sail over and around us like so many spectres. I almost despaired of procuring any more. The tide was now rising, and when we met with the other boat we were told, that if we had waited until we could have shot at them while perched, we might have killed several; but that now we must remain until full tide, for the birds had gone to their feeding grounds.

The boats parted again, and it was now arranged that whenever a Heron was killed, another shot should be fired exactly one minute after, by which each party would be made aware of the success of the other. Mr EGAN, pointing to a nest on which stood two small young birds, desired to be landed near it. I proceeded into a narrow bayou, where we remained quiet for about half an hour, when a Heron flew over us and was shot. It was a very fine old male. Before firing my signal shot, I heard a report from afar, and a little after mine was discharged I heard another shot, so I felt assured that two birds had been killed. When I reached the Captain's boat I found that he had in fact obtained two; but Mr EGAN had waited two hours in vain near the nest, for none of the old birds came up. We took him from his hiding place, and brought the Herons along with us. It was now nearly high water. About a mile from us, more than a hundred Herons stood on a mud-bar up to their bellies. The pilot said that now was our best chance, as the tide would soon force them to fly, when they would come to rest on the trees. So we divided, each choosing his own place, and I went to the lowest end of the key, where it was separated from another by a channel. I soon had the pleasure of observing all the Herons take to wing, one after another, in quick succession. I then heard my companions' guns, but no signal of success. Obtaining a good chance as I thought, I fired at a remarkably large bird, and distinctly heard the shot strike it. The Heron merely croaked, and pursued its course. No another bird came near enough to be shot at although many had alighted on the neighbouring key, and stood perched like so many newly finished statues of the purest alabaster, forming a fine contrast to the deep blue sky. The boats joined us. Mr. EGAN had one bird, the Captain another, and both looked at me with surprise. We now started for the next key, where we expected to see more. When we had advanced several hundred yards along its low banks, we found the bird at which I had shot lying with extended wings in the agonies of death. It was from this specimen that the drawing was made. I was satisfied with the fruits of this day's excursion. On other occasions I procured fifteen more birds, and judging that number sufficient, I left the Herons to their occupations. . . .

When I left Key West, on our return towards Charleston, I took with me two young birds that had been consigned to the care of my friend Dr B. STROBEL, who assured me that they devoured more than their weight of food per day. I had also two young birds of the *Ardea Herodias* alive. After bringing them on board, I placed them all together in a very large coop; but was soon obliged to separate the two species, for the white birds would not be reconciled to the blue, which they would have killed. While the former had the privilege of the deck for a few minutes, they struck at the smaller species, such as the young of *Ardea rufescens* and *A. Ludoviciana*, some of which they instantly killed and swallowed entire, although they were abundantly fed on the flesh of green Turtles. None of the sailors succeeded in making friends with them.

On reaching Indian Key, I found those which had been left with Mrs EGAN, in excellent health and much increased in size, but to my surprise observed that their bills were much broken, which she assured me had been caused by the great force with which they struck at the fishes thrown to them on the rocks of their enclosure,—a statement which I found confirmed by my own observation in the course of the day. It was almost as difficult to catch them in the yard, as if they had never seen a man before, and we were obliged to tie their bills fast, to avoid being wounded by them while carrying them on board. They thrived well, and never manifested the least animosity towards each other. One of them which accidentally walked before the coop in which the Blue Herons were, thrust its bill between the bars, and transfixed the head of one of these birds, so that it was instantaneously killed.

When we arrived at Charleston, four of them were still alive. They were taken to my friend JOHN BACHMAN, who was glad to see them. He kept a pair, and offered the other to our mutual friend Dr SAMUEL WIL-SON, who accepted them, but soon afterwards gave them to Dr GIBBES of Columbia College, merely because they had killed a number of Ducks. My friend BACHMAN kept two of these birds for many months; but it was difficult for him to procure fish enough for them, as they swallowed a bucketful of mullets in a few minutes, each devouring about a gallon of these fishes. They betook themselves to roosting in a beautiful arbour in his garden; where at night they looked with their pure white plumage like beings of another world. It is a curious fact, that the points of their bills, of which an inch at least had been broken, grew again, and were as regularly shaped at the end of six months as if nothing had happened to them. In the evening or early in the morning, they would frequently set, like pointer dogs, at moths which hovered over the flowers, and with a well-directed stroke of their bill seize the fluttering insect and instantly swallow it. On many occasions, they also struck at chickens, grown fowls and ducks, which they would tear up and devour. Once a cat which was asleep in the sunshine, on the wooden steps of the veranda, was pinned through the body to the boards, and killed by one of them. At last they began to pursue the younger children of my worthy friend, who therefore ordered them to be killed. . . .

American Avocet

(*Recurvirostra americana*)

THE fact of this curious bird's breeding in the interior of our country accidentally became known to me in June 1814. I was at the time travelling on horseback from Henderson to Vincennes in the State of Indiana.
As I approached a large shallow pond in the neighbourbood of the latter
town, I was struck by the sight of several Avosets hovering over the margins and islets of the pond, and although it was late, and I was both fatigued and hungry, I could not resist the temptation of endeavouring to
find the cause of their being so far from the sea. Leaving my horse at liberty, I walked toward the pond, when, on being at once assailed by four
of the birds, I felt confident that they had nests, and that their mates
were either sitting or tending their young. The pond, which was about
two hundred yards in length, and half as wide, was surrounded by tall
bulrushes extending to some distance from the margin. Near its centre
were several islets, eight or ten yards in length, and disposed in a line.
Having made my way through the rushes, I found the water only a few
inches deep; but the mud reached above my knees, as I carefully advanced towards the nearest island. The four birds kept up a constant
noise, remained on wing, and at times dived through the air until close
to me, evincing their displeasure at my intrusion. My desire to shoot
them however was restrained by my anxiety to study their habits as
closely as possible; and as soon as I had searched the different inlets, and
found three nests with eggs, and a female with her brood, I returned to
my horse, and proceeded to Vincennes, about two miles distant. Next
morning at sunrise I was snugly concealed amongst the rushes, with a fair
view of the whole pond. In about an hour the male birds ceased to fly
over me, and betook themselves to their ordinary occupations, when I
noted the following particulars.

On alighting, whether on the water or on the ground, the American Avoset keeps its wings raised until it has fairly settled. If in the
water, it stands a few minutes balancing its head and neck, somewhat in
the manner of the Tell-tale Godwit. After this it stalks about searching
for food, or runs after it, sometimes swimming for a yard or so while passing from one shallow to another, or wading up to its body, with the wings

partially raised. Sometimes they would enter among the rushes, and disappear for several minutes. They kept apart, but crossed each other's path in hundreds of ways, all perfectly silent, and without shewing the least symptom of enmity towards each other, although whenever a Sandpiper came near, they would instantly give chase to it. On several occasions, when I purposely sent forth a loud shrill whistle without stirring, they would suddenly cease from their rambling, raise up their body and neck, emit each two or three notes, and remain several minutes on the alert, after which they would fly to their nests, and then return. They search for food precisely in the manner of the Roseate Spoonbill, moving their heads to and fro sideways, while their bill is passing through the soft mud; and in many instances, when the water was deeper, they would immerse their whole head and a portion of the neck, as the Spoonbill and Red-breasted Snipe are wont to do. When, on the contrary, they pursued aquatic insects, such as swim on the surface, they ran after them, and on getting up to them, suddenly seized them by thrusting the lower mandible beneath them, while the other was raised a good way above the surface, much in the manner of the Black Shearwater, which however performs this act on wing. They were also expert at catching flying insects, after which they ran with partially expanded wings.

I watched them as they were thus engaged about an hour, when they all flew to the islets where the females were, emitting louder notes than usual. The different pairs seemed to congratulate each other, using various curious gestures; and presently those which had been sitting left the task to their mates and betook themselves to the water, when they washed, shook their wings and tail, as if either heated or tormented by insects, and then proceeded to search for food in the manner above described. Now, Reader, wait a few moments until I eat my humble breakfast.

About eleven o'clock the heat had become intense, and the Avosets gave up their search, each retiring to a different part of the pond, where, after pluming themselves, they drew their heads close to their shoulders, and remained perfectly still, as if asleep, for about an hour, when they shook themselves simultaneously, took to wing, and rising to the height of thirty or forty yards, flew off towards the waters of the Wabash River.

I was now desirous of seeing one of the sitting birds on its nest, and leaving my hiding place, slowly, and as silently as possible, proceeded toward the nearest islet on which I knew a nest to be, having the evening before, to mark the precise spot, broken some of the weeds, which were now withered by the heat of the sun. You, good Reader, will not, I am sure, think me prolix; but as some less considerate persons may allege that I am tediously so, I must tell them here that no student of Nature ever was, or ever can be, too particular while thus marking the precise situation of a bird's nest. Indeed, I myself have lost many nests by being less attentive. After this short but valuable lecture, you and I will do our best to approach the sitting bird unseen by it. Although a person can advance but slowly when wading through mud and water knee-deep, it does not take much time to get over forty or fifty yards, and thus I was soon on the small island where the Avoset was comfortably seated on her nest. Softly and on all four I crawled toward the spot, panting with heat and anxiety. Now, Reader, I am actually within three feet of the unheeding creature, peeping at her through the tall grasses. Lovely bird! how innocent, how unsuspecting, and yet how near to thine enemy, albeit he be an admirer of thy race! There she sits on her eggs, her head almost mournfully sunk among the plumage, and her eyes, unanimated by the sight of her mate, half closed, as if she dreamed of future scenes. Her legs are bent beneath her in the usual manner. I have seen this, and I am content. Now she observes me, poor thing, and off she scrambles,—running, tumbling, and at last rising on wing, emitting her clicking notes of grief and anxiety, which none but an inconsiderate or callous-hearted person could hear without sympathizing with her.

The alarm is sounded, the disturbed bird is floundering hither and thither over the pool, now lying on the surface as if ready to die, now limping to induce me to pursue her and abandon her eggs. Alas, poor bird! Until that day I was not aware that gregarious birds, on emitting cries of alarm, after having been scared from their nest, could induce other incubating individuals to leave their eggs also, and join in attempting to save the colony. But so it was with the Avosets, and the other two sitters immediately rose on wing and flew directly at me, while the one with the four younglings betook herself to the water, and waded quickly off, followed by her brood, which paddled along swimming, to my astonishment, as well as ducklings of the same size.

How far such cries as those of the Avoset may be heard by birds of the same species I cannot tell; but this I know, that the individuals which had gone toward the Wabash reappeared in a few minutes after I had disturbed the first bird, and hovered over me. But now, having, as I thought, obtained all desirable knowledge of these birds, I shot down five of them, among which I unfortunately found three females. . . .

Trumpeter Swan

(*Olor buccinator*)

. . . The Trumpeter Swans make their appearance on the lower portions of the waters of the Ohio about the end of October. They throw
themselves at once into the larger ponds or lakes at no great distance
from the river, giving a marked preference to those which are closely surrounded by dense and tall cane-brakes, and there remain until the water
is closed by ice, when they are forced to proceed southward. During mild
winters I have seen Swans of this species in the ponds about Henderson
until the beginning of March, but only a few individuals, which may
have staid there to recover from their wounds. When the cold became
intense, most of those which visited the Ohio would remove to the Mississippi, and proceed down that stream as the severity of the weather increased, or return if it diminished; for it has appeared to me, that neither
very intense cold nor great heat suit them so well as a medium temperature. I have traced the winter migrations of this species as far southward
as the Texas, where it is abundant at times, and where I saw a pair of
young ones in captivity, and quite domesticated, that had been procured in the winter of 1836. They were about two years old, and pure
white, although of much smaller size than even the younger one represented in the plate before you, having perhaps been stinted in food, or
having suffered from their wounds, as both had been shot. The sound of
their well-known notes reminded me of the days of my youth, when I
was half-yearly in the company of birds of this species.

At New Orleans, where I made the drawing of the young bird here
given, the Trumpeters are frequently exposed for sale in the markets,
being procured on the ponds of the interior, and on the great lakes leading to the waters of the Gulf of Mexico. This species is unknown to my
friend, the Rev. JOHN BACHMAN, who, during a residence of twenty
years in South Carolina, never saw or heard of one there; whereas in
hard winters the *Cygnus Americanus* is not uncommon, although it does
not often proceed farther southward than that State. The waters of the
Arkansas and its tributaries are annually supplied with Trumpeter
Swans, and the largest individual which I have examined was shot on a
lake near the junction of that river with the Mississippi. It measured

nearly ten feet in alar extent, and weighed above thirty-eight pounds. The quills, which I used in drawing the feet and claws of many small birds, were so hard, and yet so elastic, that the best steel-pen of the present day might have blushed, if it could, to be compared with them.

Whilst encamped in the Tawapatee Bottom, when on a fur-trading voyage, our keel-boat was hauled close under the eastern shore of the Mississippi, and our valuables, for I then had a partner in trade, were all disembarked. The party consisted of twelve or fourteen French Canadians, all of whom were pretty good hunters; and as game was in those days extremely abundant, the supply of Deer, Bear, Racoons, and Opossums, far exceeded our demands. Wild Turkeys, Grous, and Pigeons, might have been seen hanging all around; and the ice-bound lakes afforded an ample supply of excellent fish, which was procured by striking a strong blow with an axe on the ice immediately above the confined animal, and afterwards extricating it by cutting a hole with the same instrument. The great stream was itself so firmly frozen that we were daily in the habit of crossing it from shore to shore. No sooner did the gloom of night become discernible through the grey twilight, than the loud-sounding notes of hundreds of Trumpeters would burst on the ear; and as I gazed over the ice-bound river, flocks after flocks would be seen coming from afar and in various directions, and alighting about the middle of the stream opposite to our encampment. After pluming themselves awhile they would quietly drop their bodies on the ice, and through the dim light I yet could observe the graceful curve of their necks, as they gently turned them backwards, to allow their heads to repose upon the softest and warmest of pillows. Just a dot of black as it were could be observed on the snowy mass, and that dot was about half an inch of the base of the upper mandible, thus exposed, as I think, to enable the bird to breathe with ease. Not a single individual could I ever observe among them to act as a sentinel, and I have since doubted whether their acute sense of hearing was not sufficient to enable them to detect the approach of their enemies. The day quite closed by darkness, no more could be seen until the next dawn; but as often as the howlings of the numerous wolves that prowled through the surrounding woods were heard, the clanging cries of the Swans would fill the air. If the morning proved fair, the whole flocks would rise on their feet, trim their plumage, and as they started with wings extended, as if, racing in rivalry, the pattering of their feet would come on the ear like the noise of great muffled drums, accompanied by the loud and clear sounds of their voice. On running fifty yards or so to windward, they would all be on wing. If the weather was thick, drizzly, and cold, or if there were indications of a fall of snow, they would remain on the ice, walking, standing, or lying down, until symptoms of better weather became apparent, when they would all start off. One morning of this latter kind, our men formed a plot against the Swans, and having separated into two parties, one above, the other below them on the ice, they walked slowly, on a signal being given from the camp, toward the unsuspecting birds. Until the boatmen had arrived within a hundred and fifty yards of them, the Swans remained as they were, having become, as it would appear, acquainted with us, in consequence of our frequently crossing the ice; but then they all rose on their feet, stretched their necks, shook their heads, and manifested strong symptoms of apprehension. The gunners meanwhile advanced, and one of the guns going off by accident, the Swans were thrown into confusion, and scampering off in various directions took to wing, some flying up, some down the stream, others making directly toward the shores. The muskets now blazed, and about a dozen were felled, some crippled, others quite dead. That evening they alighted about a mile above the camp, and we never went after them again. I have been at the killing of several of these Swans, and I can assure you that unless you have a good gun well loaded with large buck-shot, you may shoot at them without much effect, for they are strong and tough birds.

To form a perfect conception of the beauty and elegance of these Swans, you must observe them when they are not aware of your proximity, and as they glide over the waters of some secluded inland pond. On such occasions, the neck, which at other times is held stiffly upright, moves in graceful curves, now bent forward, now inclined backwards over the body. Now with an extended scooping movement the head becomes immersed for a moment, and with a sudden effort a flood of water is thrown over the back and wings, when it is seen rolling off in sparkling globules, like so many large pearls. The bird then shakes its wings, beats the water, and as if giddy with delight shoots away, gliding over and beneath the surface of the liquid element with surprising agility and grace. Imagine, Reader, that a flock of fifty Swans are thus sporting before you, as they have more than once been in my sight, and you will feel, as I have felt, more happy and void of care than I can describe. . . .

I kept a male alive upwards of two years, while I was residing at Henderson in Kentucky. It had been slightly wounded in the tip of the wing, and was caught after a long pursuit in a pond from which it could not escape. Its size, weight, and strength rendered the task of carrying it nearly two miles by no means easy; but as I knew that it would please my wife and my then very young children, I persevered. Cutting off the tip of the wounded wing, I turned it loose in the garden. Although at first extremely shy, it gradually became accustomed to the servants, who fed it abundantly, and at length proved so gentle as to come to my wife's call, to receive bread from her hand. "Trumpeter," as we named our bird, in accordance with the general practice of those who were in the habit of shooting this species, now assumed a character which until then had been unexpected, and laying aside his timidity became so bold at times as to give chase to my favourite Wild Turkey Cock, my dogs, children, and the servants. Whenever the gates of our yard happened to be opened, he would at once make for the Ohio, and it was not without difficulty that he was driven home again. On one occasion, he was absent a whole night, and I thought he had fairly left us; but intimation came of his having travelled to a pond not far distant. Accompanied by my miller and six or seven of my servants, I betook myself to the pond, and there saw our Swan swimming buoyantly about as if in defiance of us all. It was not without a great deal of trouble that we at length succeeded in driving it ashore. Pet birds, good Reader, no matter of what species they are, seldom pass their lives in accordance with the wishes of their possessors; in the course of a dark and rainy night, one of the servants having left the gate open, Trumpeter made his escape, and was never again heard of. . . .

Part 🌿 Three

LETTERS AND JOURNALS

As noted in the Introduction, Audubon kept a journal from 1820 until the mid-1840s, and during those same years he maintained a steady correspondence with family, friends, business associates, and customers. Because he carried on these two sorts of writing simultaneously, often casting his journal in the form of letters to Lucy or his sons, I have chosen to interweave the letters and journal entries, arranging them chronologically. The letters from the period 1826–1840 and the journals from 1820–21 and 1826 have come down to us in their original form, reflecting Audubon's wayward spelling, grammar, and punctuation. I have modernized the spelling, but the grammar and punctuation I have left alone, for their eccentricity is one of the pleasures in reading Audubon. The remaining journals survive only in the versions published by his granddaughter Maria Audubon, who edited them with a prim and ruthless hand. I have marked omissions in the middle of passages with ellipses, and have made the listing of dates and locations uniform.

Down the Ohio and Mississippi in Search of Birds, 1820–1821

After the failure of his investments in 1819, Audubon declared bankruptcy, and was briefly jailed for debt. That same year his second daughter died at the age of seven months. Lucy and his two sons were thrown on the charity of friends and relations. In 1820, at the age of thirty-five, without work or prospects, he left his family and undertook a journey down the Ohio and Mississippi rivers to New Orleans, imagining that he might be able to earn a living by seriously pursuing his longtime hobby, the painting of birds.

Ohio River, Oct. 12, 1820 I left Cincinnati this afternoon at half past 4 o'clock, on board of Mr. Jacob Aumack's flatboat—bound to New Orleans—the feeling of a husband and a father, were my lot when I kissed my beloved wife & children with an expectation of being absent for seven months—

I took with me Joseph Mason a young man of about 18 years of age of good family and naturally an aimiable youth, he is intended to be a companion, & a friend; and if God will grant us a safe return to our families our wishes will be congenial to our present feelings leaving home with a determined mind to fulfill our object—

Without any money my talents are to be my support and my enthusiasm my guide in my difficulties, the whole of which I am ready to exert to keep, and to surmount.

Nov. 2 We started about 5 and floated down slowly within 2 miles of Henderson when we experienced quite a *gale* and put to on the Indiana shore opposite Henderson—the wind blew so violently that I could only make a very rough drawing of that place—I can scarcely conceive that I stayed there 8 years and passed them comfortably for it undoubtedly is one [of] the poorest spots in the western country according to my present opinion. . . .

So warm tonight that bats are flying near the boats—extremely anxious to be doing something in the drawing way—

Nov. 3 We left our harbour at daybreak and passed Henderson about sunrise, I looked on the mill perhaps for the last time, and with thoughts that made my blood almost cold bid it an eternal farewell—

Nov. 5 The weather fair this morning, the thermometer down at 30—the sun rose beautiful and reflected through the trees on the placid stream much like a column of lively fire—the frost was heavy on the decks and when the sun shone on it it looked beautiful beyond expression.

Nov. 16 My dear children if ever you read these trifling remarks pay your attention to what follows—

Never be under what is called obligations to men not aware of the value or the meanness of their *conduct*

Never take a passage in any state or vessel without a well understood agreement between you & the owners or clerks & of all things never go for nothing if you wish to save mental troubles & bodily vicissitudes.

Nov. 17 We left early—I took the skiff and went to the mouth of the Ohio, and round the point up the Mississippi—

Eleven years ago on the 2 of January I ascended that stream to St. Genevieve Ferdinand Rozier of *Nantes* my partner in a large keel boat loaded with sundries to a large amount *our* property

The 10th of May 1819 I passed this place in an open skiff bound to New Orleans with two of my slaves—

Now I enter it *poor* in fact *destitute* of all things and relying only on that providential hope the comforter of this wearied mind—in a flat boat a passenger—

The meeting of the two streams reminds me a little of the gentle youth who comes in the world, spotless he presents himself, he is gradually drawn in to thousands of difficulties that make him wish to keep apart, but at last he is overdone mixed, and lost in the vortex. . . .

I saw here two Indians in a canoe they spoke some French, had bear traps, uncommonly clean kept, a few venison hams a gun and looked so independent, free & unconcerned with the world that I gazed on them, admired their spirits, & wished for their condition—here the traveller enters a new world, the current of the stream about 4 miles per hour, puts the steersman on the alert and awakes him to troubles and difficulties unknown on the Ohio, the passenger feels a different atmosphere, a very different prospect. . . .

I bid my farewell to the Ohio at 2 o'clock P.M. and felt a fear gathering involuntarily, every moment draws me from all that is dear to me my beloved wife & children—

Mississippi River, Nov. 19 When we left Cincinnati, we agreed to shave & clean completely every Sunday—and often have been anxious to see the day come for certainly a shirt worn one week, hunting every day and sleeping in buffalo robes at night soon becomes soiled and disagreeable.

Nov. 28 Ever since [I was] a boy I have had an astonishing desire to see much of the world & particularly to acquire a true knowledge of the birds of North America, consequently, I hunted whenever I had an opportunity, and drew every new specimen as I could, or dared *steal time* from my business and having a tolerably large number of drawings that have been generally admired, I concluded that perhaps I could not do better than to travel, and finish my collection or so nearly that it would be a valuable acquisition—my wife hoped it might do well, and I left her once more with an intention of returning in seven or eight months. . . .

We moved from our landing of last night and only crossed the river for the rain lowered the *smoke* so much that it was impossible to see, beyond 20 or 30 yards; played great deal on the flutes, looked at my drawings, read as much as I could and yet found the day very long and heavy for although I am naturally of light spirits and have often tried to keep these good, when off from my home, I have often dull moments of anguish—

Dec. 7 Caught a nice *cat fish* weighing 29 lb. at 3 o'clock this morning—stabbed him . . . but it did not die for one hour—at daybreak the wind stiff ahead, a couple of light showers lulled it, and we put off—Mr Aumack winged a *white headed eagle*, brought it alive on board, the noble fellow looked at his enemies with a contemptible eye. I tied a string on one of its legs this made him jump overboard. My surprise at seeing it swim well was very great, it used its wings with great effect and would have made the shore distant there about 200 *yards* dragging a pole weighing at least 15 *lbs*—Joseph went after it with a skiff, the eagle defended itself—I am glad to find that its eyes were corresponding with my drawing—this specimen rather less than the one I drew—the female hovered over us and shrieked for some time, exhibiting the *true sorrow* of the *constant mate*. . . .

Our eagle ate of fish freely about one hour after we had him, by fixing a piece on a stick and putting it to its mouth—however while I was friendly Indian toward it it lanced one of its feet and caught hold of my right thumb, made it feel very sore—

Dec. 10 After breakfast we left the post of Arkansas with a wish to see the country above, and so *strong* is my enthusiasm to enlarge the ornithological knowledge of my country that I felt as if I wished myself *rich again* and thereby able to leave my family for a couple of years. . . . We travelled fast—reached the cutoff and landed our skiff. . . . The Indians still at their canoes, we hailed, and gave them a drachem of whiskey, and as they could not speak either French or English, I *drew a deer* with a stroke across its hind parts, and thereby made them know our wants of venison hams—

They brought 2 we gave them 50 *cts* and a couple loads of gun powder to each, brought out smiles, and a cordial shaking of hands—a squaw with them a *handsome woman* waded to us as well as the men and drank freely—whenever I meet *Indians* I feel the greatness of our Creator in all its splendor, for there I see the Man naked from His hand and yet free from acquired sorrow—

Natchez, Dec. 27 I found few men interested towards ornithology except those who had heard or pleased to invent wonderful stories respecting a few species.

. . . having not one cent when I landed here I immediately looked for something to do in the likeness way for our support (unfortunately naturalists are obliged to eat and have some sort of garb) I entered the room of a portrait painter naming himself *Cook* but I assure you he was scarcely fit for a scullion, yet the *gentleman* had some politeness and procured me the drawing of two sketches for $5 each, this was fine sauce to our empty stomachs

. . . the awkwardness I felt when I sat to dinner at the hotel was really justified to me; having not used a fork and scarcely even a plate since I left Louisville, I involuntarily took meat and vegetables with my fingers several times; on board the flatboats we seldom ate together and very often the hungry cooked, this I performed when in need by plucking & cleaning a duck, or a partridge and throwing it on the hot embers; few men have eaten a teal with better appetite than I have dressed in this manner—

Others preferring bacon would cut a slice from the *side* that hung by the chimney and chew that raw with a hard biscuit—Such life is well intended to drill men gradually to hardships to go to sleep with wet muddy clothing on a buffalo skin stretched on a board—to hunt through woods filled with fallen trees, entangled with vines, briars, canes, high rushes and at the same time giving under foot; produces heavy sweats strong appetite, & keeps the imagination free from worldly thoughts, I would advise many *citizens* particularly our Eastern *dandies* to try the experiment—leaving their high-heeled boots, but not their *corsets*, for, this would no doubt be serviceable whenever food giving way, they might wish to depress their stomachs for the occasion—

Dec. 31 I drew this afternoon—and here I have to tell a sad misfortune that took place this morning—having carried under my arm my smallest portfolio and some other articles I laid the whole on the ground and ordered Mr Berthow's servant to take them on board

I unfortunately went off to Natchez again to breakfast the servant forgot my folio on the shore and now I am without, any silver paper, to preserve my drawings, have lost some very valuable drawings, and my beloved wife's likeness—the greatest exertions I now must make to try to find it again, but so dull do I feel about it that I am nearly made sick

Jan. 1, 1821 This day 21 years since I was at *Rochefort* in France. I spent most of that day at copying letters of my father to the Minister of the Navy—

What I have seen, and felt since, would fill a large volume—the whole of which would end at *this day January 1st 1821. I am on board a keelboat going down to New Orleans the poorest man on it*—

New Orleans, Jan. 7 At New Orleans at last—We arrived here about 8 o'clock this morning; hundreds of fish crows hovering near the shipping and dashing down to the water like gulls for food. . . .

Arrived at the House of Mr Arnauld. . . . We had a good dinner and great deal of mirth that I call *French gaiety* that really sickened me. I thought myself in Bedlam, everybody talked loud at once and the topics dry jokes—Yet everyone appeared good, well disposed, gentlemen, and were very polite to us—a monkey amused the company a good deal by his gambols and pranks—formerly I would have been able as well as anxious to go to the theatre but now I can only partake of the last, and after having paid a short visit to Mr Gordon I retired to the keelboat; with a bad headache occasioned by drinking some wine—

Jan. 13 I rose early tormented by many disagreeable thoughts, nearly again without a cent, in a bustling city where no one cares a fig for a man in my situation—I walked to *Jarvis* the painter and showed him some of my drawings—he overlooked them, said nothing then leaned down and examined them minutely but never said they were good or bad—merely that when he drew an eagle for instance, he made it resemble a lion, and covered it with yellow hair and not feathers—some fools who entered the room, were so pleased at seeing my eagle that they prized it, and Jarvis whistled—

Jan. 14 Dressed I went to Jarvis—he took me immediately in his painting room, and asked me many questions, until *I thought* that he *feared* my assistance; he very simply told me he could not believe that I might help him in the least—I rose, bowed, and walked out without one word, and no doubt he looked on me as I did on him as an original, and a cracked man—

Feb. 22 We at last have the keelboat off and have moved on the earth again—Our present situation is quite a curious one to me, the room we are in and for which we pay $10 per month is situated . . . between two shops of grocers and divided from them and our yellow landlady by mere board partitions, receiving at once all the new matter that issues from the thundering mouths of all these groups—

Mar. 16 I had the pleasure of receiving a letter this morning from Mr. A. P. Bodley dated Natchez 8th instant informing me of my portfolio having been found and . . . that I could have it by writing. . . .

I took a walk with my gun this afternoon to see the passage of millions of *golden plovers* coming from the northeast and going nearly south—the destruction of these innocent fugitives from a winter storm above us was really astonishing—the sportsmen are here more numerous and at the same time more expert at shooting on the wing than anywhere in the United States on the first sight of these birds early this morning assembled in parties of from 20 to 100 at different places where they knew by experience they told me the birds pass and arranged themselves at equal distances squatted on their hams, as a flock came near every man called in a masterly astonishing manner, the birds immediately lowered and wheeled and coming about 40 or 50 yards run the gantlet every gun goes off in rotation, and so well aimed that I saw several times a flock of 100 or more plovers destroyed at the exception of 5 or 6—the dogs after each volley while the shooters charged their pieces brought the same to each individual—this continued all day, when I left one of those lines of sharpshooters then the sun setting, they appeared as intent on killing more as when I arrived at the spot at 4 o'clock—

A man near where I was seated had killed 63 dozens—from the firing before & behind us I would suppose that 400 gunners were out. Supposing each man to have killed 30 dozen that day 144,000 must have been destroyed—

May 8 . . .seldom before my coming to New Orleans did I think that I was looked on so favorably by the *fair* sex as I have *discovered* lately—

June 16 . . .should you ever be employed as a teacher to any ostentatious opulent person—*flatter*, keep flattering and end in flattery or else expect no pay—

My misfortunes often occur through a want of attention to that maxim in similar cases after having with assiduity attended on a gentleman's lady (whose name I will not at present mention) for forty days, I received the rudest of dismissal and my pride would not admit me to the house—to even ask any compensation—how agreeable the first lessons were I shall always remember. *She thought* herself endowed with superior talents, and her looking glass pleasing her vanity I dare say made her believe she was a star dropped from the heavens to ornament this earth—but difficulties augmented and of course drawing ceased to please, I could not well find time to finish every piece that I had begun for her, and constancy the lady said was never to be found the companion of genius—toward the last she would be unwell when I walked in, yawned and postponed to the morrow—I believe the husband saw her weakness, but the good man like *one* or *two* more of my acquaintances was weaker still. . . .

I had attended a Miss Perrie to enhance her natural talent for drawing, for some days when her mother whom I intend noticing in due time, asked me to think about my spending the summer and fall at their farm near Bayou Sarah; I was glad of such an overture, but would have greatly preferred her living in the Floridas—We concluded the bargain promising me 60 dollars per month for one half of my time to teach Miss Eliza all I could in drawing music dancing &c &c furnishing us with a room &c for Joseph & myself—so that after the one hundred different plans I had formed as opposite as could be to this, I found myself bound for several months on a farm in Louisiana.

Bayou Sarah, July 29 I had the pleasure of meeting with several red cockaded woodpeckers yesterday during a walk we took to the pine woods and procured two beautiful males, both alive, being slightly wounded each in the wing. . . .

Confined in my hat on my head, they remained still and stubborn. I looked at them several times, when I found them trying to hide their heads as if ashamed to have lost their liberty—the report of my gun alarmed them every time I shot when they both uttered a plaintive cry—

Through pain of the wound or the heat felt in my hat one died before we reached Mr Perrie's house—the other I put in a cage. . . .

This afternoon having finished my drawing of the red cockaded woodpecker and satisfied of its correctness by a close comparison to the living original I gave it its liberty, and was glad to think that it most likely would do well as it flew 40 to 50 yards at times and seemed much refreshed by its return to liberty—

New Orleans, Oct. 20 I had perceived that my long flowing buckled hair was looked on with astonishment by the passengers on board and saw that the effect was stronger in town—My large loose dress of whitened yellow nankeen and the unfortunate *cut* of my features made me decide to be dressed as soon as possible like other folks and I had my chevelure parted from my head. . . .

Oct. 27 Dressed all new, hair cut, my appearance altered beyond my expectations, fully as much as a handsome bird is when robbed of all its feathering, the poor thing looks, bashful dejected and is either entirely neglected or looked upon with contempt; such was my situation last week—but when the bird is well fed, taken care of, suffered to enjoy life and dress himself, he is cherished again, nay admired—such my situation this day—Good God that 40 dollars should thus be *enough* to make a *gentleman*—Ah my beloved country when will thy sons value more intrinsically each brother's worth? Never!!

Dec. 18 My wife & my two sons arrived at 12 o'clock all in good health . . . after 14 months' absence the meeting of all that renders life agreeable to me, was gratefully welcomed and I thanked my maker for this mark of mercy.

To England in Search of a Publisher, 1826

Frustrated in his attempts to find a publisher for his bird portraits in America, Audubon sailed to England in the summer of 1826, bearing letters of introduction from such worthies as Senator Henry Clay, Andrew Jackson, and General William Clark.

At Sea, July 9, 1826 My leaving the United States had for some time the appearance and feelings of a dream. I could scarce make up my mind fixedly on the subject. I thought continually that I still saw my beloved friend [Lucy] and my dear children. I still believed, when every morning I awaked, that the land of America was beneath me, that I would in a moment throw myself into her shady woods, and watch for and listen to the voice of her many lovely warblers. But now that I have positively been at sea since *fifty-one days*, tossing to and fro, without the sight nor the touch of those objects so dear to me, I feel fully convinced, and look forward with anxiety that I do not believe ever ruffled my mind.

At Sea, July 15 The same dull, cold, damp weather still prevails. Still the wind is northwest and propitious as can be. On a passage like this, how much a man may find to think upon! I am pretty sure that few memorable events of my life, (if I dare call any of them memorable), have not been recalled to memory, weighed, disarranged, and improved (in thought only, not, unfortunately, in action), until the whole of my life has been surveyed with scrutiny, and all the lines, landmarks, beacons, branding places, &c., &c., have been examined fairly or unfairly. The days have been brought before my sight and bodily feelings. Yes, I have had time enough, I assure thee, to consult on all points. There can exist no doubt that had I been fortunate enough whenever I have erred, (and I have no doubt erred enough), had I had an equal opportunity to think before I acted, I would have committed but few errors, and probably never a sin. . . .

"A whale! A whale! Run, Mr. Audubon, there's a whale close alongside." The pen, the book, were abandoned, the mice frightened. I ran up, and lo! there rolled most majestically the wonder of the oceans. It was of immense magnitude. Its dark auburn body fully overgrew the vessel in size. One might have thought it was the God of the Seas beckoning us to the shores of Europe. I saw it and therefore believed its existence. . . .

Many people speak lightly of leaving America to go and visit Europe. Many indeed, when returned, who have not found Europe what they wished, speak lightly of the whole. I cannot touch the subject so superficially. I spoke for many years of this, my present voyage, always dreaded it before I undertook it; and after being swung about, rolled, heaved, bruised and shifted around probably around half a million times within the first sixty days of a voyage that I moderately calculated to last full fifteen months, have I not good substantial reasons for thinking of it *rationally?*

Liverpool, England, July 22 The noise of pattens [on the flagstones] startles me very frequently. Indeed I generally turn my head . . . , expecting to see a horse [running] full speed, with open mouth, intent on taking my head for fresh grass. I am sure my eyes are then quite full, but the moment that they meet those of a neat, plump-looking maid tripping as briskly by as a Killdeer, they soon compose again to their regular size, and—Lucy, thy countrywomen are very beautiful! Yes indeed, they are to my eyes very beautiful! It is not only the freshness of their complexions, nor, added to this, their lovely rosy hue, nor (continuing to add) their well shaped forms but it is—*all about them* I admire so much.

Liverpool, July 31 This day, Lucy, was one of trial to me, believe thy friend. This was Monday, and it was appointed to exhibit my collection partially to the public and my kind Liverpool friends. At 9 this morning I was quite busy, arranging and disposing in sets my drawings to be fairly inspected by the public, the connoisseurs, the critics. This last word has something very savage in its nature, as well as in its orthography or its pronunciation. I know not why. Yet I know that I dread this very casting askance of a single eye of those dangerous personages of whom I have so much heard, but whom, fortunately, thus far, I have only met in scanty form, and of little value.

I drew my new watch and in five minutes, by its regular movements, it proved to be at the meridian. The doors of the Royal Institution were thrown open and the ladies flocked in; I, however, saw but one: Mrs. Rathbone. Then I was in view of the world. How many glances to meet—questions to answer and repeat! *"La, that's beautiful,"* again and again repeated, made me wish to be in the forests of America, to be able myself to say at meeting a new specimen, *"Ah, how beautiful!!"*

Liverpool, Aug. 5 From the time I was up this morning until the moment I reached the Institution, my head was full of Lord Stanley, and indeed so much so that I believe thy sweet name did not come forth to my senses for perhaps an hour at a time. I am a very poor fool, to be sure—to be troubled and disturbed in mind at the idea of meeting an *English gentleman* called, moreover, *a Lord!* Yes, and particularly the bigger fool am I, as the English lords are not only more like others but are superior men—in manners, in interests, in kindness—to strangers, and generally the upholders of science in their country. But that confounded feeling is too deeply rooted ever to be extricated from my nature; and with a sense of pity toward myself I must get more and more accustomed to the disagreeable thoughts of dying with it.

Liverpool, Aug. 6 [E]ntered *Lodge Lane* and Mr. Roscoe's habitation. It was full of ladies and gentlemen, all of his *own family*, and, as I knew almost the whole I was soon at my ease.

A great deal was said about Lord Stanley, his bird [drawings], and my Birds. I was asked to imitate the Wild Turkey call, and I did, to the surprise of all the circle. Hooted like a Barred Owl, and cooed like the doves. I am glad, really, that I was not desired to bray! "Why?" Why! Because an ass is an ass and it would have been rude even in an ass to bray in such company. . . .

A beautiful young lady, called here a *miss*, is at my side, and asks with the volubility of interesting youth and enthusiasm many, many questions about America. But they all appear very much surprised that I have no wonderful tale to relate; that, for instance, *I*, so much in the woods, have not been devoured at least six times by tigers, bears, wolves, foxes, or—a rat. No, I never was troubled in the woods by any animal larger than ticks and mosquitoes; and that is quite enough, is it not, Dearest Lucy?

I must acknowledge, however, that I would like to have rode a few hundred miles on a Wild Elk or a Unicorn—or an Alligator.

Liverpool, Aug. 21 By 6 . . . I was at work on my painting of the "Wild Turkey Cock," my neck uncovered as usual, my sleeves up to my shoulders, my hair all flowing and the colors also—on canvas measuring 4'8⁄12" by 5'8⁄12", [which] I covered completely in twenty-three hours time. Mr. Melly, Dr. Traill, Mr. William Rathbone, and many other persons were in my painting room the while, talking, and wondering how I managed to conceive and finish [so] fast; and I believe their presence made me work still faster and better. The fact is that on the two days after I began this large and beautiful painting, it was framed and hung in the Exhibition Room.

To Victor Audubon, from Liverpool, Sept. 1 I have been in England now upward of a month and am quite well—I have been received most kindly and I think that I have much in my favor now toward enabling me to do well with my collection. The letters that I brought . . . have been all received with a due regard I assure thee—& I am in miniature in Liverpool what Lafayette was with us on our great scale plan and habit of doing everything. My drawings are exhibited at the Liverpool Royal Institution and will continue so this week—the proceeds are far beyond my expectations and it seems that I am considered unrivaled in the art of drawing even by the most learned of this country. The newspapers have given so many flattering accounts of my productions and of my being a superior ornithologist that I dare no longer look into any *of them*—

I shall continue to exhibit my works through the three kingdoms and then proceed to the Continent—I have no doubt that this method will pay well and that it will not prevent me from my publication. . . .

You would be surprised to see the marked attentions paid me wherever I go by the first people of Liverpool—My exhibition attracts the *beau monde* altogether and the Lords of England look at them with wonder more so I assure thee than at my flowing curling locks that again loosely are about my shoulders—The ladies of England are ladies indeed—Beauty, suavity of manners and the most improved education render them desirable objects of admiration.

Manchester, England, Sept. 11 About twenty persons came to see my Birds, of course called them very beautiful, &c., &c. I had to stand the brunt of all this; and the eyes of the ladies were again, I perceived, searching the lines of my face and the undulations of my locks.

But my style puzzles all. Not a soul can ever guess how I proceed— a great proof that a simplicity of a thing proves the difficulty of its discovery.

Manchester, Sept. 12 When at Liverpool I found the streets full of annoyances, but compared with Manchester it is nothing. I thought that the gentleman that accompanied me from Piccadilly to King Street and myself would be carried by force off the pavement. Groups of those abandoned females of from twenty to thirty stood watching for prey at all the corners we passed. The appearance of the feminine sex is not so prepossessing here as it is at Liverpool. The women in the streets have none of that freshness of coloring nor the fullness of breasts that I remarked at the sea port. I conceive this is the result of the confinement they have to [undergo] in the manufactories.

Manchester, Sept. 14 I cannot sleep, and I have got out of my bed, dressed and washed myself, and walked the room for upwards of one hour to try to be benefited by Franklin's advice. But all this won't do. I cannot sleep. A man awake and alone in a bed is a most stupid animal in creation. What the feelings of females are on such occasions, it will be best for thee to say. I am writing again. For although I am lodging at a circulating library, the books below will not come by themselves to my assistance, and I cannot, in good conscience, [rouse] the house because I alone in it cannot sleep.

Manchester, Sept. 23 I concluded to-day to have a book of subscriptions, open to receive the names of all persons inclined to have the *best American illustrations of birds of that country ever yet transmitted to posterity.* And *I* will do so. I have also thought of a plan to procure lookers-on by putting up a few drawings of mine in the most conspicuous shops here, to invite the public to call upon me, with each their shillings, and perhaps out of twenty [win] a name for my support in publication. Indeed I feel as inclined, if not more so, to do all in my power to push forward at a round pace and prove the test of my value, from the penny's worth to the capital now in the Bank of England!!

In Edinburgh, he found an engraver, William Home Lizars, who was eager to publish the bird drawings. Lucy, left behind in Louisiana to look after and support the two boys, would not say whether she would eventually join him in England.

Edinburgh, Scotland, Nov. 2 Mr. Lizars had not seen one of my largest drawings. He had been enamoured with the "Mocking Bird and Rattlesnake," but Lucy, the "Turkey"—her brood—the "Cock Turkey"—the "Hawk" pouncing on seventeen partridges—the "Whooping Crane" devouring alligators newly born—all were, he said, wonderful productions. According to his say so, I was a most wonderful compositor. He wished to engrave the "Partridges," but when the "Great-footed Hawks" came with bloody rage at their beak's ends and with cruel delight in the glance of their daring eyes, he stopped mute for perhaps an instant. His arms fell (if so, he was not squeezing me), then he said, "I will engrave and publish this." . . .

[Lizars] said to me, "Mr. Audubon, the people here don't know who you are at all. But depend on it, they shall know." We talked of the engraving of the "Hawks," and it seems they will be done.

Then Fame, expand thy unwearied pinions, and far, far and high,

high soar away! Yet smoothly circle about me wherever I go, and call out with musical mellowness the name of this child of Nature, her humble but true admirer. Call out, call out, call out—LOUD, LOUD, *LOUD*, *AUDUBON!!!!*

Edinburgh, Nov. 29 Mrs. Fletcher sent for me just as I was setting to my dinner. Ladies, however, having the right to command, I went immediately and saw a woman not handsome but good looking, more characterful in her features than women are generally. Her eyes were penetrating and her words powerful. I was struck with the strength of all she said, although nothing seemed to be studied. It certainly was and is the fruit of a long, well fed round of general information. She, of course, praised my works but I scarce thought her candid. Her eyes reached my very soul, and I feared her presence. I know that at one glance she had discovered my great inferiority. . . .

Lucy, I feared her probably too much to like her. I felt her elevated mind bearing on my feeble intelligence more and more forcibly, the longer I tried to steal a glance at her face. But this was not permitted. She positively riveted me to my blushes, and never before have I felt more stupid. I was glad I had met with her, and yet still better pleased that I was at liberty to go.

Edinburgh, Dec. 3 I came to this Europe fearful, humble, dreading all, scarce daring to hold up my head and meet the glance of the learned, and I am praised so high. It is quite unaccountable and I still fear it will not last. These good people certainly give me more merit than I am entitled to. It is only a mere glance of astonishment or surprise operating on them, because my style is new and different from what has preceded me.

Edinburgh, Dec. 12 A man who never looked into an English grammar and very seldom, unfortunately, into a French or a Spanish one, a man who has always felt awkward and very shy in the presence of a stranger, one habituated to ramble alone with his thoughts, always bent on the beauties of *Nature herself*—this man, *me*, in Edinburgh, seated opposite Dr. Brewster, reading one of my puny efforts at describing habits of birds that none but an Almighty Creator can ever know! was so ridiculously absurd, all the while, in my estimation. Also whilst I felt the riveting looks of observation of the learned personage before me, to say that a cold sweat ran over my body much worse than when I dined with the Antiquarians, and that to say this to thee is only to give thee one of the ten thousand tormenting thoughts that crossed my mind whilst my eyes and mouth were reading.

Edinburgh, Dec. 16 Since Napoleon became, from the ranks, an Emperor, why should not Audubon be able to leave the woods of America a while and publish and sell a *book?* No, no. I will try by heavens until each and every hair about me will have dropped from my body, dead grey from old age!!

To Lucy, from Edinburgh, Dec. 21 After postponing day after day for the last two weeks writing to thee full of hopes that each new day would bring some tiding of thee or of some one connected with me in America I am forced to sit and write filled with fear and sorrow. Many of the vessels I have wrote by have returned from America with full cargoes but nothing from thee—it is the more surprising because a fortnight since De Witt Clinton answered a letter of mine dated Manchester and enclosed one of recommendation to General Lafayette—My situation in Edinburgh borders almost on the miraculous without education and scarce one of those qualities necessary to render a man able to pass through the throng of the learned here I am positively looked on by all the professors & many of the principal persons here as a very extraordinary man. . . .

It is now a month since my work has been begun by Mr. W. H. Lizars of this city—it is to come out in numbers of 5 prints all the size of life and in the same size paper of my largest drawings that is called double elephant—they will be brought up & finished in such superb style as to eclipse all of the kind in existence. . . . I cannot yet say that I will ultimately succeed but at present all bears a better prospect than I ever expected to see I think this under the eyes of the most discerning people in the world—I mean Edinburgh—if it takes here it cannot fail anywhere it is not the naturalist that I wish to please altogether I assure thee it is the wealthy part of the community the first can only speak well or ill of me but the latter will fill my pockets. . . . I am now better aware of the advantages of a family in unison than ever and I am quite satisfied that by acting conjointly and by my advice we can realize a handsome fortune for each of us—it needs but industry & perseverance—going to America is mere song and I now find that most valuable voyages could be made by procuring such articles as are wanted here and most plentiful there—It is now about time to know from thee what thy future intentions are. I wish thee to act according to thy dictates but wish to know what those dictates are—think that we are far divided and that either sickness or need may throw one into a most shocking situation without either friend or help for as thou sayest thyself "the world is not indulgent." Cannot we move together and feel and enjoy the natural need of each other—Lucy my friend think of all this very seriously—not a portion of the earth exists but will support us amply and we may feel happiness anywhere if careful—When you receive this sit and consider well . . . then consult thyself and in a long plain explanatory letter give me thy own heart entire.

To Lucy, from Edinburgh, Dec. 22 I herein send thee the result of Mr. Combes the phrenologist about my skull—It proves to resemble that of Raphael very much and I have been astounded at the merit of the science through some particular observations that the gentleman and others have made about my propensities and faculties. . . . I want thee to send me by first opportunity as much of thy hair as will make me a cord for my watch. . . . I have come to fine dressing again—silk stockings and pumps, shave every morning and sometimes dress twice a day—My hairs are now as beautifully long and curly as ever and I assure thee do as much for me as my talent for painting.

At Work on *The Birds of America,* 1827–1832

With publication of The Birds of America *under way, Audubon set about canvassing for subscribers, a task that would occupy the better part of the next twelve years. After Lizars proved unable to continue work on* The Birds, *Audubon found in London a new engraver, Robert Havell, Jr., who went on to complete the mammoth project.*

Edinburgh, Scotland, Jan. 7, 1827 I have labored hard, but my work is bad; some inward feeling tells me when it is good. No one, I think, paints in my method; I, who have never studied but by piecemeal, form my pictures according to my ways of study. For instance, I am now working on a Fox; I take one neatly killed, put him up with wires, and when satisfied of the truth of the position, I take my palette and work as rapidly as possible; the same with my birds. If practicable, I finish the bird at one sitting,—often, it is true, of fourteen hours,—so that I think they are correct, both in detail and composition.

Jan. 28 Yesterday I had so many visitors that I was quite fatigued; my rooms were full all the time, yet I work away as if they were so many cabbages, except for a short time taken to show them a few drawings, give them chairs, and other civil attentions.

Feb. 9 I have been, and am yet, greatly depressed, yet why I am so it is impossible for me to conceive, unless it be that slight vexations, trifling in themselves, are trying to me, because, alas! I am only a very, very common man.

March 4 I was trundled into a sedan chair to church. I had never been in a sedan chair before, and I like to try, as well as see, all things on the face of this strange world of ours; but so long as I have two legs and feet below them, never will I again enter one of these machines, with their quick, short, up-and-down, swinging motion, resembling the sensations felt during the great earthquake in Kentucky.

March 14 I have been drawing all day, two Cat-birds and some blackberries for the Countess of Morton, and would have finished it had I not been disturbed by visitors. Mr. Hays came with his son; he asked me if it would not be good policy for me to cut my hair and have a fashionable coat made before I reached London. I laughed, and he laughed, and my hair is yet as God made it.

March 19 This day my hair was sacrificed, and the will of God usurped by the wishes of man. As the barber clipped my locks rapidly, it reminded me of the horrible times of the French Revolution when the same operation was performed upon all the victims murdered at the guillotine; my heart sank low.

York, April 24 How doleful has this day been to me! It pleased to rain, and to snow, and to blow cold all day. I called on Mr. Phillips, the curator of the Museum, and he assured me that the society was too poor to purchase my work. I spent the evening by invitation at the Rev. Wm. Turner's in company with four other gentlemen. Politics and emancipation were the chief topics of conversation. How much more good would the English do by revising their own intricate laws, and improving the condition of their poor, than by troubling themselves and their distant friends with what does not concern them. I feel nearly determined to push off to-morrow, and yet it would not do; I may be wrong, and to-morrow may be fairer to me in every way; but this "hope deferred" is a very fatiguing science to study. I could never make up my mind to live and die in England whilst the sweet-scented jessamine and the magnolias flourish so purely in my native land, and the air vibrates with the songs of the sweet birds.

London, May 21 I should begin this page perhaps with a great exclamation mark, and express much pleasure, but I have not the wish to do either; to me London is just like the mouth of an immense monster, guarded by millions of sharp-edged teeth, from which if I escape unhurt it must be called a miracle. I have many times longed to see London, and now I am here I feel a desire beyond words to be in my beloved woods.

To Victor, from London, Aug. 25 I cannot say that I admire England much. My habits here are cramped and confined quite too much . . . but the ultimate comfort of your good Mamma, the hope of having her, yourself and John nearer together is so urgent on my mind that I abandon without reluctance the less necessary pleasure of trailing a bass or of bringing down a wild turkey from the lofty top of a poplar—

It is thus my dear son that I am now situated and (barring accidents) will write to your good Mamma about January next to come again to her native clime!—What a difference of countries neither you nor any other man can conceive; the more I live in this, the more I wonder at all that I see. The *superfluity of refinement* here is of itself a source of wonder inexhaustible, but the unbounded freedom of our beloved America will be for ever preferred by me.

To Lucy, from Liverpool, Nov. 25 Now thou must not think me flighty, and abandoning my dear America, rough as it is yet; and, swelled in thought in favor of all & everything in England. No, indeed, my Lucy, not even the metaphoric name of "Sir John," as Sir Wm Jardine was pleased to call me at Twizel, could make me relinquish the idea of knowing that in *my universe* of America, the deer runs free, and the hunter as free forever.—No—America will always be my land. I never close my eyes without travelling thousands of miles along our noble streams; and traversing our noble forests. The voice of the thrush and the rumbling noise of the alligator are still equally agreeable to my sense of recollection.—

My health is good, and I wear well; indeed I am, I think, as active as ever.—I rise as always, at daylight, walk whenever I have time to spare, keep as regular in all my habits as when in the woods, and have only suffered once in attempting to dry my clothes on me, instead of changing them, on my way to Scotland. I have had a few fits of the ague, but quinine and port wine soon recovered me, & I will try to become more prudent.

Liverpool, Nov. 30 I walked into town with Richard Rathbone, who rode his horse. I kept by his side all the way, the horse walking. I do not rely as much on my activity as I did twenty years ago, but I still think I could kill any horse in England in twenty days, taking the travel over rough and level grounds. This might be looked upon as a boast by many, but, I am quite satisfied, not by those who have seen me travel at the rate of five miles an hour all day. Once indeed I recollect going from Louisville to Shippingport in fourteen minutes, with as much ease as if I had been on skates.

Dec. 10 I received a letter from Thomas Sully telling me in the most frank and generous manner that I have been severely handled in one of the Philadelphia newspapers. The editor calls all I said in my papers read before the different societies in Edinburgh "a pack of lies." Friend Sully is most heartily indignant, but with me my motto is: "*Le temps decouvrira la verité.*" It is, however, hard that a poor man like me, who has been so devotedly intent on bringing forth facts of curious force, should be brought before the world as a liar by a man who doubtless knows little of the inhabitants of the forests on the Schuylkill, much less of those elsewhere. It is both unjust and ungenerous, but I forgive him. I shall keep up a good heart, trust to my God, attend to my work with industry and care, and in time outlive these trifles.

Manchester, Jan. 1, 1828 Now, my Lucy, when I wished thee a happy New Year this morning I emptied my snuff box, locked up the box in my trunk, and will take *no more*. The habit within a few weeks has grown upon me, so farewell to it; it is a useless and not very clean habit, besides being an expensive one. Snuff! farewell to thee. Thou knowest, Lucy, well that when I will *I* will.

London, Jan. 20 Oh! how dull I feel; how long am I to be confined in this immense jail? In London, amidst all the pleasures, I feel unhappy and dull; the days are heavy, the nights worse. Shall I ever again see and enjoy the vast forests in their calm purity, the beauties of America? I wish myself anywhere but in London. *Why* do I dislike London? Is it because the constant evidence of the contrast between the rich and the poor is a torment to me, or is it because of its size and crowd? I know not, but I long for sights and sounds of a different nature.

Cambridge, March 6 A cold snowy day; I went to the library of the University and the Philosophical Society rooms, and dined again in "Hall," with Professor Sedgwick. There were four hundred students, and forty "Fellows;" quite a different scene from Corpus College. Each one devoured his meal in a hurry; in less than half an hour grace was read again by *two* students, and Professor Whewell took me to his own rooms with some eight or ten others. My book was inspected as a matter of courtesy. Professor Sedgwick was gay, full of wit and cleverness; the conversation was very animated, and I enjoyed it much. Oh! my Lucy, that I also had received a university education! I listened and admired for a long time, when suddenly Professor Whewell began asking me questions about the woods, the birds, the aborigines of America. The more I rove about, the more I find how little known the interior of America is; we sat till late.

London, May 4 I have been summing up the pros and cons respecting a voyage to America, with an absence of twelve months. The difficulties are many, but I am determined to arrange for it, if possible. I should like to renew about fifty of my drawings; I am sure that now I could make better compositions, and select better plants than when I drew merely for amusement, and without the thought of ever bringing them to public view. To effect this wish of mine, I must find a true, devoted friend who will superintend my work and see to its delivery—this is no trifle in itself. Then I must arrange for the regular payments of twelve months' work, and *that* is no trifle; but when I consider the difficulties I have surmounted, the privations of all sorts that I have borne, the many hairbreadth escapes I have had, the times I have been near sinking under the weight of the enterprise—ah! such difficulties as even poor Wilson never experienced—what reasons have I now to suppose, or to make me think for a moment, that the omnipotent God who gave me a heart to endure and overcome all these difficulties, will abandon me now. No! my faith is the same—my desires are of a pure kind; I only wish to enjoy more of Him by admiring His works still more than I have ever done before. He will grant me life, He will support me in my journeys, and enable me to meet thee again in America.

Paris, Sept. 15 France, my dearest friend, is indeed poor! This day I have attended at the Royal Academy of Sciences, and had all my plates spread over the different large tables, and they were viewed by about one hundred persons. "Beau! bien beau!" issued from every mouth, but, "Quel ouvrage!" "Quel prix!" as well. I said that I had thirty subscribers at Manchester; they seemed surprised, but acknowledged that England, the little isle of England, alone was able to support poor Audubon. Poor France! thy fine climate, thy rich vineyards, and the wishes of the learned avail nothing; thou art a destitute beggar, and not the powerful friend thou wast represented to be. Now I see plainly how happy, or lucky, or prudent I was, not to follow friend Melly's enthusiastic love of country. Had I come first to France my work never would have had even a beginning; it would have perished like a flower in October.

Oct. 1 The book opened accidentally at the plate of the Parrots, and Gerard, taking it up without speaking, looked at it, I assure thee, with as keen an eye as my own, for several minutes; put it down, took up the one of the Mocking-Birds, and, offering me his hand, said: "Mr. Audubon, you are the king of ornithological painters; we are all children in France and in Europe. Who would have expected such things from the woods of America?" My heart thrilled with pride at his words. Are not we of America men? Have we not the same nerves, sinews, and mental faculties which other nations possess? By Washington! we have, and may God grant us the peaceable use of them forever.

London, Nov. 4 I travelled from Paris to Boulogne with two nuns, that might as well be struck off the calendar of animated beings. They stirred not, they spoke not, they saw not; they replied neither by word nor gesture to the few remarks I made. In the woods of America I have never been in such silence; for in the most retired places I have had the gentle murmuring streamlet, or the sound of the Woodpecker tapping, or the sweet melodious strains of that lovely recluse, my greatest favorite, the Wood Thrush.

To Victor, from London, Dec. 22 You would stare were you to enter my study at the number of books, portfolios, pictures, easels, and *trash* that forms an artist's laboratory, those are my principal companions by day & by night. In looking at them I remove in idea to sceneries in America, I see the very spot where my gun felled such or such a bird and I almost enjoy my life in the woods a second time. . . . Write to me my Dear Victor not so much as to a Father as you would do to a friend connected in links of dearest, & best congeniality—write sheets after sheets. Your letters, those of your Mother, and those of my excellent friend *Wam* Rathbone, are the only ones tendant to drive away that state of despondency connected with my habits and my nature—

After three years in England, Audubon still had not persuaded Lucy to join him there; so he returned to the United States to continue his suit from nearer at hand. While in America, he collected new birds and made new drawings, to keep his great work going. He begged Lucy to come from Louisiana to join him, but she stayed put.

To Lucy, from New York, May 10, 1829 I wish to . . . receive as *true* and as *frank* an answer *as I know my Lucy will give me,* saying whether or no, the facts and the prospects, will entice her to join her husband and go to Europe with him; to enliven his spirits and assist him with her kind advices—the "no" or the "yes" will stamp my future years—if a "no" comes *I never will put the question again* and *we probably* never will meet again—if a "yes," a kindly "yes" comes bounding from thy heart my heart will bound also, and it seems to me that it will give me nerve for further exertions!—We have been married a good time, circumstances have caused our voyage to be very mottled with incidents of very different nature but our *happy days* are the only days *I now remember.*

To Lucy, from Philadelphia, Oct. 11 I live alone and see scarcely anyone besides those belonging to the house I am at—I rise before day, take a walk, return and set to my work until night fall—take another walk equally short—hot water time comes on—I drink my grog, read some, think of thee and of tomorrow and lay my head to rest with the hopes of rendering thee happy for ever hereafter!—

I am delighted with what I have accumulated in drawings this season—indeed I am surprised when sometimes I spread them on the carpet and look to see their effect—42 drawings in 4 months, 11 large, 11 middle size and 20 small comprising 95 birds from eagles downwards, with plants, nests, flowers and 60 different kinds of eggs.

Audubon finally had to fetch Lucy from Louisiana in person, then returned with her to England in the spring of 1830. A year later he again ran short of subjects for his work. So the couple sailed back to the United States, and Audubon undertook a southern journey. In Charleston, South Carolina he met a Lutheran minister and avid naturalist named John Bachman, who would become his closest friend and most reliable correspondent. The two men later collaborated on The Quadrupeds of North America. *Audubon's sons eventually married Bachman's daughters.*

To Lucy, from Charleston, Oct. 23, 1831 I found a man of learning, of sound heart and willing to bear the "American Woodsman" a hand— he walked with me and had already contrived to procure us cheaper lodgings &c when he presented me in the street to the Reverend Mr. Bachman!—Mr. Bachman!! why my Lucy Mr. Bachman would have us all to stay at his house—he would have us to make free there as if we were at our own encampment at the head waters of some unknown rivers— he would not suffer us to proceed farther south for 3 weeks—he talked— he looked as if his heart had been purposely made of the most benevolent materials granted to man by the Creator to render all about him most happy—Could I have refused his kind invitation? No!—It would have pained him as much as if grossly insulted. We removed to his house in a crack—found a room already arranged for Henry to skin our birds—another for me & Lehman to draw and a third for thy husband to rest his bones in on an excellent bed! An amiable wife and sister-in-law, two fine young daughters and 3 pairs more of cherubs all of whom I already look upon as if brought up among them—

Out shooting every day—skinning, drawing, talking ornithology the whole evening, noon, and morning—in a word my Lucy had I thee and our dear boys along I certainly would be as happy a mortal as Mr. Bachman himself is at this present moment.

To Lucy, from St. Augustine, Florida, Nov. 29 We have been uncommonly busy shooting & drawing—have drawn 13 different species amongst which a *new one* which proves to be a *new genera* for the United States—a kind of exotic bird probably very common in South America but quite unknown to me or to anyone else in this place—it is a mixture of buzzard and hawk. . . . The transition of idleness to hard labour has operated upon me as if the electric fluid and I was very nearly *knocked up* last Sunday when I certainly drew faster than ever I have done in my Life.

To Lucy, from St. Augustine, Dec. 5 Do not despond my Lucy, depend upon it we must yet see better days and I think as I believe in God that *he* will grant me life and health to enable me to finish my tremendous enterprise and grant us a happy old life.—I feel as young as ever and I now can undertake and bear as much hardship as I have ever done in my life.—Industry and perseverance joined to a sound heart will carry me a great ways—indeed *nothing* but an *accident* can destroy me in this tedious journey. . . .

My name is now ranging high and our name will stand still higher should I live through my present travels therefore the name of our sons will be a passport through the world—I have now great confidence in what I have undertaken and indeed feel so light hearted and willing to follow all my plans to the last that I only pray for your health and comfort until I have the satisfaction of joining you all again.

To Lucy, from St. Augustine, Jan. 16, 1832 What will my Philadelphia friends say or think when they read that Audubon is on board of the U.S. Schooner of war the Spark going around the Floridas after *birds*!? I assure thee my Sweet Girl I begin to be proud of myself when I see that my industry, perseverance and honesty has thus brought me so high from so low as I was in 1820 when I could not even procure through my relations and former partners the situation of a clerk on board an Ohio steamer.—now they prize me—nay wish me well—very good I wish them the same and may God grant them peace and plenty. . . .

Nothing less than the total loss of the vessel in great distance from the shore can injure me for I can swim well and far thou knowest and my heart and cause are equally good with my bodily strength. . . .

Thou wilt be surprised to read that I have *abandoned snuff for ever!* . . . I came to that determination on the 1st of this month—I am So tanned and burnt that thou might easily take me for an Indian.

To Labrador and Back, 1833

During Audubon's long absences in America, his older son, Victor, remained in England, overseeing the production and shipping of new portions of The Birds *of America. Despite Victor's efforts, Audubon still felt moved to exhort the engraver from a distance.*

To Robert Havell, from New York, Apr. 20, 1833 The success of my work depends much on your own exertions in the finishing of the plates as accurately as you are able to do, and in seeing that the colorers do their duty.—Knowing you as I do, I naturally expect all your attention—I might speak otherwise had I not known you so well as I do—*Americans are excellent judges* of work particularly of such as are drawn from their country's soil—they are proud of every thing that is connected with America, and feel mortified whenever any thing is done that does not come up to their sanguine expectations. . . .

My youngest son and I are going a long & tedious journey this spring & summer.—I intend to visit the whole coast of Labrador into Hudson's Bay and reach Quebec by returning overland—No white man has ever tramped the country I am about to visit, and I hope the result will prove profitable to all concerned.—I am heartily glad that my son and you agree and go on so well.—All I regret is the unquiet state of England with Ireland—it seems that this in a very great measure puts a stop to our business in England at least.—

After I leave this which will be on the 1st of May I shall have no opportunities at all to hear from England until my return—there are *no post offices in the wilderness before us*—I therefore ask of you to do your best and consult my son who is my right arm and hand in everything connected with my publication—he will pay you punctually as I have done myself and I am sure the more you know him the more you will like him and be pleased with him

Do not think for a moment that I am *lecturing* you.—I have no such thoughts—but merely wish to enjoin you to keep a master's eye over the Work in each of its departments.—Who knows but that your name if not your fortune is now connected with mine and with my family?

In Maine, Audubon and John prepared for a birding expedition into Labrador.

To Lucy, from East Port, Maine, May 22 We will be comfortably fixed as to clothes &c a strange figure indeed do we cut in our dresses I promise thee—fishermen boots, the soles of which are all nailed to enable us to stand erect on the sea weeds—pantaloons of fearnought so coarse that our legs look more like bear's legs than any thing else; oil jackets & overtrousers for rainy weather and round white wool hats with a piece of oil cloth dangling on our shoulders to prevent the wet running down our necks.—a coarse bag strapped on the shoulder to carry provisions during inland excursions, hunting knife at our sides and guns on the back—add to these the full grown beard which thy friend will have on his return and form an idea of his looks next autumn.

Gannett Rocks, near Labrador, June 14 We rose at two o'clock with a view to proceed to the eastern extremity of these islands in search of certain ponds, wherein, so we were told, wild geese and ducks of different kinds are in the habit of resorting annually to breed. . . . About ten a speck rose on the horizon, which I was told was the Rock; we sailed well, the breeze increased fast, and we neared this object apace. At eleven I could distinguish its top plainly from the deck, and thought it covered with snow to the depth of several feet; this appearance existed on every portion of the flat, projecting shelves. Godwin said, with the coolness of a man who had visited this Rock for ten successive seasons, that what we saw was not snow—but Gannets! I rubbed my eyes, took my spy-glass, and in an instant the strangest picture stood before me. They were birds we saw,—a mass of birds of such a size as I never before cast my eyes on. The whole of my party stood astounded and amazed, and all came to the conclusion that such a sight was of itself sufficient to invite any one to come across the Gulf to view it at this season.

June 17 I looked on our landing on the coast of Labrador as a matter of great importance. My thoughts were filled, not with airy castles, but with expectations of the new knowledge of birds and quadrupeds which I hoped to acquire. . . . The air was now filled with Velvet Ducks; *millions* of these birds were flying from the northwest towards the southeast. The Foolish Guillemots and the *Alca torda* were in immense numbers, flying in long files a few yards above the water, with rather undulating motions, and passing within good gunshot of the vessel, and now and then rounding to us, as if about to alight on the very deck. . . . The shores appeared to be margined with a broad and handsome sand-beach;

our imaginations now saw Bears, Wolves, and Devils of all sorts scampering away on the rugged shore.

June 22 The Wild Goose is an excellent diver, and when with its young uses many beautiful stratagems to save its brood, and elude the hunter. They will dive and lead their young under the surface of the water, and always in a contrary direction to the one expected; thus if you row a boat after one it will dive under it, and now and then remain under it several minutes, when the hunter with outstretched neck, is looking, all in vain, in the distance for the *stupid* Goose! Every time I read or hear of a stupid animal in a wild state, I cannot help wishing that the stupid animal who speaks thus, was half as wise as the brute he despises, so that he might be able to thank his Maker for what knowledge he may possess. . . . Last year upwards of twenty sail were engaged in "egging;" so some idea may be formed of the birds that are destroyed in this rascally way. The eggers destroy all the eggs that are sat upon, to force the birds to lay again, and by robbing them regularly, they lay till nature is exhausted, and few young are raised. In less than half a century these wonderful nurseries will be entirely destroyed, unless some kind government will interfere to stop the shameful destruction.

June 23 Fur animals are scarce, yet some few Beavers and Otters are caught, a few Martens and Sables, and some Foxes and Lynx, but every year diminishes their numbers. The Fur Company may be called the exterminating medium of these wild and almost uninhabitable climes, where cupidity and the love of gold can alone induce man to reside for a while. Where can I go now, and visit nature undisturbed?

July 2 A beautiful day for Labrador. Drew another M. *arcticus*. Went on shore, and was most pleased with what I saw. The country, so wild and grand, is of itself enough to interest any one in its wonderful dreariness. Its mossy, gray-clothed rocks, heaped and thrown together as if by chance, in the most fantastical groups imaginable, huge masses hanging on minor ones as if about to roll themselves down from their doubtful-looking situations, into the depths of the sea beneath. Bays without end, sprinkled with rocky islands of all shapes and sizes, where in every fissure a Guillemot, a Cormorant, or some other wild bird retreats to secure its egg, and raise its young, or save itself from the hunter's pursuit. The peculiar cast of the sky, which never seems to be certain, butterflies flitting over snowbanks, probing beautiful dwarf flowerets of many hues pushing their tender stems from the thick bed of moss which everywhere covers the granite rocks. Then the morasses, where you plunge up to your knees, or the walking over the stubborn, dwarfish shrubbery, making one think that as he goes he treads down the *forests* of Labrador. The unexpected Bunting, or perhaps Sylvia, which perchance, and indeed as if by chance alone, you now and then see flying before you, or hear singing from the creeping plants on the ground. The beautiful fresh-water lakes, on the rugged crests of greatly elevated islands, wherein the Red and Black-necked Divers swim as proudly as swans do in other latitudes, and where the fish appear to have been cast as strayed beings from the surplus food of the ocean. All—all is wonderfully grand, wild—aye, and terrific.

July 6 By dint of hard work and rising at three, I have drawn a *Colymbus septentrionalis* and a young one, and nearly finished a Ptarmigan; this afternoon, however, at half-past five, my fingers could no longer hold my pencil, and I was forced to abandon my work and go ashore for exercise. The fact is that am growing old too fast; alas! I feel it—and yet work I will, and may God grant me life to see the last plate of my mammoth work finished.

July 8 Rainy, dirty weather, wind east. Was at work at half-past three, but disagreeable indeed is my situation during bad weather. The rain falls on my drawing-paper, despite all I can do, and even the fog collects and falls in large drops from the rigging on my table; now and then I am obliged to close my skylight, and then may be said to work almost in darkness.

July 18 On leaving the wood we shot a Spruce Partridge leading her young. On seeing us she ruffled her feathers like a barnyard hen, and rounded within a few feet of us to defend her brood; her very looks claimed our forbearance and clemency, but the enthusiastic desire to study nature prompted me to destroy her, and she was shot, and her brood secured in a few moments; the young very pretty and able to fly.

July 21 We talked of the country where we were, of the beings best fitted to live and prosper here, not only of our species, but of all species, and also of the enormous destruction of everything here, except the rocks; the aborigines themselves melting away before the encroachments of the white man, who looks without pity upon the decrease of the devoted Indian, from whom he rifles home, food, clothing, and life. For as the Deer, the Caribou, and all other game is killed for the dollar which its skin brings in, the Indian must search in vain over the devastated country for that on which he is accustomed to feed, till, worn out by sorrow, despair, and want, he either goes far from his early haunts to others, which in time will be similarly invaded, or he lies on the rocky seashore and dies. We are often told rum kills the Indian; I think not; it is oftener the want of food, the loss of hope as he loses sight of all that was once abundant, before the white man intruded on his land and killed off the wild quadrupeds and birds with which he has fed and clothed himself since his creation. Nature herself seems perishing. Labrador must shortly be depeopled, not only of aboriginal man, but of all else having life, owing to man's cupidity. When no more fish, no more game, no more birds exist on her hills, along her coasts, and in her rivers, then she will be abandoned and deserted like a worn-out field.

Aug. 4 It is quite surprising to see how quickly the growth is attained of every living thing in this country, either animal or vegetable. In six weeks I have seen the eggs laid, the birds hatched, their first moult half over, their association in flocks, and preparations begun for their leaving the country. That the Creator should have commanded millions of delicate, diminutive, tender creatures to cross immense spaces of country to all appearance a thousand times more congenial to them than this, to cause them to people, as it were, this desolate land for a time, to enliven it by the songs of the sweet feathered musicians for two months at most, and by the same command induce them to abandon it almost suddenly, is as wonderful as it is beautiful.

Aug. 5 The migration of birds is perhaps much more wonderful than that of fishes, almost all of which go feeling their way along the shores and return to the very same river, creek, or even hole to deposit their spawn, as birds do to their former nest; but the latter do not *feel* their way, but launching high in air go at once and correctly too, across vast tracts of country, yet at once stopping in portions heretofore their own, and of which they know by previous experiences the comforts and advantages.

Aug. 10 I now sit down to post my poor book, while a heavy gale is raging furiously around our vessel. My reason for not writing at night is that I have been drawing so constantly, often seventeen hours a day, that the weariness of my body at night has been unprecedented, by such work at least. At times I felt as if my physical powers would abandon me; my neck, my shoulders, and, more than all, my fingers, were almost useless through actual fatigue at drawing. Who would believe this?—yet nothing is more true. When at the return of dawn my spirits called me out of my berth, my body seemed to beg my mind to suffer it to rest a while longer; and as dark forced me to lay aside my brushes I immediately went to rest as if I had walked sixty-five miles that day, as I have done *a few times* in my stronger days. Yesternight, when I rose from my little seat to contemplate my work and to judge of the effect of it compared with the nature which I had been attempting to copy, it was the affair of a moment; and instead of waiting, as I always like to do, until that hazy darkness which is to me the best time to judge of the strength of light and shade, I went at once to rest as if delivered from the heaviest task I ever performed. The young men think my fatigue is added to by the fact that I often work in wet clothes, but I have done that all my life with no ill effects. No! no! it is that I am no longer young. But I thank God that I did accomplish my task; my drawings are finished to the best of my ability. . . .

To Victor, from New York, Sept. 23 In England little can now be expected, the English are agog on emancipation reform, &c &c—here all works well—every industrious man makes and saves money—the taste for science improves daily—youth is educated with much care and books of every useful kind are sought for more than ever.—I think I now know, that the greatest success in keeping up ourselves, through the numbers of subscribers necessary for that support will be derived in the U.S.— and I shall feel proud to find this the fact.—I will now devote about six weeks for the sole purpose of adding to our list. . . .

I am growing old and will have to abandon the severe manner in which I have been obliged to travel in search of Birds and knowledge of their Habits, in a few more years.—The pleasure of seeing our vast undertaking completed would be to me the last furlough of my life. . . .

Among the several critics who attacked Audubon in print, the two most bitter and persistent were an Englishman, Charles Waterton, and a Philadelphia scientist named George Ord.

To Victor, from Charleston, Nov. 4 I am sorry that you should trouble yourself about the attacks of Mr. Waterton, and more so that you should answer to any of these attacks.—depend upon it, the world will judge for itself and I conceive, that the regular publication of our work, accompanied with well ascertained facts will sooner or later cast aside any such animadversions, and that the true cause of their appearance through such persons as Mr. Waterton will very soon be properly understood.—

The world is well aware that it is not necessary for anyone inclined to publish falsehoods or form tales of wonder, to travel as I constantly do, at an (I am sorry to say) enormous expense, keeping a regular journal of all my actions and the whole of my observations connected with the science which I am studying, when on the contrary I might with tenfold ease settle myself in some corner of London and write nolens volens all such fables as might cross my brains and publish these without caring one jot about the consequences.—but I feel greatly proud of our work, I feel greatly proud that I am the happy possessor of a most excellent wife and two sons whom I can view as my dearest and best attached friends—I am greatly proud that *I* possess the knowledge that every word which I have published or shall publish is truth and nothing but the result of my own observations in fields and forests where neither of my enemies ever have or ever will tread with as firm a foot & step as I have done and still do.—There is another thing of which I am equally very proud, that is that I have firmly attached to me, both in Europe and in our Country a large set of excellent & learned friends.—I have received unprecedented privileges at the hands of our government, as well as from that of England; I see our work progress well & steadily, in a word I feel happy within my heart. This is the palm I have always searched for, and it is the truest blessing on earth!

Finishing a Great Work, 1834–1838

Audubon carried on a long and affectionate correspondence with Bachman's sister-in-law Maria Martin, who contributed botanical drawings for some of the later bird portraits.

To Maria Martin, from New York, Apr. 6, 1834 I am delighted that you all are interesting yourselves in botany & drawing, nothing starts the blues so effectually than constant employment—for myself who have done next to nothing since I left you, have had the horrors all around me—dreams of sinking & burning ships at night.—fears of lost drawings & failures of subscribers by day have ever and anon been my companions—Not even the bustle of this large town can dissipate these unpleasant fancies—I walk the streets it is true, but neither hear nor see anything but my fancies dancing about through the atmosphere like so many winged imps resembling in shapes, colour, & capers all the *beau ideal* of the infernal regions!

Fine text I have taken up while writing to one of my best friends, and yet me thinks that it is only to such an one as yourself that I can write as I am doing at present—with you as with my wife or your excellent brother I can speak my feelings without either fear or remorse, and how grateful am I that I can thus speak to some on whom I *can* depend!

Audubon and Lucy returned to England in May 1834. There he discovered a great many natural history projects under way, most of them created, in his opinion, by men who never left their studies. The first volume of his own Ornithological Biography, *written with the assistance of the Scottish scientist William Macgillivray, had appeared in 1831. Now with the help of Macgillivray and his "Old Friend," Lucy, he pitched in to work on the second volume.*

To John Bachman, from London, Aug. 25 Now when I receive letters I write in answer at once you see; and if I receive none, I keep hammering at my friends' doors like a woodpecker on the back of some tough tree, the inside of which it longs to see. . . .

I have written so constantly for two months, that I was obliged to leave off after having finished 100 articles of Biography and 13 Episodes.—I became swelled as I was at your house &c and have been idle there 10 days to assist my recovery—McGillivray is assisting me as before, he says this volume will be much superior to the first, & larger—the fact is that my late tramps, and our *visitation* to you was of the greatest benefit imaginable to my studies—Since here I have read, Selby's & Temminck's Works, but they are I am sorry to say *not from Nature*. not a word could I find in them but what was compilation. . . .

My Old Friend mends our socks makes our shirts, reads to us at times, but drinks no brandy nowadays—she has cast off her purchased sham curls [and] wears her own dear grey locks and looks all the better.

To John Bachman, from Edinburgh, Nov. 5 Look at the place and date of this most amiable letter and see me from morn to darkness inclosed into night, and that too *inclosed*, at revising, correcting, and sending forth for "press" each successive sheet of the 2nd volume of my "delightful" Biographies of birds, and then you will have "a pretty tolerable idea I guess" of what I am about. My good Old Friend is at my side dashing away at the same work—Not labour, but most *agreeable avocation!*—If you would think my advice to you worth a jot, never set to the writing of any one *book*—but my book will be out in 4 weeks and after that date let us grant it rest. . . .

The author of the Ornithological Biographies is a most curious fellow.—I have read his introduction and *every one* of the sheets his 2nd Vol. will contain—aye I have read & reread it all, and to my surprise that same daring, adventurous fellow has in fact introduced your name throughout the book!—Now I strongly advise you to *review* him and his works, and to *give it* to him as he deserves!—

Metaphors aside, the prime object of this letter to you my dear Bachman is to *beg* of you to collect for me all the birds you can and just on your return from shooting cause at least a pair of each species to be immersed into a barrel of common whisky until that is filled up.—Anything—everything of the bird kind will be most useful to me hereafter.

To John Bachman, from Edinburgh, Dec. 10 My dear fellow "The Book" is out! yes quite done and I am relieved for a *moment* at least.—It consists of 38 *sheets* better *stuff* than the first volume and I am sure much better looking.—The reviewers are at work here—God only knows how they may trounce me but no matter the truth is the truth after all, and beyond *that* I care not a single jot.—I have replied to no one for previous abuses of me, and I think and trust that Ord and that fool Watterton will be greatly punished by my contemptuous silence. . . .

I am quite sure I never have been half so anxious as I am at this moment to do all in my power to *complete* my vast enterprise, and sorrowful
indeed would be my dying moments if this Work of mine was not finished ere my eyes are forever closed.—Nay my dear friend there is *something* within me that tells me that should I be so fortunate as to see the
close of my present publication, my name will be honourably handed to
posterity and the comforts of my sons and their families much augmented through this means.

To John Bachman, from London, Jan. 16, 1835 I must ask you in most
earnest manner to assist all you can and merely enable me to publish *no
trash.* but pure, clean, truths, and nothing but facts—which makes me
stand so proud in my own estimation for what I have already done.—My
work I feel assured will be a standard one for ages to come. for I feel certain that with the exception of some few errors, the truths & facts contained in my writings and in my figures of birds will become more
apparent to every student of nature *out* of his *closet!* . . .

You will see that though old I am as ardent as ever in my life if not
more so . . . between writing Biographies, finishing drawings, answering letters, and bothering many with some who will not write to me my
hands are as full [that] of work as I can possibly wish, and I have not a
moment to think of the blue devils. . . .

Can you send me some good stories for Episodes? Send quickly and
often.

To John Bachman, from London, Apr. 20 Works on the birds of *all the
world* are innumerable—cheap as dirt and more dirty than dirt—Sir
William Jardine will encumber the whole of God's creation with stuff as
little like the objects of the Creator's formation as the moon is unto
cheese—but who cares? as long as these miscellanies bring forth 5 shillings per volume to the pocket bag of the one who produces
them. . . . *Ornithological Times* are fast going bye—by the time my
Work will be done the world will have ceased to think that such beings
as birds exist under Heaven's canopy—bugs—fishes and reptiles are,
and will [be] the go for a time—then geology will move heavily above,
as well as through the earth—Africa will cease to be an unknown land—
for aught I know the north passage into the Pacific will become easier of
performance to steamers, than the passage of one of such vehicles is now
to the bar of Charleston—people will dive into the antipodes—fishes
will swim on earth—quadrupeds all will fly, and birds exchanging their
present natures will build *churches* and again become the rage of the
times! . . .

The world is all agog—for what? for *bugs* the size of *watermelons*.— There is in fact a bug now in Havell's shop for which the owner asked— how much? once, twice, thrice?—you give it up?—no less than 50 pounds sterling!—250 dollars for a beetle—as large as my fist it is true, but nought but a beetle after all—30 guineas have [been] offered and *refused*—I almost wish I could be turned into a *beetle* myself! . . .

My intention is to go to America with John next April or May— this time twelve months—No more subscribers are, or can be expected in this country—I hope I may gather some in our dear own land?? and take a tremendous concluding journey, the Lord knows where—but I shall certainly go through the "Ever Glades" of Florida, then to the mouth of the Sabine River and up into the broad prairies—I love the prairies! and then on to the Rocky Mountains and—

So much for an old man!

To John Bachman, from Edinburgh, Oct. 20 Now the purport of this letter is to give you notice, that I am now studying the anatomy of birds, and that in my concluding volume, my intention is to give the anatomical descriptions of at least one bird of each genus—this has never been offered to the scientific world by any author as regards our birds and my anxiety to accomplish this is extreme.—The subject is to me one of peculiar interest, and I am quite sure that when I shall have given you a few lessons in this study, you will feel as much as I do the necessity to attend to it hereafter, as thereby you will obtain the means of positively establishing any species differing from another. . . .

The nature of the internal structure of our birds is extremely instructive, nothing has been done in it, and whatever you and I do, must be kept a secret from all the world until published!

To John Bachman, from Liverpool, Dec. 27 I received *one* letter from you about ten days ago altogether *on birds*, and thank you for the contents.—but between *you* and *I* and the *post* I think you extremely lazy! frightful—horrible—disgraceful!—Why don't you know then that the older we become the more busy we ought to be *for the sake of our dear children* who I know are truly busy themselves! fie fie—stir up for the sake of yourself and that of an old friend—Climb up trees! Seek for the "rara avis" and then all will be right! . . .

But stop a while and you stand still to proceed is the maximum of all desiderata, therefore mind me and keep up to it, or . . . sure as fate the Devil will take the endmost.

To John Bachman, from London, Jan. 22, 1836 Then to you I now address myself as if the man in distress for the want of that relief which may at all times be derived from a friendly Christian!—Then take to your gun at all your *leisure hours*, go [to] the woods, and go to the shores, or if you cannot at all, send some worthy one on whom you can . . . depend—Note down every *insignificant* incident brought forth to your eye, and to your mind's eye, for of course any incident of consequence . . . I am sure you will not forget to *write down*! Measure, the depths, the diametrical width, of every nest you meet with this *coming spring*—Mark the substance of their outward and inner formation.—See to the period of the first deposits of the eggs, ennumerate them—Nay measure them as the nest themselves, save the shells if you can, but at all events describe them in *writing* and on the *spot*! Whatever younglings you meet with do describe, or put them in plain whiskey or common rum, the cheapest will answer for that as if the very best.—And now whenever you secure an adult, down with it in spirits also with a memorandum of the date of your procuring the same.—*Look not to the expense* in any portion of this for God granting me life I shall pay for all, except for your own trouble, and that must ever remain an unsettled account, which *science* may *perhaps* some day balance with you. . . .

I am extremely desirous to give such anatomical descriptions of each species, as may hereafter lead to the formation of a *positively natural system* without a word of humbug or *theory*! and depend upon it that it prove sooner or later the only way to ascertain *even species*! . . .

If fortunate enough, I shall indeed be enabled to leave behind us a memento that Audubon was not unworthy of his country!—beyond which all is trash in this world!

Back in the United States for a final collecting trip, Audubon learned that two Philadelphians—John Kirk Townsend and the ornithologist Thomas Nuttall— had just returned from the Far West with a cargo of bird skins, including species new to science.

To John Bachman, from New York, Oct. 2 I found Nuttall when he arrived at Boston from California he has given me 6 new species of birds found *within the limits* of our territories, and there most positively [are] fully 40 more new ones procured by himself and Townsend on both sides the Rocky Mountains. Nay good friend he assures me that they *saw* many more, among which were 3 species of jays! but wonders will never end—no not even in ornithology.—I have a world to say, but cannot write more just now.—indeed I feel very much fatigued, and my dangling curling grey hairs say to me—Audubon go to rest or you may not see your great task finished.—Oh when we meet and when we are once more again under your roof and amid our dear families, how we will talk, and laugh, and be merry!!

To John Bachman, from Philadelphia, Oct. 23 Now good friend open your eyes! aye open them tight!! Nay place specks on your proboscis if you choose! Read aloud!! quite aloud!!!—I have purchased *ninety-three bird skins!* Yes 93 bird skins!—Well what are they? Why nought less than 93 bird skins sent from the Rocky Mountains and the Columbia River by Nuttall & Townsend!—Cheap as dirt too—only one hundred and eighty-four dollars for the whole of these, and hang me if you do not echo my saying so when *you see them!!*—Such beauties! such rarities! Such novelties! Ah my worthy friend how we will laugh and talk over them! . . .

So you see nor do not you see how lucky the "Old Man" is *yet!* and why all this luck?—Simply because I have laboured like a cart horse for the last thirty years on a single Work, have been successful almost to a miracle in its publication thus far, and now am thought a—a—a—(I dislike to write it, but no matter here goes) a Great Naturalist!!!—That's all! oh! what a strange world we do live in, and how grateful to our God must we be, when after years of trouble, anxiety & sorrow, we find ourselves happy because true to him! him without whose assistance, and ever parental care, we poor things never could be called worthy the notice of even our own race!

To John Bachman, from New York, July 16, 1837 Oh if . . . I have good luck how I will *revise* my own Work in my fourth volume. How I will cut & slash at my own poor past ignorance; and yet how more careful than ever must I proceed not to blunder worse than I have already done. . . . What a strange realization of a dream this finishing of a Work that has cost me so many years of enjoyment, of labour and of vexations, and yet a few more months will I trust see it ended aye ended, and myself a naturalist no *longer!* No more advertisements of this poor me. No more stares at my face whilst travelling—No I have some idea of revising even myself and altering my very name, not to be pestered any more.

In England, rivals were pushing ahead with their own ornithological projects.

To John Bachman, from London, Aug. 14 London is just as I left it, a vast artificial area, as well covered with humbug, as are our pine lands and old fields with broom grass.—Swainson is publishing his incomprehensible works—Gould has just finished his Birds of Europe and now will go on with those of *Australia*. *Yarrell* is publishing the *British birds* quarto size—and about one thousand other niny tiny works are in progress to assist in the mass of confusion already scattered over the world. . . .

The 14 turtles caught by us in the Texas are now crawling about our *little back yard* in good health, the poor things have not eaten a mouthful since caught!

To John Bachman, from London, Oct. 4 Just as I had finished the last line, we heard a crash in the dining room below, Lucy went to inquire, and we soon heard that a *cat* had thrown down the cage which contained Maria's sweet grosbeak!—off John & I flew both armed with pokers, and you know what pokers can do? Mr. Puss had gone below stairs into the kitchen, and there we also made our way.—Doors all to in a crack.— Pussy like all other sinners much discomfitured—Under the tables, up towards the windows—Would not do.—the first stroke of my teaser confounded Mr. Puss; John touched (slightly) a few more times; and taking the Devil by the tail it was launched on the pavement.—And the bird is now quite safe, for I have passed a resolution that no cat shall poach on our grounds.

One of the first ornithologists to befriend Audubon was Charles Lucien Bonaparte, nephew of Napoleon. Early on, before undertaking his own book, Audubon freely shared with Bonaparte his knowledge of American birds. Later, he grew cautious.

To John Bachman, from London, Oct. 8 Charles Bonaparte returned to London a few days ago, and came to see me after I had gone to bed; but there he came, sat by my side and talked about birds for upwards of one hour, the consequences of which were that I scarcely closed my eyes afterwards that night. . . . Me thinks that he is over anxious to *pump me*, but I am now no longer a greenhorn, and will not write such accounts for him as I did when I sent him all the habits of the wild turkey from Bayou Sarah to New York, and for which *he* has received all credit, and I scarcely any.—I cannot well imagine why he should continue Wilson's Ornithology after my Work is finished, unless it is merely to arrange our fauna in squares, circles, or triangles, in the manner of Swainson and all other crazed naturalists of the closet.

To John Bachman, from London, Oct. 31 I have for some time past thought that the cottony substance, attached to the breast and rump of herons was capable of becoming *luminous* under certain circumstances, as during dark nights &c—when by the assistance of these magic lanterns being lighted at the will of the bird, as it is in certain insects; they may be enabled to detect the quarry, which otherwise would pass by unheeded!—I had it at my tongue's end to say this to you many & many a time, and yet you see it was always forgotten.—Now my means of proving that my thoughts are true, and that I have discovered the utility of this curious cottony substance in herons; are very poor indeed. to test the thing, one must have herons alive, and watch them during the *darkest night*, and in places too where the birds are engaged at their work; and the chances near Charleston are just about one thousand for one in London; and I should much like to hear from you on this particular subject as soon as you have *thought of it* and made *some experiment*. but I pray you keep this to yourself until we are satisfied, whether one way or the other.—I am going to try my experiments with the herons now in the Zoological Society's Gardens; but am apprehensive that whilst in confinement Nature may not act quite as freely as when at large. . . . At present the number of *positively* good species in my Work, and drawings amount to 459, and it is probable that it will ultimately be 470!

Back Home in America Attending to Business, 1839–1842

The final volume of The Birds of America *appeared in 1838, the final volume of the* Ornithological Biography *in 1839. Now Audubon was free to return to the United States, not just for a visit but for good. Still energetic, he immediately set out to produce and market a cheaper edition of* The Birds, *and to plan with Bachman a study of* The Quadrupeds of North America.

To John Bachman, from Boston, Dec. 8, 1839 As distance does not produce difference in the price of postage in our country, I have thought of writing to you this damp and gloomy morning for the purpose of raising my naturally inclined disposition to become when alone and away from my family, desponding if not low spirited. . . .

I found my generous friend Parkman and all acquaintances well, and since my arrival here have been in constant bustle, moving as fast as my legs could carry me, ringing at many many doors, and shaking the hands of numberless worthy men and fair ladies! I came to Boston with the double purpose to see all I know here, and again with the desire to procure subscribers for our little edition of the Birds of America. . . .

Almost all the persons to whom I speak of the publication of the Quadrupeds of our country are delighted, and a good number would at once subscribe was I prepared to say how much it will contain and the price of it; and this prompts me to hope that if well done, that Work will succeed and pay.

To John Bachman, from New York, Jan. 2, 1840 I believe that such a publication will be fraught with difficulties innumerable, but *I trust* not insurmountable, provided we join our names together, and you push your able and broad shoulders to the wheel. I promise to you that I will give the very best figures of all our quadrupeds that ever have been thought of or expected, and that you and I can relate the greatest amount of *truths* that to this time has appeared connected with their dark and hitherto misunderstood histories!—My hairs are grey, and I am growing old, but what of this? My spirits are as enthusiastical as ever, my legs fully able to carry my body for some ten years to come, and in about two of these I expect to see *the illustrations* out, and ere the following twelve months have elapsed, their histories studied, their descriptions carefully prepared and the book printed!—Only think of the quadrupeds of America being presented to the world of science, by Audubon and Bachman.

The younger son, John, was married to Maria Bachman in 1837, and in due course they presented Audubon with two grandchildren, Lucy and Harriet.

To Maria Martin, from Baltimore, Feb. 29, 1840 Only think that in the course of a short fortnight, the citizens of Baltimore have so contributed to the publication of the small edition of the Birds of America, as to have presented the American Woodsman with no less than one hundred and fifty-three names!! Unexpected as this success has been, I can even now scarcely believe the truth of this fact; and every one of these good people say to me, proceed onward and do likewise in every city of the Union! But sanguine as I have always been since the beginning of my career as a student of Nature's works, I can scarcely expect to meet another Baltimore in this respect!

Victor forwarded [to] me last evening the list of names procured at Charleston, and as in terms of old "it is pretty fair" and I trust that it will [be] still more so, as soon as my old Phiz appears through the streets of hospitable Charleston, where I hope to be bye & bye!—Do you not think my little Lucy a sweet interesting child and somewhat superior to most children of her age? To me she is everything at present, but when little Harriet can be handled without fears and caressed with equal fondness, it will be difficult for me to say whom I will love best.—You my dear friend cannot imagine how desirous I feel to see some *grandsons* perhaps you will call it vanity in me to say that I have a great desire that the name of Audubon should be handed to posterity, but as that is absolutely my present feeling I say so to you in confidence! . . .

One thing only I regret, and that is, that I have not yet *danced* in America, since I first visited Europe. Perchance when at Charleston, you will have the goodness to assist me in that pleasure.

To Lucy, from Baltimore, Mar. 1 When some years ago I did look upon my *progress* through this world, I often felt greatly surprised, and yet how puny and meagre were the *benefits* which we then received at the hands of that world compared to what those benefits are now. . . .

It is true that my name, and as Victor is pleased to say my "looks" may have some influence in the matter. . . . This success and the means through which it has occurred has however taught me a most excellent lesson which I am determined to remember and to put in use wherever else I may hereafter chance to go. i.e. to seek from the very first some of the most influential men or *ladies* of the towns I visit, and have them to *accompany* thy poor old husband, from door to door, and house to house, and to present him and to *preamble* for him, and in his behalf! . . .

Thy own dearest wishes that we should have in this country 5000 subscribers to the present publication is not quite what I wish for myself. It would prove too much for the sake of our dearest beloved children, all of whom I ever will wish to be industrious and honest, and not drones wallowing in wealth and useless to their own kind if not so to their own family circles. No. No! 2000 subscribers for instance, provided they are all good and true will suffice for us all. . . .

I have suddenly been brought here into a vortex of worldly society, which I had long hoped would never occur to me in our country, and which indeed I extremely dislike, however well intended and profitable it might prove to us. I have been to several parties, and some dinners, where with all the friendliness and kindness of the persons who did invite me, I have felt as I always do on such occasions a lost sheep; seeking for a dark corner to hide my want of that knowledge which non education calls upon me to search.—To see crowded assemblies gazing upon me I most truly despise and never will endure. Give me the woods, the prairies, the sea shores, the squatter's fireside, or the delights of *my own* dearest family circle, and then, and only then, thy husband will be happy!

Hingham, Massachusetts, Aug. 19 I was up at 4 this morning; the weather was beautiful and cool, my breakfast was ready at ½ past five and at 6 I was in a very coach indeed on my way to Hingham! My companions at first were only 2 of both sex and extremely talkative;—Poor I took my snuff and gazed on the Nature spread around me.—How delightful I thought was the refreshing air, and the green grass and foliage and the trees of the orchards bending beneath their loaded bows! How oft I thought of those at *home* and of my Johnny and his Maria at Charleston, and of the beloved angels of theirs, my little Lucy and still smaller babe Harriet; of my Lucy, my Victor and my beloved Eliza! Yet the coach proceeded on and I with it; travellers one after another assisted in the filling of the benches, frequently the driver stopped to exchange letters for letters, until at last we reached the very wharf from which a steamer is ready thrice a day to carry passengers to Boston, and at the sound of that word, I as if by magic was conveyed there, and amid the dear friends whom I do know in that friendly city!

Portsmouth, New Hampshire, Sept. 15 This day has been a beautiful one, but although I delivered all my letters and have seen many individuals, not a *name* have I procured. I found the people good & kind but I fear not quite rich enough to meet my views or wishes. . . . My large plates were shown at the Atheneum and perhaps admired, but $1000 is *here* quite a sum! I visited the Navy Yard and saw several gentlemen there &c. If tomorrow is not better than today, I shall not as Wilson did Louisville, damn Portsmouth, but bid it my adieus!

I was astonished last evening when I had had my supper at the table d'hote, to hear the answer returned by my host to several gents who asked him who and what I was? "Why I guess that he is a scientific gentleman of some sort or other, for he is very polite and talks to no one that does not talk to him." I was highly tickled at this as I heard it somewhat distinctly.

Boston, Nov. 21 Called at the U.S. Hotel to see Daniel Webster, not in left a card. Called upon him at his office corner of Court and Tremont Streets, found him. He was greatly surprised that I have not received a dollar yet on account of what he owes us for the copy of the large work to which he subscribed years ago and said that he would attend to that business at once, and indeed settle it to my satisfaction by Wednesday next. Nous verrons! he bought a copy of the five volumes of my Ornithological Biographies for which he would pay me also.

Boston, Nov. 27 Called on Daniel Webster twice, and finally got $100 Dollars from him on account of the large work, and a memorandum authorizing me to draw upon him at three different dates for the balance he now owes us. To my astonishment he subscribed to the little work; and Mr. Little of Little & Brown, guaranteed me the payment thereof! He moreover, (D. Webster) promised me to send me letters of introduction for several places by next Sunday. Nous verrons!

Boston, Nov. 28 Went to Mr. Almy who walked with me in different parts of the city until ¼ past 1 and we procured 12 subscribers, my self 3, he and I together the rest. I procured another at the shop of C. Little & Brown after dinner.—Much fatigued dined at Docr. Shattuck. Called on Docr. Parkman, not in, saw his daughter who was playing on the harp.—Had the lock of my green box picked, having left the key at home or lost it.—Took 7 copies out of it . . . , and carried them to Little & Brown, where the young men assisted me in arranging them into sets of 20 numbers each. Went to tea to David Eckley, and there heard of the suicide of Mr. Prince Senior at New York, and on my return at 7 to Doctor Shattuck heard of the like act, having been committed this day in this city. Surely those men must have both been mad! Wrote home, and sent a check to Johnny, value $200. I have done remarkably well today, and although I feel much fatigued, I am contented. God bless you all, good night!

Worcester, Massachusetts, Dec. 12 Weather fair and *very cold*. Rose early and walked a good deal around the village to judge of its tout-en-semble, very handsome place, and in the summer must be quite beautiful. I felt in good spirits for a wonder, and after breakfast went to Mr. Harris, and we started in search of subscribers at once, and sure enough I have procured 12! Almost all the houses are of wood, painted white and look well. . . . We visited the lunatic asylum and found it kept in the very best of order; it is a large brick building standing on an eminence and commanding the view of Worcester.—Afterwards we went to the Antiquarian Library, and saw its curious old books, paintings, etc. . . . The Librarian told me that the famous learned blacksmith *Burritt* wished to see me and to subscribe to our Work, and off to his shop we went. He came into his office, with his sleeves turned up, his arms bare and full of sinew, his eyes sparkling bright, his forehead smooth and high, his person manly, his demeanor modesty itself! We shook hands as I am sure with sincerest good will, and talked for a while, and strange as it may appear, his opinions of our success in regard to mental improvement coincide precisely with my own; i.e. that *We are what we make ourselves*. He asked for my autograph and I wrote a few lines. Being a very poor exchange for his signature on my subscription list.—I can write a famous episode upon my friend Burritt and will do so.

Hartford, Connecticut, Dec. 17 This morning at 8, the weather fair and somewhat cold, I left Springfield for Hartford in a stage, having an Irish dyer (by trade) for my only companion. The road was very bad, but the sight of the Connecticut River, here and there peeping, now in the distance, and again at our feet rendered the journey pleasant. The sun was out brightly shining, and the snow lightly wafting from the branches and twigs towards mother earth.—The valley through which we passed is beautiful during the summer months and I pictured the scenery anew as if again in my youthful days! About 2 o'clock, the several steeples of this beautiful village came to our view, and anon I was deposited at the United States Hotel. How curious it is to me to see how eagerly the non employed loungers about taverns peep in to the *book of names*, and again stare at the poor but honest, and I would almost say *modest* "American Woodsman." There are indeed times when I wish I could leave the earth and fly away from the staring gaze of these idlers, but as I cannot fly, I must sit still & silent and give them the fairest of chances to gratify their appetites.

Washington, D.C., July 16, 1842 I reached the Capitol. . . . I entered the Library, and was immediately presented to many new members of Congress (the time not up for sitting) and the 4 plates were gazed upon with wonder.—But only think how mean my drawings must be, when I tell you that even this day after having told the names of each animal represented to the librarian who is a man of sense and who generally speaks instead of me at my request—the Great Folks call the rats squirrels, the squirrels flying ones, and the marmots, poor things, are regularly called beavers or musk rats! I will have to amend my style and touches and *drawing* greatly before the world knows "*what's what*"!

Quebec, Sept. 24 This day was very beautiful, though this morning was *cold* as well as this evening. To me it has been one of sorrow and mortifying disappointment. First I received a letter from Victor with the sad news of our Caroline's newly born babe having died almost instantly after birth. A boy too; but God has his will and we must obey with constant contentedness! . .

Several notices of my being in Quebec finally appeared in this and yesterday's journals (at last) and some persons told me not to be out of heart. Now I should like to know when, notwithstanding the thousand and one disappointments I meet in this life, have I felt cast down for more than a few moments. When the rats destroyed my drawings at Henderson is an exception and the losing of my own sweet little daughters and daughters-in-law exceptions.

Up The Missouri to the Yellowstone Country, 1843

In the spring of 1843, at the age of fifty-eight, Audubon undertook his last wilderness journey, into the region of the Upper Missouri and Yellowstone Rivers. Failing health prevented him from crossing the Rocky Mountains and from reaching his long-sought destination, the Pacific.

Mississippi River, April 25, 1843 Having conveyed the whole of our effects on board the steamer, and being supplied with excellent letters, we left St. Louis at 11.30 A.M., with Mr. Sarpy on board, and a hundred and one trappers of all descriptions and nearly a dozen different nationalities, though the greater number were French Canadians, or Creoles of this State. Some were drunk, and many in that stupid mood which follows a state of nervousness produced by drinking and over-excitement. . . .

I forgot to say that as the boat pushed off from the shore, where stood a crowd of loafers, the men on board had congregated upon the hurricane deck with their rifles and guns of various sorts, all loaded, and began to fire what I should call a very disorganized sort of a salute, which lasted for something like an hour, and which has been renewed at intervals, though in a more desultory manner, at every village we have passed.

Missouri River, May 1 The four [gophers] which I kept alive never drank anything, though water was given to them. I fed them on potatoes, cabbages, carrots, etc. They tried constantly to make their escape by gnawing at the floor, but in vain. They slept wherever they found clothing, etc., and the rascals cut the lining of my hunting-coat all to bits, so that I was obliged to have it patched and mended. In one instance I had some clothes rolled up for the washerwoman, and, on opening the bundle to count the pieces, one of the fellows caught hold of my right thumb, with fortunately a single one of its upper incisors, and hung on till I shook it off, violently throwing it on the floor, where it lay as if dead; but it recovered, and was as well as ever in less than half an hour. They gnawed the leather straps of my trunks during the night, and although I rose frequently to stop their work, they would begin anew as soon as I was in bed again.

May 10 My guide was anxious to take a short cut, and took me across several bayous, one of which was really up to the saddle; but we crossed that, and coming to another we found it so miry, that his horse wheeled after two or three steps, whilst I was looking at him before starting myself; for you all well know that an old traveller is, and must be, prudent. We now had to retrace our steps till we reached the very tracks that the squad sent after us in the morning had taken, and at last we reached the foot of the Bluffs, when my guide asked me if I "could ride at a gallop," to which not answering him, but starting at once at a round run, I neatly passed him ere his horse was well at the pace; on we went, and in a few minutes we entered a beautiful dell or valley, and were in sight of the encampment. We reached this in a trice, and rode between two lines of pitched tents to one at the end, where I dismounted, and met Captain Burgwin, a young man, brought up at West Point, with whom I was on excellent and friendly terms in less time than it has taken me to write this account of our meeting. I showed him my credentials, at which he smiled, and politely assured me that I was too well known throughout our country to need any letters. While seated in front of his tent, I heard the note of a bird new to me, and as it proceeded from a tree above our heads, I looked up and saw the first Yellow-headed Troupial alive that ever came across my own migrations. The captain thought me probably crazy, as I thought Rafinesque when he was at Henderson; for I suddenly started, shot at the bird, and killed it.

May 13 We saw this morning eleven Indians of the Omaha tribe. They made signals for us to land, but our captain never heeded them, for he hates the red-skins as most men hate the devil. One of them fired a gun, the group had only one, and some ran along the shore for nearly two miles, particularly one old gentleman who persevered until we came to such bluff shores as calmed down his spirits. . . . On a sand-bar afterwards we saw three more Indians, also with a canoe frame, but we only interchanged the common yells usual on such occasions. They looked as destitute and as hungry as if they had not eaten for a week, and no doubt would have given much for a bottle of whiskey. At our last landing for wood-cutting, we also went on shore, but shot nothing, not even took aim at a bird; and there was an Indian with a flint-lock rifle, who came on board and stared about until we left, when he went off with a little tobacco. I pity these poor beings from my heart!

May 17 We have seen floating eight Buffaloes, one Antelope, and one Deer; how great the destruction of these animals must be during high freshets! . . . The most extraordinary part of the history of these drowned Buffaloes is, that the different tribes of Indians on the shores, are ever on the lookout for them, and no matter how putrid their flesh may be, provided the hump proves at all fat, they swim to them, drag them on shore, and cut them to pieces; after which they cook and eat this loathsome and abominable flesh, even to the marrow found in the bones. In some instances this has been done when the whole of the hair had fallen off, from the rottenness of the Buffalo. Ah! Mr. Catlin, I am now sorry to see and to read your accounts of the Indians *you* saw—how very different they must have been from any that I have seen!

May 22 We started as early as usual, *i.e.*, at half-past three; the weather was fine. We breakfasted before six, and immediately after saw two Wild Cats of the common kind; we saw them running for some hundreds of yards. We also saw several large Wolves, noticing particularly one pure white, that stood and looked at us for some time. Their movements are precisely those of the common cur dog. We have seen five or six this day. We began seeing Buffaloes again in small gangs, but this afternoon and evening we have seen a goodly number, probably more than a hundred. We also saw fifteen or twenty Antelopes. I saw ten at once, and it was beautiful to see them running from the top of a high hill down to its base, after which they went round the same hill, and were lost to us.

June 7 The Mandan mud huts are very far from looking poetical, although Mr. Catlin has tried to render them so by placing them in regular rows, and all of the same size and form, which is by no means the case. But different travellers have different eyes! We saw more Indians than at any previous time since leaving St. Louis; and it is possible that there are a hundred huts, made of mud, all looking like so many potato winter-houses in the Eastern States. As soon as we were near the shore, every article that could conveniently be carried off was placed under lock and key, and our division door was made fast, as well as those of our own rooms. Even the axes and poles were put by. Our captain told us that last year they stole his cap and his shot-pouch and horn, and that it was through the interference of the first chief that he recovered his cap and horn; but that a squaw had his leather belt, and would not give it up. The appearance of these poor, miserable devils, as we approached the shore, was wretched enough. There they stood in the pelting rain and keen wind, covered with Buffalo robes, red blankets, and the like, some partially and most curiously besmeared with mud; and as they came on board, and we shook hands with each of them, I felt a clamminess that rendered the ceremony most repulsive. Their legs and naked feet were covered with mud. They looked at me with apparent curiosity, perhaps on account of my beard, which produced the same effect at Fort Pierre. They all looked very poor; and our captain says they are the *ne plus ultra* of thieves. It is said there are nearly three thousand men, women, and children that, during winter, cram themselves into these miserable hovels.

Fort Union, Upper Missouri River, June 14 [A]lthough we had lain down, it was impossible for us to sleep; for above us was a drunken man affected with a *goitre*, and not only was his voice rough and loud, but his words were continuous. His oaths, both in French and English, were better fitted for the Five Points in New York, or St. Giles of London, than anywhere among Christians. He roared, laughed like a maniac, and damned himself and the whole creation. I thought that time would quiet him, but, no! for now clarionets, fiddles, and a drum were heard in the dining-room, where indeed they had been playing at different times during the afternoon, and our friend above began swearing at this as if quite fresh. We had retired for the night; but an invitation was sent us to join the party in the dining-room. Squires was up in a moment, and returned to say that a ball was on foot, and that "all the beauty and fashion" would be skipping about in less than no time. There was no alternative; we all got up, and in a short time were amid the *beau monde* of these parts. Several squaws, attired in their best, were present, with all the guests, *engagés*, clerks, etc. Mr. Culbertson played the fiddle very fairly; Mr. Guepe the clarionet, and Mr. Chouteau the drum, as if brought up in the army of the great Napoleon. Cotillions and reels were danced with much energy and apparent enjoyment, and the company dispersed about one o'clock. We retired for the second time, and now occurred a dispute between the drunkard and another man; but, notwithstanding this, I was so wearied that I fell asleep.

June 29 Provost told me (and he is a respectable man) that, during the breeding season of the Mountain Ram, the battering of the horns is often heard as far as a mile away, and that at such times they are approached with comparative ease; and there is no doubt that it is during such encounters that the horns are broken and twisted as I have seen them, and not by leaping from high places and falling on their horns, as poetical travellers have asserted. The fact is that when these animals leap from any height they alight firmly on all their four feet.

June 30 I began drawing at five this morning, worked almost without cessation till after three, when, becoming fatigued for want of practice, I took a short walk, regretting I could no longer draw twelve or fourteen hours without a pause or thought of weariness.

July 2 Mr. Denig and I walked off with a bag and instruments, to take off the head of a three-years-dead Indian chief, called the White Cow. Mr. Denig got upon my shoulders and into the branches near the coffin, which stood about ten feet above the ground. The coffin was lowered, or rather tumbled, down, and the cover was soon hammered off; to my surprise, the feet were placed on the pillow, instead of the head, which lay at the foot of the coffin—if a long box may so be called. Worms innumerable were all about it; the feet were naked, shrunk, and dried up. The head had still the hair on, but was twisted off in a moment, under jaw and all. The body had been first wrapped up in a Buffalo skin without hair, and then in another robe with the hair on, as usual; after this the dead man had been enveloped in an American flag, and over this a superb scarlet blanket. We left all on the ground but the head. Squires, Mr. Denig and young Owen McKenzie went afterwards to try to replace the coffin and contents in the tree, but in vain; the whole affair fell to the ground, and there it lies; but I intend to-morrow to have it covered with earth.

July 12 A young dog of this country's breed ate up all the berries collected by Mrs. Culbertson, and her lord had it killed for our supper this evening. The poor thing was stuck with a knife in the throat, after which it was placed over a hot fire outside of the fort, singed, and the hair scraped off, as I myself have treated Raccoons and Opossums. Then the animal was boiled, and I intend to taste one mouthful of it, for I cannot say that just now I should relish an entire meal from such peculiar fare. . . . With great care and some repugnance I put a very small piece in my mouth; but no sooner had the taste touched my palate than I changed my dislike to liking, and found this victim of the canine order most excellent, and made a good meal, finding it fully equal to any meat I ever tasted.

July 21 We returned to the camp and saw a Wolf cross our path, and an Antelope looking at us. We determined to stop and try to bring him to us; I lay on my back and threw my legs up, kicking first one and then the other foot, and sure enough the Antelope walked towards us, slowly and carefully, however. In about twenty minutes he had come two or three hundred yards; he was a superb male, and I looked at him for some minutes; when about sixty yards off I could see his eyes, and being loaded with buck-shot pulled the trigger without rising from my awkward position. Off he went. . . . [A]s we came near Fox River, we thought of the horns of our bulls. . . . Bell's horns were the handsomest and largest, mine next best, and Harris's the smallest, but we are all contented. . . . What a terrible destruction of life, as it were for nothing, or next to it, as the tongues only were brought in, and the flesh of these fine animals was left to beasts and birds of prey, or to rot on the spots where they fell. The prairies are literally *covered* with the skulls of the victims, and the roads the Buffalo make in crossing the prairies have all the appearance of heavy wagon tracks.

July 24 I lost the head of my first bull because I forgot to tell Mrs. Culbertson that I wished to save it, and the princess had its skull broken open to enjoy its brains. Handsome, and really courteous and refined in many ways, I cannot reconcile to myself the fact that she partakes of raw animal food with such evident relish. . . . On our return Mrs. Culbertson was good enough to give me six young Mallards, which she had caught by swimming after them in the Missouri; she is a most expert and graceful swimmer, besides being capable of remaining under water a long time; all the Blackfoot Indians excel in swimming and take great pride in the accomplishment.

Aug. 5 Provost tells me that Buffaloes become so very poor during hard winters, when the snows cover the ground to the depth of two or three feet, that they lose their hair, become covered with scabs, on which the Magpies feed, and the poor beasts die by hundreds. One can hardly conceive how it happens, notwithstanding these many deaths and the immense numbers that are murdered almost daily on these boundless wastes called prairies, besides the hosts that are drowned in the freshets, and the hundreds of young calves who die in early spring, so many are yet to be found. Daily we see so many that we hardly notice them more than the cattle in our pastures about our homes. But this cannot last; even now there is a perceptible difference in the size of the herds, and before many years the Buffalo, like the Great Auk, will have disappeared; surely this should not be permitted.

Sources

The following abbreviations have been used to identify the sources for the selections in this book:

AAHJ   *Audubon and His Journals*, 2 volumes, edited by Maria R. Audubon (New York: Scribner's, 1897; reprinted New York: Dover, 1960)

1826 JOURNAL   *The 1826 Journal of John James Audubon*, edited by Alice Ford (Norman: University of Oklahoma, 1967)

1820–21 JOURNAL   *Journal of John James Audubon Made during His Trip to New Orleans in 1820–1821*, edited by Howard Corning (Boston: Club of Odd Volumes, 1929)

1840–43 JOURNAL   *Journal of John James Audubon Made While Obtaining Subscriptions to His Birds of America, 1840–1843*, edited by Howard Corning (Boston: Club of Odd Volumes, 1929)

LETTERS   *Letters of John James Audubon, 1826–1840*, 2 volumes, edited by Howard Corning (Boston: Club of Odd Volumes, 1930; reprinted New York: Kraus, 1969)

OB   *Ornithological Biography*, 5 volumes (Edinburgh, 1831–39)

In the list of sources below, the first numbers refer to the pages in this book on which a particular selection appears. This number is followed either by the title of the selection, or, in the case of letters and journals, by the date of the original.

pp. 23–26 ("The Ohio")	OB, I, 29–32
pp. 27–30 ("Louisville in Kentucky")	OB, I, 437–40
pp. 31–36 ("The Eccentric Naturalist")	OB, I, 455–60
pp. 37–40 ("The Prairie")	OB, I, 81–4
pp. 41–43 ("The Earthquake")	OB, I, 239–41
pp. 44–48 ("A Racoon Hunt in Kentucky")	OB, III, 235–9
pp. 49–51 ("Pitting of the Wolves")	OB, III, 338–41
pp. 52–54 ("Breaking Up of the Ice")	OB, III, 408–10
pp. 55–59 ("The Original Painter")	OB, I, 410–4
pp. 60–63 ("Meadville")	OB, I, 182–5
pp. 64–69 ("The Great Pine Swamp")	OB, I, 52–7
pp. 70–74 ("St. John's River, in Florida")	OB, I, 291–5
pp. 75–78 ("A Ball in Newfoundland")	OB, II, 211–5
pp. 79–82 ("The Eggers of Labrador")	OB, III, 82–5
pp. 83–86 ("Labrador")	OB, III, 584–7
pp. 89–102 ("Wild Turkey")	OB, I, 1–16
pp. 103–111 ("White-Headed Eagle")	OB, I, 160–9
pp. 112–115 ("Barred Owl")	OB, I, 242–5
pp. 116–123 ("Passenger Pigeon")	OB, I, 319–26
pp. 124–129 ("Ivory-Billed Woodpecker")	OB, I, 341–6
pp. 130–131 ("Broad-Winged Hawk")	OB, I, 461–3
pp. 132–133 ("White-Crowned Sparrow")	OB, II, 88–91
pp. 134–139 ("Pewee Flycatcher")	OB, II, 122–9
pp. 140–142 ("American Crow")	OB, II, 317–22
pp. 143–148 ("Chimney Swallow, or American Swift")	OB, II, 329–34
pp. 149–150 ("Golden Eagle")	OB, II, 464–8

Brief Bibliography

WORKS BY AUDUBON

Audubon and His Journals. Edited by Maria R. Audubon. 2 volumes. New York: Scribner's, 1897; reprint, New York: Dover, 1960. Includes "Episodes" from *Ornithological Biography*, as well as heavily edited versions of his journals from 1826–1829, 1833, and 1843.

Audubon, by Himself: A Profile of John James Audubon. Edited by Alice Ford. Garden City, New York: Natural History Press, 1969. Selections from the writings arranged to form an autobiographical sequence.

The Birds of America. Elephant folio edition, 4 volumes, London, 1827–1838. "Miniature" edition, 7 volumes, including most of text from *Ornithological Biography*, New York and Philadelphia, 1840–1844. Among modern editions, the most complete and readily available was published in New York by Macmillan, 1937; reissued, 1985. The original water-color paintings for *The Birds of America* were published by the American Heritage Publishing Company, 1966.

The 1826 Journal of John James Audubon. Edited by Alice Ford. Norman: University of Oklahoma, 1967.

Journal of John James Audubon Made during His Trip to New Orleans in 1820–1821. Edited by Howard Corning. Boston: Club of Odd Volumes, 1929.

Journal of John James Audubon Made While Obtaining Subscriptions to His Birds of America, 1840–1843. Edited by Howard Corning. Boston: Club of Odd Volumes, 1929.

Letters of John James Audubon, 1826–1840. 2 volumes. Edited by Howard Corning. Boston: Club of Odd Volumes, 1930; reprinted, New York: Kraus, 1969.

Ornithological Biography. 5 volumes, Edinburgh, 1831–39. Selections from the bird accounts have been reprinted in *The Bird Biographies of John James Audubon*, edited by Alice Ford, New York: Macmillan, 1957. The "Episodes" have been reprinted in *Delineations of American Scenery and Character*, edited by Francis Hobart Herrick, New York: Baker, 1926; and in *Audubon and His Journals* (see listing above).

The Viviparous Quadrupeds of North America, with John Bachman. 2 volumes of plates, New York, 1845–46. 3 volumes of text, New York, 1846–54. "Miniature" edition, including text and plates, in 3 volumes, New York, 1854. Modern editions include *Audubon's Animals: The Quadrupeds of North America*, compiled and edited by Alice Ford, New York: Studio Publications, 1951; and *The Imperial Collection of Audubon Animals*, edited by Victor H. Cahalane, New York: Bonanza Books, 1967.

WORKS ABOUT AUDUBON

Adams, Alexander. *John James Audubon*. New York: Putnam's, 1966. Popular biography that draws upon modern sources.

Audubon Magazine. Vol. 87, no. 3 (May 1985). Issue celebrating Audubon's bicentennial, including "In Search of the Real Mr. Audubon," by Michael Harwood and Mary Durant, pp. 58–119.

Audubon, Lucy, ed. *The Life of John James Audubon, Naturalist*. New York: Putnam's, 1869. Worshipful and frequently misleading profile by Audubon's widow.

Durant, Mary, and Harwood, Michael. *On the Road with John James Audubon*. New York: Dodd, Mead, 1980. Vivid account by a couple who retraced Audubon's American journeys.

Ford, Alice. *John James Audubon*. Norman: University of Oklahoma, 1964. Best modern biography, largely superseding that of Francis Herrick (see listing below).

Herrick, Francis Hobart. *Audubon the Naturalist*. 2 volumes. New York: Appleton, 1917. Until recently the definitive biography, and still unsurpassed for its account of Audubon's youth.

Lindsey, Alton A. et al. *The Bicentennial of John James Audubon*. Bloomington: Indiana University Press, 1985. Essays on Audubon's enduring significance.

Sanders, Scott R. *Wonders Hidden: Audubon's Early Years*. Santa Barbara: Capra Press, 1984. Short novel about Audubon's childhood, until his departure for America at age eighteen.

Editor: Jane Shelly
Book designer: Matthew Williamson
Jacket designer: Matthew Williamson
Production coordinator: Harriet Curry
Typeface: Goudy Oldstyle
Typesetter: J. Jarrett Engineering, Inc.
Printer: Maple-Vail Book
    Manufacturing Group

SCOTT RUSSELL SANDERS, Professor of English at Indiana University in Bloomington, is the author of numerous books of fiction and nonfiction, including *Wilderness Plots*, *Fetching the Dead*, *Terrarium*, *Stone Country*, and *The Paradise of Bombs*, which won the 1985 Associated Writing Programs award for nonfiction.